Hard Choices

Hard Choices

Moral Dilemmas in Humanitarian Intervention

Edited by
Jonathan Moore

OAKTON COMMUNITY COLLEGE
DES PLAINES CAMPUS
1600 EAST GOLF ROAD
DES PLAINES, IL 60016

Under the Auspices of the
International Committee of the Red Cross, Geneva

ROWMAN & LITTLEFIELD PUBLISHERS, INC.
Lanham • Boulder • New York • Oxford

ROWMAN & LITTLEFIELD PUBLISHERS, INC.

Published in the United States of America
by Rowman & Littlefield Publishers, Inc.
4720 Boston Way, Lanham, Maryland 20706

12 Hid's Copse Road
Cumnor Hill, Oxford OX2 9JJ, England

British Library Cataloguing in Publication Information Available

Library of Congress Cataloging-in-Publication Data

Hard choices : moral dilemmas in humanitarian intervention
  edited by Jonathan Moore.
    p. cm.
  Includes bibliographical references and index.
  ISBN 0-8476-9030-X (alk. paper). — ISBN 0-8476-9031-8 (pbk. :
alk. paper)
    1. Humanitarian assistance. 2. War victims—Services for.
I. Moore, Jonathan.
HV639.M67 1998
363.34'988—dc21   98-19157
                                                              CIP

Printed in the United States of America

∞ ™ The paper used in this publication meets the minimum requirements of
American National Standard for Information Sciences—Permanence of Paper
for Printed Library Materials, ANSI Z39.48–1984.

Contents

Acknowledgments

Simply put, this book would not have happened without the vision and steadfastness of the International Committee of the Red Cross (ICRC) in Geneva. It is a great privilege to have the opportunity to work with this remarkable organization.

Individual gratitude has been richly earned by Jean-François Berger, who was the ICRC's vigilant, quick-witted, and companionable principal officer on the project almost from its inception. Others at the ICRC who should be identified for their important help are Urs Boegli, Rowena Binz, Jean de Courten, Peter Fuchs (former ICRC director-general), Pierre Gassman (who started the project), Paul Grossrieder, Ceri Hammond, Gilbert Holleufer, Christophe Meier, René Kosirnik, Charles Pierrat, Jean-Daniel Tauxe, and Yves Sandoz. Also, Jose A. Aponte and Josie Martin, both vice presidents of the American Red Cross in Washington, D.C., should be mentioned.

Marvin Kalb and the staff of the Joan Shorenstein Center on the Press, Politics and Public Policy of the Kennedy School of Government at Harvard University are thanked for the generous support provided the editor during the project. Others who made deeply appreciated contributions include Richard Amdur, Bill Buford, George Demko, Louise Fréchette, Robert Gersony, Anne Griffin, Bishop Samir Kafity, Katherine Moore, Henry Scammell, and Timothy Seldes.

Foreword

Cornelio Sommaruga
President of the ICRC

I t has been quite rightly said that suffering, like light, knows no national boundaries. No matter when or where it erupts, every new conflict is a setback for civilization itself, and it is usually the weakest who pay the price. Looking the other way serves no purpose: recourse to violence always leaves us impoverished in the end, even if appearances suggest otherwise.

But the key issue lies elsewhere, beyond resignation or its deadly accessory, indifference. The essential thing is to alleviate suffering—to rely on that small flame of humanity that can light the way out of chaos. What convinces me all the more of this, after ten years at the helm of an organization that pioneered humanitarian action, is my daily realization that the more one is confronted with the suffering caused by war, the less one becomes accustomed to it.

Since the end of the Cold War, we have all had to face fresh challenges. The tension between the process of globalization and the assertion of identity has been constantly mounting during this period, which has not yet been given a label. In many cases, the tension has escalated into conflict, mostly of an internal nature. At the same time, new entities have emerged, particularly interest groups and nongovernmental organizations (NGOs) within civil society, economic operators, paramilitary groups, private armies, and networks associated with organized crime. The common denominator among all these players is that they function independently of the state, or at least with some degree of autonomy.

Against this shifting background, humanitarian action has also undergone considerable change, with a great surge in momentum and a remarkable proliferation of players and organizations. This in itself is a welcome development, even if all too frequently it is accompanied by a certain amount of confusion that can erode the coherence essential to humanitarian operations. Another major change concerns the role of states: keen to act immediately in a crisis, the most influential among them are sometimes tempted to embark on humanitarian operations at the expense of political action focusing on conflict resolution. In the global atmosphere of détente, the military forces mobilized in the context of the United Nations and regional organizations have also invested more heavily in humanitarian action on the basis of new mandates. The right to intervene on humanitarian grounds has been tried and tested on numerous occasions, with varying results. All these factors combined have brought about a profound change in the humanitarian environment, which has become more complex and at the same time more dangerous than ever for those working in it.

Inter arma caritas ("compassion in the midst of battle"): this was the motto adopted by the International Committee of the Red Cross (ICRC) and put into practice by Henry Dunant, the Swiss founder of the Red Cross, on the battlefield at Solferino in 1859. Originally the idea of the Red Cross was based on the following premise: since war is inevitable, we must try to make it less barbaric, both by laying down rules of warfare and by conducting relief operations. Declaring to the participants in the Geneva International Conference of 1863, which formally established the Red Cross, that "we will have planted a seed which may bear fruit in the future," General Dufour, the first ICRC president, demonstrated the clarity of his vision and his acute sense of the strength and extraordinary potential of the humanitarian ideal.

Since its inception over 130 years ago, the ICRC has performed a special function in that it plays a dual role in relation to the suffering caused by war. On the one hand, it acts directly on behalf of the victims of armed conflict and internal violence, largely through operations to protect and assist civilians, prisoners, the wounded, the displaced, and various other categories of vulnerable people. On the other hand, it strives to influence the conduct of all parties actually or potentially involved in war and internal violence, engaging in dialogue and raising awareness of the Fundamental Principles of the International Red Cross and Red Crescent Movement, which include humanity, impartiality, and independence. The ICRC is also the main promoter of international humanitarian law, striving to ensure its application. This body of law is also called the law of armed conflict or the law of war because its aim, ever since the adoption of the original Geneva Convention of 1864 to protect wounded soldiers on the battlefield, has been to regulate the conduct of combatants and thereby limit the pernicious effects of armed conflict. The essence of international humanitarian law is contained in the four Geneva Conventions of 1949 and their two Additional Protocols of 1977. The 1949 conventions, which are approaching their fiftieth anniversary, have been ratified in the meantime by virtually every state across the globe. Hence, it can be seen that humanitarian action and humanitarian law are inextricably linked in the work of the ICRC: each contributes to the development of the other, the benefit being reaped by the victims of conflict.

Nevertheless, a closer look at reality in the field quickly reveals how difficult it is to secure compliance with humanitarian law; indeed, its rules are all too often totally ignored. Once war has erupted, it tends to sweep all before it: it strikes our very core, with utter disregard for what is most precious in each one of us. Ethics and humanitarian values carry little weight when confronted by intolerance and hatred. As the fortunes of war ebb and flow, the magnitude of suffering and of humanitarian needs beggars belief. Faced with the running sore of war, what can be done? We believe that dialogue with all the players involved, whatever their level of authority, must be stepped up at all costs. And here our efforts must be unrelenting, for we know that humanitarian action and humanitarian law are based on values inherent in all cultures and traditions. Such values are a priceless asset; it is vital to promote them, to ensure that they are understood, and to restore them to their proper place. Regulating war also means propagating universal ethical standards by taking responsibility for them and making them a part of everyday attitudes. This is why it is important for humanitarian agencies to establish closer bonds with local cultures and make better use of the expertise and resources available on the spot. In this way, the core values of humanity can be instilled in communities at the deepest level.

The humanitarian organizations must find their way not just through the theater of operations but also into people's minds. In turning to the sixteen distinguished authors who express their views in this work, the ICRC's chief objective is to fuel the contemporary debate on the impact of humanitarian responses in internal conflicts, stressing the ethical dilemmas and all the moral issues that these responses raise. Indeed, we felt that this was the right time to focus a rich variety of expert opinion on a subject of such topical relevance, given the scope of the changes that have occurred since the end of the Cold War. This diversity of viewpoints goes far beyond the ICRC's sphere of competence and therefore does not represent the ICRC's own position. But, on the threshold of the twenty-first century, the issues discussed here seemed universal and weighty enough to be compiled under the auspices of the ICRC, so as to highlight the contradictions they contain and the ways in which they interact. Here I would like to pay tribute to the invaluable and extremely thorough work done by the indefatigable Ambassador Jonathan Moore, whom we had the happy inspiration to enlist as coordinator and editor of this volume.

Involving as it does an ever-increasing number of players, the word *humanitarian* has become an all-purpose term that can be magical and deceptive by turns: magical when every possible virtue is attributed to it in cases of success, particularly in the eyes of diplomatic circles and the media, and deceptive when it is seen as being in collusion with particular political and strategic interests or as a smokescreen for a laissez-faire attitude.

Certainly the dilemmas of humanitarian activity go back a long way. Who should receive assistance, according to what criteria, and to what extent? Who should the war surgeon operate on first? Will the siting of such and such a food distribution point uproot thousands of families and thereby contribute to "ethnic cleansing"? Should victims be abandoned if violence goes beyond a certain limit? Most of these questions have a long history and have received a variety of responses, often contradictory. On the other hand, the most constant factor in the issues considered throughout this book is the intensity of those dilemmas and the frequency with which humanitarian organizations have had to deal with them. Such ethical dilemmas and moral issues crystallize at the time of major crises, such as those in Somalia, the former Yugoslavia, and the African Great Lakes region. Today extremely difficult moral choices arise from the complexity of the current environment and from the more comprehensive approach taken to the management of crises, in which political responsibility, military operations, and humanitarian action are now more interdependent than before. Hence, the need has arisen to establish a true partnership between the various players involved in crises, with due regard for their respective responsibilities and areas of competence, in an attempt to improve the overall coherence of crisis management. A purely humanitarian organization such as the ICRC knows from experience the value of complementary roles that are clearly understood: this is a decisive factor in gaining access to all conflict victims.

It is vitally important to identify the points of divergence as well as convergence that lie at the heart of this debate. This approach is necessary to broaden general understanding, strengthen the sense of responsibility, and thus help create a sounder conceptual basis that will allow us to take greater account of day-to-day realities and the challenges ahead. We must also remain vigilant to ensure that suffering does not become accepted as inevitable. Finally, it is important to incorporate the key elements of the impressive body of humanitarian experience acquired in recent years in a common awareness and a code of practice that are more widely shared by the principal players—the better to light the way out of chaos.

Introduction

Jonathan Moore

The purpose of this book is to contribute to the public discourse about humanitarian intervention in internal conflicts
by focusing more attention on moral considerations and their
own complexity. Behind this purpose lie two broad assumptions: that
moral reasoning is not adequately integrated into political decision
making and that when moral arguments are included, they tend to be
used in an unduly singular or exclusive manner. This book arrays a
variety of authors from different countries, experiences, and perspectives who contribute chapters reflecting on a variety of moral dilemmas involved in different interventions.

The whole phenomenon of humanitarian intervention has changed
radically and grown exponentially in recent years, as the preoccupa-
tions of the Cold War have given way to both the eruption of crises
within states and the inability of the international community to ignore them. These problems have become more complex, with their
horrible combinations of poverty, competition for resources, displacement, ethnic stress, power struggles, violence, and destruction. The
means used to deal with them are also more complicated, involving
various mixtures of humanitarian aid, development, diplomacy, embargoes, and security measures including the use of force. Humanitarian intervention in the most urgent cases is driven by multiple purposes and composed of multiple components, which cannot be kept
separate from one another in theory or practice. Clearly, many moti-

vations and objectives may lie behind these operations, which in itself immediately raises questions of moral trade-offs, but the intent to alleviate humanitarian suffering is prominent among them.

At the same time, the "international community" is confused and at odds with itself as to what to do in most instances where humanitarian needs are part of internal conflict. How narrowly or broadly, consistently or erratically will our individual and collective interests be defined and executed? How much will we substitute rhetoric for action, illusion for reality, timidity for courage, indulgence for restraint? What will our moral calculus be? For the moment, political will is vulnerable to shorter attention spans, there is more impatience and uncertainty, less consensus, and fewer resources. The needs remain greater than the capacity to meet them, and the size of the challenge is greater than the effective response of the multiple actions and actors. This situation, of course, places a special premium on the careful design and exacting implementation of any given intervention.

Moral factors do not lie apart from this clutter of complexity and difficulty. They are embedded, often discordantly; moral imperatives compete not only with more material and temporal elements but also with one another. This context then requires more commitment and sophistication to incorporate them in the deliberation that should precede and accompany such acts of intervention. In its intense preoccupation with immediate pressures, political decision making cannot afford to leave out moral energy and insight; neither can its inclusion be simple-minded.

This book attempts to encourage the accommodation of both idealism and realism, each informing and illuminating rather than pre-empting the other. It does so modestly, by inviting people concerned with humanitarian intervention in various ways to reflect on the moral dimension as current interventions are examined. It is not an academic book, but it is meant to be an educational one. It is more concrete than abstract, more analytical than doctrinal, and more inquiring than judgmental. Explicitly addressing morality is not easy and can be dangerous. Hoping not to be "moralistic," the treatment of various problems and remedies in these essays is based on moral search rather than moral certainty. The book is not ideological; it does not attempt to resolve age-old philosophical debates. It simply attempts to heighten understanding by considering moral questions and implications so that we might be more competent than confounded as we pursue difficult choices, especially when different moralities attendant to given challenges confront one another.

The authors of the essays in this volume were chosen to provide a wide variety of perspectives. Aside from some serious exposure to the subject matter, the only common characteristics sought were that each of them had an individual moral pulse of his or her own and that none were narrow-minded or soft-headed. The authors represented here come from a diversity of geography and culture, vocation, status, role, and exposure to specific interventions of different kinds, in different countries and at different phases. Not a rounding up of the usual suspects, this volume includes academics, lawyers, policy makers, religious leaders, military men, diplomats, NGO members, aid workers, and recipients. Few are writers by profession. Many were so currently engaged in interventions that their availability and accessibility were constricted. While working on their chapters, some suffered coups, gag orders, job shifts, serious illness, or cold feet. The book both captures a broad range of insights and at the same time makes the point that moral reflection must come at all levels and in all roles—not just from priests, moral philosophers, or policy makers, and not just in private but in the open.

The authors have each been asked to focus on a given set of issues, assigned according to expertise and experience as well as by the desire for the book to cover as much substantive ground as possible. They offer very different approaches. Some make choices, others lay out the options, some raise dilemmas, and others attempt to define the complexity that challenges action. Some are more philosophical, others more operational. Some criticize failures, others issue alerts. But all attempt in their own style to comprehend the moral dimensions and consequences involved, and all demonstrate the importance of combining this sensitivity with other knowledge, skills, and demands in the humanitarian interventions they are addressing. Collectively, they demonstrate the value of exercising moral imagination and awareness in dealing with the ambiguities of such circumstances and encourage the rest of us to do so. If they do feel that many humanitarian interventions are seriously flawed, they believe it important to try to improve them.

The book's first two chapters lay historical and theoretical groundwork. Pierre Hassner traces the evolution of earlier thinking about the morality of war and peace to his own thoughts about the contemporary construct of violence and intervention. Bryan Hehir analyzes new moral and political configurations in recasting the relationship of military intervention and national sovereignty. Kofi Annan then moves the book into the realm of practical experience in the third chapter, addressing the intervention and sovereignty issue from the perspective of United Nations peacekeeping.

The next four chapters examine the ambiguities of mixed interventions focusing on specific countries. Romeo Dallaire relates his experience as a military commander of U.N. forces in Rwanda during and after the genocide. Mohamed Sahnoun recounts the interactions of the local population, culture, and leadership with the humanitarian and military intervenors in Somalia. Colin Granderson analyzes the complexities of local political instability, economic embargo, civil-military relations, and human rights in Haiti. Mu Sochua tells the story of a woman and her family on the receiving end of international management of refugee camps, repatriation, resettlement, and elections in Cambodia.

Chapters 8, 9, and 10 focus on three policy arenas of intervention. Mary Anderson emphasizes the need for rehabilitation and development, for assistance providers to come to terms with the causes of emergencies. Ian Martin reveals the intense difficulties in protecting human rights amidst rebuilding and repatriation. Rony Brauman examines issues of refugees and displaced populations from an NGO perspective.

Chapters 11 and 12 look at how the international community and the countries so ravaged deal with war crimes and the aftermath of massive killing. Richard Goldstone discusses the tensions inherent in the imposition of justice prior to the establishment of peace, especially in the former Yugoslavia. José Zalaquett extracts some principles from the experience of several countries in their efforts to achieve reconciliation following prolonged periods of widespread official torture, disappearance, and murder.

The book's final four chapters address particular instruments of intervention. Larry Minear assesses the impact of sanctions. Roger Williamson analyzes the complications of dealing with weapons manufacture and movement. Elizabeth Reid identifies the unique problems of programs to combat the HIV epidemic. Michael Ignatieff concludes with an examination of television's mediating role between the world's safe and danger zones.

The chapters, all of which were written in the authors' personal capacities and completed before April 1998, are self-contained, each standing on its own. They achieve continuity and coherence by common subject, by a structure designed to accomplish an integrated treatment, by different ideas and perspectives focusing on the same phenomena—and by a degree of unplanned redundancy and overlapping. That themes reappear and points are reinforced throughout the book is reassuring, given our modest hope that such a diverse examination would result in something other than moral fragmentation.

A few examples of this convergence can be mentioned here—without relegation of the singular insights and differing views contributed by our authors.

Several chapters articulate and prescribe for the lost innocence of humanitarian assistance, its managers no longer able to easily operate alone or in a neutral manner. A shared theme appears that perceiving the truth, and speaking it publicly, is at least an important tool if not a sacred principle in dealing with ambiguous and competing forces, when ethical tensions are intense and ethical choices are murky; evading or obscuring the truth is felt to be a bad idea. The use of force in humanitarian interventions also unsurprisingly emerges as a key target of reflection here: none of our authors would ban it; some bemoan its absence; others criticize its inefficiency or insufficiency; others condemn its domination.

Frequently noted as well is the tendency of different entities—intervening governments, U.N. agencies, or NGOs—to behave in acquisitive, imperialistic, and programmatically aggressive ways, unmindful of the role and contribution of others and of their own limited capacity. Next is the repeated admonition for greater respect in interventions for the culture and contribution of the target country and peoples and for greater industry to be devoted to configuring the most redemptive working relationship between the outside and inside actors. There is some agreement that more time is needed for interventions to be successful, at least that their duration should not be arbitrarily confined.

Finally, in this short list, is the theme of constraint. Various authors emphasize the need, with regard to all facets of intervention, to be careful not to do too much or go too far lest the effort be counterproductive—lest programs collapse of their own overweening ambition or other interests, parties, needs or imperatives be wrongly harmed. And this priority explicitly includes the capability to withhold or withdraw the humanitarian action when the intervention does more harm than good.

In addition to such evident themes, to this reader there is a strong implicit signal, a moral clue, to be distilled from this volume. In its chapters a key commitment emerges to embrace the full complexity of the challenge, rather than to avert the admittedly appalling whole in favor of some narrower, partial vision or strategy. And there can be found three prerequisites, essential principles, to be served in order to consider humanitarian interventions in their complexity: understanding, integration, and pragmatism. These may be so basic as to be painfully obvious, yet our current history of humanitarian interventions reflects their paucity rather than prominence.

First, there is the need to understand as fully as possible what the realities are, the need to avoid making untested assumptions or relying on superficial information but to comprehend respectfully and seriously the interrelationships of the various forces and actors in play, and most of all to comprehend the situation in the country that is being targeted to receive the tender mercies of intervention. Second, it follows that the various elements of intervention—humanitarian, economic, political, military, multilateral, bilateral, regional, local— have to be mobilized and implemented together; they have to fit integrally for the maximum benefit and so that weak or missing links are avoided. Capricious or obstreperous factors cannot simply be banished; somehow they must be included, reconciled. Third, there is an inherent truth here that if all the best motivations, intentions, and policies cannot be put to work effectively, cannot be applied and implemented fruitfully, then their moral vitality is merely an abstraction, only a dream. To be moral is to be operational, one might say, and this pragmatic purpose requires compromise and flexibility.

These gleanings would seem to combine moral absolutism and moral relativism, not statically opposed but dynamically joined. The moral imperatives cannot be given or give life unless they are applied relatively, with respect and allowance for other absolutes and for the requirements of bringing into being. For the integrity of the ideal to remain intact, it should not be defined reductively by competition or context, but neither can it be exercised in a rigid or dogmatic way. And implementation requires the courage of moral interpretation, which we hope this volume will affirm.

1

From War and Peace to Violence and Intervention

Permanent Moral Dilemmas under Changing Political and Technological Conditions

Pierre Hassner

Beyond War? The Decline of the Interstate Model

No relationship is more paradoxical than that between force, in particular war, and morality. There is no society that does not threaten, and sometimes use, force against domestic and foreign enemies and that does not honor the heroism and sacrifice of those who have given their life fighting for it. Yet there is no society in which taking human life does not raise a moral problem, in which war does not need a special justification, whether based on religion, on the right or duty of revenge, or on the necessities of survival.

Of course, for most societies in history war was the central normal activity of men before becoming the *ultima ratio regum,* the last resort of kings. Of course, too, some thinkers and some ideologies have glorified violence and war, seeing in them man's noblest chance for greatness, or characterizing even modern politics as the continuation of war by other means.

This latter reversal of Clausewitz's dictum seems to fit the politics of the twentieth century, dominated by world wars and totalitarian revolutions, particularly well. Yet the long-term trend, brought about first by Christianity and then by bourgeois liberalism, seems to go in the direction of the outlawing of war or of its becoming obsolete as an institution and a means of acquiring wealth, domination, or fame.

Within societies, the process of civilization has consisted in progressively eliminating violent institutions—from slavery to the duel, through feudality and private armies—and establishing restraint as a norm for relations among citizens and by the same token the state as the only legitimate user of force. Today, the process seems to go further. On the one hand, wars of conquest have become delegitimized, and our moral sensitivity no longer accepts the horrors and destructions of war with the same fatalism as our ancestors. On the other hand, moral or idealistic pacifism has found a powerful support, as eighteenth and nineteenth century thinkers had predicted, in the spirit of commerce and industry, in privatization and interdependence, in the growth of individualism and globalization.

However, whereas war and revolution seem equally distant possibilities in the Western, developed world, elsewhere the most traditional conflicts over the succession of empires, the creation or collapse of states, ethnic hatred and fears, or, simply, the looting or displacement of populations seem to persist or even to multiply. The peaceful center itself is not immune to terrorism, especially of the ethnic or religious variety, and violence, especially as a reaction to immigration. Even more disturbing is that the less immediately or directly violent our democratic and individualistic societies have become, the more they seem at a loss in dealing with violent minorities at home and with violent conflicts abroad. What seems in question is their ability and willingness to run risks in order to stop inhumane violence as long as it does not take the form of a direct attack against themselves.

The question, then, is less that of conflicts between states than that of distance between societies. The difference in attitudes and problems between relatively stable or secure societies and others whose borders, unity, and identity are in question, or between societies in which law and order are more or less kept by the state and those in which they have collapsed under the action of particularistic transnational forces, makes it difficult for the former to understand and help the latter, even though, ultimately, both may be vulnerable to the same threats. This is only one example of the ambiguities of force in a world in which not only the opposition of the blocs but also the clear distinctions between the national and the international, between state and society, between the public and the private, between the political and the economic, the military and the civilian domains, between organized crime, civil war, and interstate war, tend to become blurred. In such a world, the more general concepts of violence and *conflict,* on the one hand, may be more useful than that of war. On the other hand, the structuring concept replacing that of war as "the continuation of politics by other means" is less one of deterrence, such as during the Cold War, than one of *intervention.* At stake is not so much the negative threat of an apocalyptic force to deter an unlikely attack against the national territory, but rather the effective use of limited force to stop distant conflicts characterized by anarchy as much as by aggression. This intervention is justified less by the immediate necessity of survival, or even by the dictates of national interest, than by the ambiguous and disputed imperative of universal principles or international order.

It is still above all the states that have to follow these imperatives, and the situation in which they are called to act is caused above all by the failure of other states. However, instead of the situation envisaged by modern political philosophers from Hobbes to Aron through Clausewitz and Weber—that of states imposing law and order domestically but free to wage war among themselves because of the absence of a superior international authority—we still have the states occupying center stage but increasingly challenged by the political reappearance of world community, on the one hand, and of domestic and transnational anarchy, on the other.

In a sense, this double development can be seen as a return to the Middle Ages, which, in turn, can be seen either as the reemergence of positive factors such as a universal community or at least legitimacy and of multiple types of actors and allegiances, or as the reemergence of precisely the private violence and the religious conflicts against which the modern secular state was invented.

Whether one adopts the more optimistic or the more pessimistic view, it does look as if a historic compromise had come unstuck.

After the multiple loyalties and conflicts, invasions and crusades, pirates and bandits, aristocratic duels and peasant revolts of the Middle Ages, both political thought and historical reality had reached a solution through division. The rise of the secular state, with its monopoly of legitimate force over a given territory, had put an end to domestic anarchy and religious wars; but, by the same token, the state, successor of the princes, which was the *defensor pacis* inside, kept the freedom to make war outside. The idea of a universal spiritual authority deciding whose cause was justified was replaced by modern public international law, based on the mutual recognition and voluntary agreement of sovereign states. It eliminated the traditional question of the *jus ad bellum,* or of the moral justification of war, in favor of the question of *jus in bello,* or of the rules limiting violence (e.g., the immunity of noncombatants) during war itself.

The contradiction between the rule of law within and the state of nature, hence of war, outside created a situation that, though violently criticized by Rousseau and Kant, could nevertheless be made relatively tolerable by the Clausewitzian primacy of political authority, the mechanism of the balance of power, the cooperation of great powers within the Concert of Europe, the acceptance of international hierarchy on the part of the small ones, and, finally, the fledgling and tentative acceptance of common rules and the banning of certain weapons and practices.

The French Revolution and Napoleon brought a powerful disturbance to this system, yet it can be said, by and large, to have persisted until 1914, and at least partially until the technological and ideological revolutions of our century. Some elements of it survive and may yet flourish today and tomorrow, particularly in Asia, which has been said to be reaching its Victorian age, that of rising empires and great power rivalry. But this system does presuppose a certain number of conditions that have become more than doubtful.

Militarily, it presupposes a professionalization of war, the distinction between armies proper and civilians or irregulars, the technological ability of the state to wage war against other states and to prevail over domestic resistance.

Morally, this system presupposes a double distinction between private and public morality, and between duties toward one's own community (one's state, one's subjects, or one's fellow citizens) and toward others. Lying and killing, forbidden to private persons, are permissible or mandatory for the defense of the country, for "reasons of state," for the national interest. Covenants are to be kept among states, but, according to Spinoza and Hegel, only as long as they correspond to the state's interests. One should add that historically, the system has implied a different morality for relations between great powers, between them and small states, and above all between legitimate states and other peoples, subject to slavery, colonization, or conquest.

Hence, the ultimate condition is political: it presupposes the existence of great powers, or at any rate of states capable of enforcing their joint or respective conceptions of order on their own territory, between themselves and toward external enemies, challenges, or victims.

All these conditions have changed, and with them the relevance of the traditional historical and philosophical wisdom incorporated in the Western state system has also changed.

And so has, to some extent, the Clausewitzian definition of war as an instrument of politics. Or has it?

What takes place is what I have called the dialectic of the bourgeois and the barbarian (Hassner 1996). It is the encounter between two types of societies. On the one hand is an essentially civilian, post-heroic society that relies on technology and, ultimately, economic power for the minimum use of force indispensable for its political interests and tolerable by its population. On the other hand are societies in which the subordination of force to politics, or the social contract itself, has been broken; in which the passions of cruelty and greed, fear and hatred, sometimes artificially provoked or manipulated by cynical power-hungry leaders with the use of modern means of propaganda, no longer are held in check by any ethical, legal, or political framework.

Of course, this opposition should not be construed as a simple black-and-white one, even less as permanent or fixed, least of all as a geographic division between a civilized West and a barbaric South or East. The two poles have both very important common features and no less important interactions, and possible role reversals.

Modern societies are less and less easy to mobilize for external war, which is on the decline anyway. But governments are not separated from the people, since their main preoccupation is a domestic one, and their use of force is conditioned either by the priority of avoiding casualties that would translate negatively in opinion polls and electoral results, or by their ability to create moods of fear or hostility in their own population toward domestic or external enemies, so as to silence criticism or revolt against their own failures. The authority of the democratic state is, in both cases, replaced less by old-fashioned militarism than by demagogic populism that may cater either to the people's desire for private tranquility and the refusal of sacrifice or to their feeling of insecurity and need for scapegoats.

Western societies, contrary to some fears expressed in the late forties and early fifties, have survived the Cold War without becoming totalitarian garrison states. They now face the challenge of surviving the post–Cold War era without, if not police states, at least repressive or authoritarian ones.

More immediate than these long-range speculations is the interaction between bourgeois and barbarian within the same society or across the borders between states and between center and periphery. This intersection is increasingly taking the place of classical confrontations between states. More than the rivalry between states, the problem of war and peace lies increasingly in the interaction, interdependence, and interpenetration between societies that are, at the same time, separated by economic, social, religious, or cultural differences within nations and continents, and across the borders between them. The international system is both more fragmented and more interpenetrated than before. Classical mechanisms of escalation and generalization through alliances are blocked (hence the difference between Sarajevo 1914 and Sarajevo 1992), but transnational forces and trends make the isolation of national societies impossible.

States are still at the center of the international system and are overwhelmingly the main possessors of destructive power, at least for the time being, but they are increasingly challenged by the transnational and domestic dimensions. The first has the double face of, on the one hand, what could be called "Trevi Transnationalism" (from the name of the European Union's Working Group on terrorism, radicalism, ecology, and violence) and, on the other, that of an incipient and nascent hesitant world community, which challenges state sovereignty in the name of world peace and justice. The domestic dimension, too, can be seen in terms of anarchic conflicts challenging the state's monopoly of power and the nation's unity, or as an increasing obligation to respect the rights of individuals and groups and to take the reactions of a more informed public opinion into account.

Beyond Violence? The Dilemmas of Humanitarian Intervention

What all these dimensions have in common is the decline of interstate warfare. Whether its successor will be violent anarchy or a restrained but disciplined force in the service of the world community fighting domestic and transnational violence, they all point to the declining utility of concepts such as war and peace and to the importance of controlling anarchic violence as the main task for an emerging world community.

Hence, they raise anew the classical problems of who decides to act, against whom, for what ends, with what means, and in what context. The moral and the practical (or, if one prefers the current philosophic terminology, the deontological and the consequentialist) justifications of action and inaction, and of military versus other, diplomatic or economic, means, will look different according to one's assumptions over institutions (global or international) and societies (anarchic or tyrannical). One can put it another way: the basic moral question is that of ends and of means. But in today's international relations the question of the identity of the moral agent or subject and that of the structure of international order take a special importance, and with it that of international institutions and political regimes. If the distinction between public and private morality or that between domestic rule of law and international state of war are no longer valid, or at least no longer decisive, does it mean that we are faced with a continuum of moral subjects from the individual to the world community, through groups, state alliances, and international organizations? Similarly, should we replace the war and peace dichotomy by a continuum of violence, from structural violence, exemplified by the lack of livable conditions; through private, domestic, social, and political violence; to war and genocide? By the same token, one can envisage a continuum of *intervention,* from indirect or lateral intervention exercised by the very way of life and consumption of developed societies; through direct intervention, positive or negative, verbal, diplomatic, or economic, administrative or judicial; to military intervention. The latter, in turn, may be aimed at protecting or assisting, deterring or compelling, overturning criminal governments or consolidating or managing collapsing societies. The term *intervention* can be limited to military interventions in a state without the approval of its authorities (Roberts 1996: 1159) or extended to actions carried out without coercion and with the consent of local authorities.

The term *humanitarian* in the notion of "humanitarian intervention" is itself open to a whole spectrum of interpretations. The broadest one includes any form of intervention against any form of human suffering, whether caused by flood, famine, war, civil conflict, or tyranny. The narrowest one implies staying away from the political and the military dimensions, from states and coercion altogether. It postulates that an intervention ceases to be humanitarian if its motives include a selfish calculus of economic or strategic interests, or if its means or consequences lead it to choose sides, to be selective among its beneficiaries, or, even worse, to threaten or inflict suffering or death in the name of protection and peace. None of these pluralities of definitions can be eliminated by an objective, clear-cut distinction such as the classical one of international and internal affairs. All have given rise to vigorous controversies that oppose various schools of thought and various practical experiences, with sometimes paradoxical results when the same humanitarian organizations alternatively blast governments for not intervening militarily, such as in Yugoslavia, or for doing so, such as in Somalia (Brauman 1991), or when they demonstrate the logical impossibility of the very practice for which they exist and for which their members risk their lives (Destheixe 1993). They are all the more pressing since the two opposite dangers of, on the one hand, laxity authorizing any imperial use of force in the name of humanitarianism and, on the other hand, puritanical narrowness, intolerant of ambiguity and leading to inaction, are only too real.

These polemics are all based on real dilemmas that concern moral legitimacy and practical effectiveness as much as semantic hairsplitting. The remainder of this chapter will try to explore these dilemmas rather than to solve them and will almost invariably conclude in favor of case to case pragmatism. But there is one distinction that, to this writer, should serve to establish at least a minimal consensus. It is that between *normal* and *extreme* cases. Although there is no absolutely clear separation between them, it is nevertheless true that the pervasiveness, complexity, and ambiguity of violence must not blind us to some massive realities that characterize our century and that can be apprehended only in terms of moral absolutes.

Rudolf Rummel (1995: 3) has pointed out that the number of people (about 150 million) who have been killed in cold blood by their own government far exceeds that of the victims of all twentieth-century wars, including both world wars and all civil wars (about 35 million). This startling finding can lead us to fascinating meditations about the economy of violence in our century, about the link among totalitarianism, war, and pharaonic development, especially if one accepts Rummel's interpretation that ties "democide" to absolute power and hence peace, domestic as well as international, to democracy. It can lead to hasty practical conclusions, such as justifying war to make the world safe for democracy or, on the contrary, to a radical form of pacifist anarchism, the magnitude of the crimes and dangers being seen as depriving any use of force and any government of any moral legitimacy.

One does not have to share any of these opposite conclusions, but one has to accept the insight of the German philosopher Karl Jaspers about the two twentieth-century interventions that put humankind face to face with extreme situations: totalitarianism and nuclear weapons. For the problem of intervention, they impose absolute limits to our moral reasoning, but in two opposite directions (Hassner 1991).

On the one hand, who does not recognize today that it would have been legitimate and desirable to intervene in the 1930s in order to overthrow Hitler, because of the monstrous nature and dynamic of his regime, leading to the extermination of Jews, Gypsies, and homosexuals? Nobody thinks that this extermination was simply a matter of internal affairs and that only Germany's expansionism toward other states was a valid motive to oppose it—by force, if necessary. On the other hand, who argues that the West should have launched a nuclear attack against Stalin's Soviet Union (who killed, according to Rummel, many more people than Hitler's Germany) in order to put an end to the Gulag? Does the horror of totalitarian oppression, or even of genocide, justify unleashing another horror, another genocide—those of atomic death—thus accepting the risk of destroying the planet and the certainty of killing the millions of victims one wanted to liberate? These two imperatives—the duty of intervention in front of totalitarian crimes and the duty not to start a nuclear war—would be impossible to reconcile in the extreme case when one would have to choose between humankind's physical annihilation through the Bomb and its spiritual destruction through totalitarian domination. This supreme and supremely hypothetical case does not concern us here as such. What does concern us, however, is its relation with the actual dilemmas of "normal" politics, in which extreme situations, such as genocide in Bosnia and Rwanda, keep reappearing and facing us with the limits of pragmatism and compromise.

For the political leader the whole problem is precisely how to avoid the extreme case by distinguishing, on the one hand, among degrees of tyranny or violation of human rights (the principle of nonintervention being legitimately cast aside only for the extreme case, close to the reality or the clear and present danger of either "democide" or uncontrollable violence) and, on the other hand, between forms of intervention and even forms of military action so as to achieve precisely what the extreme case makes almost impossible: a reasonable proportionality between means and ends, between risks and stakes.

Apocalyptically oriented minds, on the contrary, tend to focus on the extreme case and to question the very notion of normality and the authority of the institutions and the norms that rule over politics.

Without going so far, one must recognize that the extreme cases of genocide, on the one hand, and nuclear war, on the other, project their shadow on whatever exists in terms of common moral consciousness. They make a great contribution to the awareness of themes such as human rights and humanitarian morality. Through the effective or imagined experience of absolute evil, the individual is face to face with universality, that of morality and the fate of the human race and planet, beyond the authorities and communities, the divisions and the rivalries, of particular societies. Hence the idea elaborated by the French doctor Bernard Kouchner (founder of Médecins sans Frontières and, later, French minister for humanitarian affairs) and the philosopher André Glucksmann of an "ethics of extreme urgency" that would no longer leave it to states and ideologies to react against inhumanity, be it under the form of famine or torture (Bettati and Kouchner 1987: 17–22, 217–23).

It appeared fairly quickly, however, that, paradoxically, centering everything on evil ran the risk of leading to an angelism without borders. To reach suffering populations, one needs the agreement or tolerance of the states that are oppressing them; to twist the arm of recalcitrant states, one needs the engagement of other states or the acceptance of common rules. This engagement or agreement has to be negotiated politically, which makes it necessary to look for allies without, however, choosing among victims.

In short, one cannot totally evade either compromise or violence, or domestic and international law, or the states, their sovereignty and their power relations, their balance or their concert. John Stuart Mill (1859), in his essay "A Few Words on Non-intervention," is opposed to intervention, even in favor of a people fighting for self-determination, except in two cases: The first is counterintervention in order to oppose the intervention of another state that threatens to tip the balance in favor of one side in a civil war or in favor of a tyrannical government against the revolt of its people. The second is a civil war in which both sides are so equally balanced that their fight threatens to continue indefinitely and to jeopardize the very existence of the given society. The first case reminds us that the morality of intervention cannot be divorced from the international context and that civil war, outside intervention, and interstate conflict are hard to disentangle. The second raises, again, the specter of the extreme case, but this time it does not involve the total power of an oppressive government but the total stalemate of opposed domestic forces. Total paralysis or total anarchy, on the one hand, total tyranny or total "democide," on the other, are the extreme cases in which morality seems to make intervention imperative, and the only question is who should implement it and what means should be used.

The minimal consensus about "doing something" in the extreme case carries with it, however, an equally extreme counterpart—that of a maximum model, in which "the international community" would protect the physical integrity, the moral dignity, and the political freedom of all individuals. Certainly the logic of humanitarian intervention would point in that direction, as indicated by Bernard Kouchner's vision of the four stages of humanitarianism: (1) the Red Cross stage, strictly limited to relief of suffering and careful not to take sides and not to bypass existing authorities; (2) the "borderless doctors" trying to reach the victims, from Biafra to Afghanistan, even against the opposition of governments; (3) the new right of governments legally based on U.N. resolutions to intervene in order to open or guarantee access to the victims and their protection through "humanitarian corridors" or "safety zones"; and (4) intervention to free oppressed people from their tyrants. But this approach would presuppose a world government. It overlooks humankind's division not only in states but also in communities, whether religious, cultural, linguistic, social, or political, who can claim the right to maintain their identities, as long as they do not conflict with the rights of individuals and those of humankind.

Kant, the philosopher who gave the greatest priority and the most rigorous basis to the rights of man as a moral being and to the cosmopolitan point of view, that of man as an inhabitant of the planet, also emphasized the plurality of states and the value of diversity. Hence, he found it necessary to compromise between the unique legitimacy of the republican government and the prohibition against establishing it by force, as well as between the logical necessity of world government and the practical limitation to a loose alliance between states (Kant 1795).

Thus, from the point of view of both legitimacy and effectiveness, the duality between universalism and particularism and the possible contradiction between them, expressed in the fact that what may be just or merciful from the point of view of one state, group, or individual may be unjust or harmful to another, leads to unsolvable dilemmas, which are compounded when one confronts the relation between legitimacy and effectiveness themselves. We shall briefly examine them from the four points of view of ends, of means, of the identity of the actors and the structure of the context. But our main point is that, precisely, none of the dilemmas raised by one of these four dimensions can be managed, let alone solved, without taking into account the three others.

In examining the goals of objectives of humanitarian intervention, one has to distinguish between ultimate general goals and intermediate specific ones. At the first level, the word *humanity* itself points toward compassion and dignity, toward fighting physical and moral injuries to human beings. But a host of questions are immediately raised: Should the goal of humanitarian intervention be the positive but potentially indefinite one of aiding development and democracy? Or should it be the more modest and immediate, negative one of fighting the evils that jeopardize them, like famine and genocide, of ending or alleviating humanitarian catastrophes, whether natural or man-made?

Two aspects are involved here: first, the nature of the intervention—providing *assistance* or *protection;* second, its scale from three points of view: in terms of functional dimensions, space, and time. Should one stop a given massacre or famine, or should one see it as part of a complex situation that requires to be treated as a whole and attacked at its very roots? Should the objectives of intervention be local, regional, or global? Perhaps most centrally, should objectives be limited in time, in terms of emergencies removing an immediate danger, reestablishing a minimum of security and stability, and then letting the parties themselves carry on from there, part of the objective being, precisely, to give them a chance to take care of themselves rather than being permanently under assistance or control? Or should intervention, particularly by force, be only one element in a continuum going from relief to rehabilitation, from stopping the war to establishing a durable peace?

Common sense tells us that neither horn of the dilemma can be carried to its logical extreme, that isolated actions can make things worse in other respects, or in other places, or in the longer run, whereas trying to take on all the evils of the world at the same time is a recipe for inaction. Obviously the solution lies in compromises, trade-offs, and prudential judgment. But it is still useful to point at two general dilemmas for which the desirable direction may not be the one dictated by common sense.

First, emergencies (let alone long-range development) being more often than not complex, it would seem that the answer to complex emergencies lies in multifunctional interventions. As Weiss (1966: 1) puts it, "The United Nations increasingly deploys multifunctional operations that combine military, civil administration (including election and human rights monitoring and police support) and humanitarian expertise with political negotiations and mediations." This scenario obviously poses, as we shall see, practical problems of compatibility and coordination at the level of means. But at the level of objectives themselves, one could do worse than to listen to Haas's (1993: 77–78) warning, according to whom complex interventions are unlikely to be sustainable financially or psychologically or even intellectually, in the long run, and hence "ambitious multilateral coercion is wrong" because "to promise the unattainable is immoral."

But here a dialectic between ends and means obviously sets in. Who defines the unattainable? The two propositions "ambitious multilateral coercion is wrong" and "the immorality of ineffective multinational coercion" are equivalent only if "ambitious" means "ineffective." While Haas is obviously right against the verbal commitments not backed by serious intent, resources, or perseverance, of which recent crises such as Yugoslavia have given so many examples, what is at fault is the lack of adequacy between ends and means, objectives and resources. But is this gap to be overcome only by lowering the goals or by escalating the means or increasing the resources? Obviously it is a matter of priorities, and these priorities can change over time, the initial commitment becoming an incentive to persevere or to get more involved. This is the "slippery slope" against which Haas warns, with ample justification based on Vietnam as well as on the post-Vietnam syndrome. Certainly the intervenor—whether it be a state or an international organization—is both immoral and ineffective if it does not plan for the next steps in case of failure. But the intervenor would deprive itself of a powerful instrument if those it wants to influence were certain in advance that it will not increase both its commitment and its objectives rather than lower both.

Hence the second counterintuitive observation: although certainly, in principle, Christoph Bertram (1997: 141–44) is right to count the clarity of goals (along with an institutional framework, the availability of relevant means of pressure, the choice of the right moment, and a feeling of urgency) among the conditions of a successful multilateral intervention, there is a good moral use of ambiguity, just as Talleyrand said that a constitution should be short and obscure. This is all the more so to the extent that, as Bertram points out in spite of his insistence on the necessity of multilateralism, "the international community gets into existence only when a few states are ready to act together" (133). These states must obviously have a minimum of consensus, but (especially if this is not to be reduced to the lowest common denominator, hence in most cases to ineffective action) it must be an unspoken compromise between differing motives, agendas, or at least priorities.

But this point leads to an ambiguity even more serious than that concerning degrees of commitment and the choice of means. Obviously different states driven by different traditions, public opinions, and interests will have different solidarities and different incentives or criteria for intervention.

The latter will, therefore, seldom be based exclusively on objective criteria concerning the situation of the country in crisis. In particular, some of the so-called "Providence principles"—such as the principle of appropriateness and the principle of proportionality, according to which "humanitarian action should correspond to the degree of suffering, wherever it occurs" (Minear and Weiss 1995: 63)—and, even more, the calculus recommended by the French philosopher Paul Ricoeur (1994: 23–27)—which compares the amount of suffering alleviated with the amount of suffering inflicted in the process—will always be modified by the different priority assigned by governments and peoples, to human life and suffering according to whether they concern their fellow citizens or strangers, groups with which they have historical, cultural, and religious ties or not, or, of course, groups whose plight has been publicized by the presence of television.

It is, indeed, one of the main functions of international organizations, governmental and nongovernmental, and other moral authorities or opinion makers to try to redress the balance and plead for the priority of universal justice and brotherhood over special interests and ties. But if the universalistic point of view is to be the only legitimate one, if any intervention whose motives are partly self-interested is disqualified, the Pol Pots and the Amin Dadas of this world will stay in power as long as a "global humanitarian community" is not ready to act instead of the Vietnamese and the Tanzanians whose motives had little to do with the defense of human rights but who did rid the Cambodian and Ugandan peoples of their mad tyrants.

The interventions and noninterventions in Rwanda, Burundi, and Zaire between 1994 and 1998 are another example of the interplay between humanitarian and power politics, and of the need for the former to insert itself in the calculations of the latter if it wants to get a hearing, without sacrificing its message.

The question also arises of the means, of the identity of the humanitarian interventionists, and of the overall structure of international order.

As far as the morality of means is concerned, clearly persuasion is preferable to coercion, positive sanctions to negative ones, diplomatic pressure to embargoes and blockades, economic sanctions to war, warning shots or attacks on criminal leaders to indiscriminate bombing on their population. But it is no less clear that, in some cases, negotiation or persuasion cannot succeed without the threat or the reality of coercion, that the refusal or withdrawal of positive rewards can be perceived as a negative sanction, that economic sanctions can be effective in the long run rather than in an emergency, that they can do more unjust harm to more people over more time than a swift and timely military action, but that the latter can never be guaranteed not to lead to escalation or not to strike innocent victims.

The diversity of means (with the exclusion of some extreme ones) is, then, both desirable and inevitable. The question is whether they can be used at the same time, in the same place and by the same organs. Clearly economic assistance and economic sanctions do not go well together, any more than peacekeeping and peace enforcement. Many humanitarian organizations condemn the "state humanitarianism" defended by Bernard Kouchner. They would like doctors and humanitarian organizations to help the victims without compromising their neutrality by taking sides politically, governments to pursue their political interests without dressing them in humanitarian clothes, soldiers to be soldiers rather than nurses or police officers, the job of dealing with crimes against humanity to be left to the International Tribunal. Such a world would certainly raise fewer moral dilemmas than the real one. In the latter, however, though it is certainly desirable that the various missions using the various means should run in parallel but separately, humanitarian assistance may need military protection, and the interests of states include a more humane international order. Conversely, the humanitarian, the political, and the military, which sometimes can complement each other harmoniously, may also in other circumstances embarrass or jeopardize each other. At some points in some conflicts, ending the massacre must take precedence over alleviating its consequences. Finally, in some cases the various dimensions overlap.

Was stopping Hitler and the genocide a humanitarian, a political, or a strategic action? The answer is less important than the fact that lives were saved, crimes were stopped, and criminals were tried. Who achieved this result? Democratic powers, but allied with a criminal one and guilty themselves of criminal or antihumanitarian practices such as the terror bombing of German cities. And this point raises again the problem not only of means but of the authors of interventions.

Today, as compared with the World War II era, democracy and international organization have made huge progress; Russia is no longer a totalitarian country; the Hague Tribunal is morally more legitimate (if politically less powerful) than the Nuremberg one. Yet it does remain true that, even in the case of civil wars, intervention—whether humanitarian or political or both—may involve military force and that, by definition, force can be guaranteed neither to prevail militarily nor to remain clean morally. Unless the United Nations becomes a world government endowed with the monopoly of force that today escapes nation-states, can it intervene in ongoing conflicts without taking sides? Can it engage in a war, which means risking military defeats or at least setbacks, having its forces commit crimes, or at least involuntarily inflicting suffering on populations?

It does seem that, for the time being at least, the military task of international organization proper should be confined to preventive presence or peacekeeping and that coercion should be left to "coalitions of the willing" among states, for the sake not only of effectiveness but also of moral credibility. Yet, already today, the only generally accepted legitimation for the use of force is multilateral. The twin pillars indicated by Haas for justifiable intervention ("global moral consensus" and "reasonable effectiveness") or his three conditions ("multilateral authorization, probable effectiveness, good chance that it will not be abused") seem to be in potential conflict with each other. The United Nations seems to have the legitimacy and the states the effectiveness.

There are, of course, compromises. In the former Yugoslavia, it seemed at one point that only the Security Council could legitimize the use of force, only the United States could apply it effectively, and only the European Union could lead the reconstruction and integration that must follow military intervention if the latter is not to be counterproductive. Since then, the gap between the three dimensions has been partly bridged, at least temporarily, with NATO for all practical purposes replacing the United Nations and the United States getting more involved in a policing role on the ground. But delegation, subcontracting, authorization, and legitimation through mandate remain fragile bridges between several logics—that of universal law and morality, that of a concert of states, and that of the integrating and disintegrating dynamics of social and economic interdependence. These logics may be reconciled most of the time through compromise, but, as Max Weber recognized, situations arise when even the most prudent and responsible statesman has to make a radical choice and take an absolute stand.

We are back, then, to the contradictory character of international order in the present period. We are no longer in the interstate, Clausewitzian modern world. We are back to the medieval questions of legitimate authority, just cause, proportionality, and discrimination but without a pope and an emperor, although the secretary-general of the United Nations and the United States sometimes seem reluctantly and fleetingly to fill part of the two roles. And we are under the influence of globalization and modernization, which seem to heal old tensions and create new ones, to make classical war obsolete but a global, regional, and local police more necessary than ever.

In this situation, as Kant foresaw, a progress in moral consciousness is making its way as a consequence of economic and cultural
progress, but not enough to transform a solidarity of interest and,
sometimes, compassion into a real moral conversion that would eliminate violence. As he indicated through the three articles of his *Project
for Perpetual Peace,* hope lies in three directions that are distinct, and
sometimes conflicting, but basically complement each other: constitutional government, an alliance of states against war, and "cosmopolitan law" (i.e., universal hospitality) (Kant 1795). Politics continues
to be ruled by the self-interest of individuals and states, but awareness
of people's common dignity and basic humanity can increasingly
make a difference. Kant would have subscribed, as we should, to Hil-
lel's famous interrogation: "If I don't speak for myself, who will? But
if I speak only for myself, who am I? And if *we* don't speak up, who
will? And if not now, when?"

References

Arendt, Hannah. *On Revolution.* New York: Viking, 1963.
Aron, Raymond. *War and Peace.* New York: Doubleday, 1966.
Bertram, C. "Die Völkergemeinschaft als Konfliktverhüter." In *Frieden Ma-
chen,* ed. O. Senghaas Suhrkamp, 1997.
Bettati, M., and B. Kouchner, eds. *Le Devoir d'ingérence.* Paris: Denoel,
1987.
Brauman, Rony. "Contre l'Humanitarisme." *Esprit,* December 1991.
———. *L'Action humanitaire.* Paris: Flammarion, 1995.
Chaunu, Pierre. "Violence, guerre et paix." *Politique étrangère* 4 (Winter
1996–1997): 887–98.
Destheixe, A. *L'Humanitaire impossible.* 1993.
Haas, Ernst. "Beware the Slippery Slope: Notes towards the Definition of
Justifiable Intervention." In *Emerging Norms of Justified Intervention,* ed.
Laura Reed and Carl Kaysen. Cambridge, Mass.: American Academy of
Arts and Sciences, 1993.
Hassner, Pierre. "Devoirs, dangers, dilemmes." *Le Débat,* November–
December 1991, 16–24.
———. "Bürger und Barbar Gewalt und Krieg in Philosophie und Gesch-
ichte." In *Immanuel Kant und der internationale Frieden,* ed. E. Crome
and L. Schrader. Brandeburgische Zentrale für Politische Bildung, 1996a.
———. "Relations Internationales." In Monique Canto-Sperber ed., *Dic-*

tionnaire d'Ethique et de Philosophie Politique. Paris: Presses universitaire de France, 1996b.

————. *Violence and Peace*. Central European University Press, 1997.

Holst, Kalevi J. *The State, War and the State of War*. Cambridge: Cambridge University Press, 1996.

Kant, I. *Eternal Peace*. In *The Philosophy of Kant*, ed. K. Friedrich. New York: Modern Library, 1949. (Original work published 1795.)

Keegan, John. *A History of Warfare*. London: Hutchinson, 1993.

Mill, John Stuart. *"A Few Words on Non-intervention." Fraser's Magazine*, December 1859.

Minear, Larry, and Weiss, Thomas G. *Mercy under Fire: War and the Global Humanitarian Community*. Boulder, Colo.: Westview, 1995.

Mueller, John. *Retreat from Doomsday: The Obsolescence of Major War*. New York: Basic Books, 1989.

Ricoeur, Paul. Académie Universelle des cultures: *Intervenir? Droits de la personne et raisons d'État*. Paris: Grasset, 1994.

Roberts, Adam. *Humanitarian Action in War*. London: Adelphi Paper, 1996.

Rummel, R. J. *Death by Government*. New Brunswick, N.J.: Transaction, 1995.

Weiss, Thomas G. ed. *The United Nations and Civil Wars*. Boulder, Colo.: Lynne Rienner, 1996.

2

Military Intervention and National Sovereignty

Recasting the Relationship

J. Bryan Hehir

T he design of this book involves a formidable objective: the
study of intervention from the perspective of the moral conflicts and consequences posed by the decision to intervene in
an internal conflict of another state. Neither the history of international relations nor the expectations of moral theory provides encouragement about this topic. Theorists of world politics constantly return to the problem of the "logic of anarchy," which is the basis of
interstate relations, a world lacking both a common power and common security. Moral theory has long understood the gap between personal or societal behavior, on the one hand, and the competition of
states, on the other; the moral order should apply at all three levels,
but the logic of anarchy poses challenges of a qualitatively different
kind from other forms of relationships. That logic is particularly evident when intervention means military intervention, as it does in this
chapter.

Humanitarian Intervention: The State of the Question

The issue of military intervention has a long history in international
politics and a present status that is strikingly different from the past.

29

The historical narrative reaches back to Thucydides and runs with consistent logic through the religious wars of the sixteenth century, the balance of power politics of the eighteenth and nineteenth centuries, and the imperial politics of the twentieth century. The content of this historical narrative is crisply captured in Thucydides' commentary: "They that have odds of power exact as much as they can, and the weak yield to such conditions as they can get."[1] In this context intervention is about major powers, acting from reasons of interest, intervening when necessary in pursuit of their political objectives. It is a realist tale in which normative considerations of ethics or law are regarded as irrelevant.

The contemporary interest in military intervention (much to the dismay of realists) is driven by normative concerns. It is focused on the conflict of values—state autonomy versus state responsibility for human suffering—that a multiplicity of internal conflicts within states pose for world politics in the 1990s. The debate of this decade about intervention challenges the norm of nonintervention, but it does so cautiously, remembering not only the realist's fear that intervention disrupts the order of states but also the liberal's fear that intervention forecloses the exercise of self-determination by individuals and groups within states. Those pressing the contemporary debate about the ethics of military intervention do not have a secure theoretical home. Their proposals challenge both classic realist and liberal theory in world politics, and they seek to revise, reform, or overturn the prevailing norm of nonintervention in international law.

The realist perspective on intervention is determined by its classical concerns of security and order in the relations among states. These twin ideas yield the counsel that interventions should be rare, interest driven, and effective. The interest may be eliminating a hostile regime, stabilizing the balance of power, or maintaining discipline within an alliance, but it is always related to the permanent objectives of state policy. Intervention is too costly and unpredictable to be driven by compassion or commitment to normative goals that are rarely achieved or achievable in the games of states; intervention makes sense only in pursuit of self-interest, not as an instrument of universal goals or values.[2]

Liberal theory is not a secure foundation, either, for those seeking to revise prevailing norms of nonintervention. As Stanley Hoffmann has observed, "The issue of intervention for Liberalism turned out to be deeply divisive. Kant's scheme was resolutely noninterventionist— among liberal states. Mill saw a fundamental difference between interventions for self-government (which he rejected) and interventions for self-determination (which he endorsed). The gamut ranged from what we today would call isolationism on the one side to moral crusades on the other."[3]

The split in liberal theory is generated by two of its foundational ideas. On the one hand, it seeks to preserve autonomy and freedom, primarily of individuals but also, as one can see in the Michael Walzer of *Just and Unjust Wars,* the autonomy of states; intervention threatens autonomy and freedom. Yet, intervention can be a way to protect basic values and principles in world politics, an objective that distinguishes the liberal tradition in the history of international relations. Liberal responses to proposals to enhance the possibility of military interventions for normative reasons will not be as skeptical or resistant as classical realism, but they will likely be ambivalently supportive.

At the level of international legal theory and practice, Lori Fisler Damrosch, with support from Tom Farer, makes the point that "one cannot legitimize humanitarian intervention *while remaining within the idiom of classical international law*."[4] This is not to say that international law is devoid of foundation or resources that might lead to such legitimation, but it is a case to be made, not simply received from the legal tradition—even when it finds expression in the U.N. Charter.[5] In brief, neither the political theory nor the legal theory of international politics will yield a conclusion of the kind the contemporary debate on military intervention asserts.

The split between the historical and contemporary debates on intervention reflects the distinction Marc Trachtenberg draws between two traditions of discourse on military intervention. The first looked to instances of intervention in support of maintaining a secure balance of power among the major states of the system. Such a view of intervention, as noted earlier, is virtually indistinguishable from the story of Great Power politics. The second tradition, as Trachtenberg defines it, was about "imposing European values" on others; it had "to do with relations between 'civilized nations' at the core of the system and other states, viewed as less civilized, whose sovereignty was viewed as more problematic."[6] The contemporary debate is not about the balance of power, and it does not depend on the invidious distinctions of nineteenth-century colonialism, but aspects of both of these traditions find their way into the arguments of the 1990s. Focus is put on what the major powers should be expected to do or prohibited from doing, and there is a pervasive suspicion on the part of states and their citizens who were the "imposed upon" of the last century and who see the contemporary debate as a possible rerun of a past they thought would not be repeated.

Trachtenberg's distinction is not primarily a normative one, but it has a normative counterpart, which I have described in other writings as the difference between the moral and legal traditions of intervention.[7] The distinguishing characteristics of these two normative traditions involve their conception of political community, their understanding of the use of force, and their conclusions about military intervention. The moral tradition stressed the solidarity of bonds within the political community, the use of force as an instrument of justice, and the *obligation* of intervention as a *duty* of solidarity to those endangered or under attack. The legal tradition stressed the autonomy of states, the right to use force as an attribute of sovereignty, and the necessity of nonintervention as a principle of order in international relations.

Each tradition corresponded to an earlier conception of international relations (the medieval and modern systems, respectively), and they illustrate the need to develop normative prescriptions and prohibitions in light of the changing character of politics. The shape and structure of the international system do not by themselves produce a normative guide to intervention, but the system presents the historical context and the empirical challenge to which a normative theory must respond.[8] Moments of deep structural change in the system highlight the gaps, limits, and fragilities of norms that have not addressed the consequences of change. These same challenges of change often call for the creative adaptations of ancient principles to new configurations of power.

In retrospect, the sixteenth and seventeenth centuries appear as one of those fault lines in the history of international relations, marking a time of lasting change in the way the world is understood. It was at this time that three major figures in the moral tradition—Francisco de Vitoria, Francisco Suarez, and Hugo Grotius—struggled to adapt the moral doctrine of Just War to the new reality of the sovereign state.[9] The ending of the Cold War and the powerful processes of increasing interdependence and economic globalization converge to create a time of comparable importance in world politics. The Yale historian John Lewis Gaddis, whose work during the Cold War defined its character and logic, has made the following assessment about the passing of the Cold War era:

> We are at one of those rare points of leverage in history when familiar constraints have dropped away; what we do now could establish the framework within which events will play themselves out for decades to come.[10]

Military power holds the ambiguous role in world politics of being simultaneously the decisive threat to life and order and the instrument of protecting both. The determining factor of which role it plays lies with the political-moral vision that restrains, directs, and guides the use of force. In the era of Grotius and his contemporaries, newly sovereign princes resisted attempts to limit the purposes for which the *droit de guerre* was exercised, and the moralists turned their principal attention to setting limits on how force was used—an ethic of means. In contrast to this pattern of focusing on means but taking the ends of war as a given, the contemporary debate on intervention must return to the question of what moral purposes call states to use force, particularly in the difficult case of using force because of the domestic character of another state's conduct and policy.

From the normative perspective two characteristics of this contemporary problem need to be noted. First, the ethic of the use of force has been principally concerned with the conduct of states (or empires) in relation to other states; the literature is primarily an ethic of war, not an ethic of intervention. I will need to return to this distinction later in this chapter. Second, insofar as intervention has been part of the policy debate, neither the moral nor the legal tradition's view of intervention seems adequate for the contemporary dynamic of international politics.

The moral tradition's view of intervention was an extension of its ethic of war; it was an instrument of police power, and the tendency was to endorse intervention broadly. The legal tradition was shaped post-Grotius, and it held a highly restrictive position on the legitimacy of intervention precisely because the autonomy of sovereign states posed a threat of constant war if intervention was taken as normal or legitimate.[11]

Both traditions are reflected in the contemporary debate, but neither corresponds to the way the intervention question is posed in the post–Cold War order. The remainder of this chapter will seek to draw on both the moral and legal traditions to fashion an ethic and policy of intervention. Involved in this task is the need to ask why intervention has become so central in world politics, then the need to propose criteria for an ethic of intervention, and finally to determine the policy implications of such an ethic for actors in world politics today.

The Politics of Intervention

John Lewis Gaddis identified the significance of the transition from the Cold War to the post–Cold War international system, but the specific impact of this change for intervention still has to be defined. Debates about intervention have assumed an importance that they did not have during the Cold War, yet intervention was a pervasive fact of life during the era of bipolar competition. Cold War interventions were of the Great Power kind; they were not humanitarian in motive or purpose. The pattern of Cold War interventions followed a symmetrical logic. Within the sphere of influence of either superpower, interventions were a constant possibility: the Soviets in Hungary and Czechoslovakia; the United States in Guatemala, the Dominican Republic, Panama, and Grenada. These interventions were relatively risk-free because the threat of nuclear conflict made counterinterventions virtually unthinkable; the Soviet gamble at the time of the Cuban Missile Crisis left a lasting memory for both superpowers. The undefined problematic area during the Cold War was intervention in the "third world." From Nikita Khrushchev's declaration of the legitimacy of "wars of liberation" in 1961 to John F. Kennedy's promise "to pay any price" to resist them, the dynamic was initiated that led to vast havoc in the countries of the Southern Hemisphere and to major humiliations for each superpower in Vietnam and Afghanistan. These interventions were also of the Great Power variety, seeking advantage in a global contest by subjecting local conflicts to the larger struggle of ideology and power that defined world politics for forty years after World War II. Both superpowers sought to justify and legitimize these interventions, but neither the moral nor the legal traditions provided a rationale for them.

Indeed, the intensity of the ideological struggle left little time, energy, or moral vision for truly humanitarian intervention when it was needed. The lasting example of failure to address the humanitarian challenge when it arose was Cambodia in the 1970s. The conflict of Great Power interests in Southeast Asia meant that neither China, nor the Soviet Union, nor the United States was a suitable candidate to prevent the unspeakable destruction of a people and a society that was carried out while the world watched.

The Cold War pattern of power was so stark and clear that its sudden collapse has generated a plethora of proposals about what structure of power will finally emerge to replace superpower bipolarity.[12] The analysis differs about the kind of change expected in international relations as well as in the consequences predicted for policy makers. Following up on his original description of the significance of the collapse of the Cold War, Gaddis attempted an interpretation of world politics that focused on dynamics of integration and fragmentation at work in the international system.[13] This perspective on world politics stresses the transnational character of political interaction and moves away from a more traditional statecentric view. Samuel Huntington, long respected for his assessment of states and power, moved even farther away from the traditional model of analysis by locating the crucial dividing line of political analysis at the level of grand civilizations: "It is my hypothesis that the fundamental source of conflict in this new world will not be primarily ideological or primarily economic. The great divisions among humankind and the dominating source of conflict will be cultural . . . the principal conflicts of global politics will occur between nations and groups of different civilizations."[14]

Both Gaddis's and Huntington's moves change the focus and structure of political analysis; both have implications for thinking about intervention. Gaddis's view, with its stress on forces that cut across the life of states, promises a plethora of cases in which intervention will be a possibility precisely because disintegration will mark the life of some states. Huntington's prescriptions for policy would suggest caution about humanitarian intervention, not only because his realist instincts make him sensitive to questions of order but because his more recent preoccupation with cultural conflict makes him reticent to invoke any Western influences as a useful response to other civilizations.[15]

Other responses to the collapse of the Cold War have argued the necessity for a change in analysis from the past, but not so substantial a change in method of analysis. Henry Kissinger's prediction is a post–Cold War system of multiple centers of power in which traditional balance of power politics will prevail.[16] The world moves from bipolarity to multipolarity, and traditional concepts such as national interest take on renewed significance, but in a more complex setting than the nineteenth-century balance of power ever manifested. In light of his conviction about the direction of change in international politics, Kissinger is critical of those who would distinguish between strategic and humanitarian intervention and highly dubious of political or ethical arguments in support of humanitarian intervention as a staple of U.S. foreign policy:

> "Humanitarian intervention" asserts that moral and humane concerns are so much a part of American life that not only treasure but lives must be risked to vindicate them. . . . No other nation has ever put forward such a set of propositions.[17]

Dean Joseph Nye of Harvard's Kennedy School of Government sees a more complex pattern of relationships arising than Kissinger's shift from bipolarity to multipolarity. Power is a multidimensional reality today, which means that no single lens can capture the dynamic of world politics. The international system is irreducibly three-dimensional, containing political-military, political-economic, and transnational actors, each of whom contributes to the dynamic of world politics.[18] In this complex mix Nye identifies three possible forms of conflict: Great Power Wars (e.g., World Wars I and II), regional conflicts (e.g., the wars of the Middle East, particularly the Gulf War), and communal conflicts (within states). The third form of war, communal conflicts, is the one most likely to occur in the immediate future, and it is the one the international system is least ready to address.[19] These conflicts are precisely the ones that invite intervention. Unlike Kissinger, Nye does not take a position against U.S. involvement, but he lays stress on how rudimentary existing multilateral mechanisms are for addressing internal conflicts. The argument about complexity carries the hint of a warning about early, major, or frequent responses to such conflicts.

The positions surveyed here about how and why intervention has assumed such a visible role in policy debates are primarily political assessments, with none of the authors proposing moral arguments for or against intervention. But the mix of complexity and caution that mark most of the analysis points to a feature of the emerging order of international relations that has, in my view, decisive significance for an ethical analysis of intervention.

Each of these analysts seeks to plot the new distribution of power and influence in the world. While no unified theory is in sight, one characteristic that is decisively different than the Cold War order is the fragmentation of interests that already prevails today. The competition of the Cold War imposed an artificial but influential unity on the world, making every region and almost every country an asset to be "won" or "lost" in the Cold War struggle. The idea of a unified theater of competition was contrived, and trying to secure superpower interests led to some disastrous policies, but there was a sense among the major powers that no area fell outside the scope of their interests.[20] The competitive quality of the Cold War led to a language of duress and necessity for policy: if one's interests were not global, a price would ultimately be paid.

The fragmentation of power (among actors and issues) in the emerging system has dispelled the conceptual unity that gave Cold War politics a tight inner coherence. One need not be nostalgic for

the previous model to recognize that in the emerging system large
parts of the globe may be very distant from the interests and attention
of major powers. If one alters Joseph Nye's three-dimensional world
just a bit, the following pattern of politics and interests emerges. First,
a circle of Great Power interests and relations: China, Russia, the
United States, Europe, Japan, and the Middle East. Second, a sphere
of tight economic interdependence: Europe, Japan, the United States,
and East Asia—with China a certain future participant. These two
circles involve at most sixty countries. The third circle—containing
Nye's communal conflicts—involves over a hundred countries that
are more or less related in some fashion to the first two. But the relationships to the third circle do not have the Cold War character of
necessary linkages that one must address. They are much closer to
relationships of choice, not necessity. Hence, the degree of engagement on issues as diverse as economic relations, human rights, foreign
assistance, and political ties will depend on the vision that informs
the policy of major states.

The relevance of this dynamic to intervention illustrates the new
setting for this issue in world politics. The usually vulnerable states
of the third circle have been major supporters of the nonintervention
principle, since it was seen as a hedge against imperialism. The perception was accurate and remains a valid reason to be cautious about
reshaping the principle. But the post–Cold War system may not be
primarily threatened by imperialism. The first decade of the new
order of power has witnessed two genocidal conflicts (Bosnia and
Rwanda) in which even the traditional exception to nonintervention
(the fact of genocide) did not stimulate effective international action.
The danger of political, psychological, and moral disengagement as a
premise of policy may be as much of a threat to the third circle as a
new brand of interventionary imperialism.

Disengagement is not old-fashioned isolationism; such a posture is
virtually impossible in the interdependent character of the modern
world. Disengagement is selective, purposeful, and varies among issues and parts of the globe. Disengagement can establish a foundation
for policy that would make humanitarian intervention very unlikely.
The contemporary debate about humanitarian intervention is driven
by the twofold sense that Nye's prediction about communal conflict

is accurate, and disengagement by the major powers of the world could be as devastating as imperialism ever was.[21] Because political arguments about interests are unlikely to address this threat of potential disengagement, the ethical arguments about humanitarian intervention are an alternative source of policy guidance. Alone they will not alter policy, but as a dimension of the policy debate they may help put humanitarian intervention in a different perspective than existing patterns of power yield.

The Ethics of Intervention

If normative arguments about intervention are to have any influence on policy choices about intervention, two requirements must be met: first, a clarification of what an ethic of military intervention ought to say in the conditions of the post–Cold War era; second, an examination of how the structure of the ethic of intervention should relate to the substance of policy choices. It is useful at this point to return to distinctions invoked earlier in this chapter, primarily the distinction between the moral and the legal traditions of intervention; these constitute two stages of development in normative thinking about intervention. Both seek to limit and restrain, yet they use force in the world when it will act as an instrument of justice in the service of protecting human life and social order. But they reach different conclusions, partly because of the political context each tradition sought to shape and direct. The moral tradition is interventionist in the sense that it lays stress on the duty of public authorities to act in the face of aggression and injustice. The legal tradition—confronted with newly emergent sovereign states—saw greater danger in legitimizing the use of force than in ignoring evil within other societies. It takes historical perspective to surface this tension within the normative tradition on intervention, because the legal position is securely in possession in the twentieth century. Drawing on the Westphalian legacy in international relations theory (with its strong stress on protecting state sovereignty as the foundation of the political order), along with the dominant position in positive international law (which developed from the seventeenth century) and the institutionalization of the legal perspective in the U.N. Charter, it is accurate to portray the prevailing ethical position as that embodied in the norm of nonintervention. While the rationale sustaining the norm is a pluralist position, the conclusion derived from it rules out intervention in the internal affairs ("domestic jurisdiction") of other states except for the case of genocide.

The pluralist rationale corresponds to three different functions the nonintervention norm has fulfilled. First is the Westphalian emphasis on prohibiting intervention in order to reduce or prevent conflict among major states; the objective arose as a necessity to halt the interventionary pattern of war rooted in the sixteenth-century wars of religion. Second, what might be termed the liberal emphasis seeks to prevent intervention in the name of protecting self-determination and/or communal autonomy. Third, the anti-imperialist or postcolonial emphasis seeks to prevent the subordination of small states to the policy interests of major powers. The rationale of the nonintervention norm, therefore, reflects the experience of diverse moments in the history in international politics since the sixteenth century. What ties these diverse themes together is the objective of containing the actions of powerful states that acknowledge no supreme authority.

In contrast to the moral tradition's emphasis on the duties of political authorities to exercise care for the common good, the legal tradition saw its primary objective in preventing actions undertaken to pursue state interests without regard for the rights of lesser powers. Although they frame the question in different fashion, both the Trachtenberg and Damrosch articles reflect the tension expressed here as the moral versus legal traditions. Trachtenberg begins with a generalized norm of nonintervention, then traces two exceptions to the norm: interventions to support an existing balance of power and interventions "to correct" the cultural or political practices of nations outside the orbit of European diplomacy. Damrosch focuses on the differences between seeing intervention as unilateral action that must be restrained and as positive collective actions that should be mandated. The latter is precisely what is at the heart of the moral tradition, but conceptions of sovereignty, cultural and religious pluralism, and national interest make direct transposition of the moral tradition impossible today. The legal tradition, however, has its own limitations; in a world marked by the degree of socioeconomic and political interdependence that the contemporary system exhibits, a normative vision governed *only* by the maxim "Do no harm," understood as restraining state action, fails to address the most likely source of conflict—within states—that faces the world today. Writing only about the legal tradition, Damrosch notes, "The term 'intervention' not only lacks a shared meaning but invites profound normative confusion."[22]

In my view, one way to define the potential for confusion is to distinguish between the problems of Great Power interventions and the problem of humanitarian intervention. The legal tradition has built a strong, if still breachable, wall against Great Power interventions, combining arguments of self-interest (which realists support) with arguments of respect for others (which liberals support) under the rubric of nonintervention. The term *Great Power* has an anachronistic ring to it and some invidious overtones. In the most recent period of world politics, it had been supplanted by the category of "superpowers." Signs indicate, however, that the end of the superpower conflict returns the world significantly in the direction of the Security Council assuming the "Great Power" role. One need not endorse the return of the language to admit the need to think in the logic of Great Power relationships. One fundamental restraint needed is what the tradition of nonintervention supplies. There is clearly a need to reinforce the triple prohibition that governs Great Power actions. The normative confusion, which Damrosch rightly identifies, arises when the logic of restraint is then extended to the problems posed by communal war, civil conflict, and humanitarian intervention as a response to them. Trachtenberg struggles with this question, not primarily in legal but political terms, and concludes that "no firm legal principle separating 'legitimate' from 'illegitimate' intervention has yet emerged in the post–Cold War period,"[23] thus leaving the boundary between humanitarian and other forms of political intervention undefined.

Damrosch, Trachtenberg, and I agree on the state of the question, but we move in different directions to resolve the normative confusion. The paths are not incompatible, but different resources are used and different conclusions emphasized in the search for a political and normatively coherent position. Damrosch seeks resolution by an effort of reinterpretation of the legal tradition itself.[24] Trachtenberg stresses the importance of a politically systemic view of the function of intervention, stressing that "the sole test of the legitimacy of intervention should not be narrow, apolitical and legalistic."[25]

I propose to support the three purposes of the nonintervention norm found in the legal tradition and then to revise the norm using the principal resource of the moral tradition, the just war ethic. Although this normative theory was designed primarily to legitimate and limit some forms of conflict between states, its structure of reasoning can be used analogically to provide criteria for "just" or "legitimate" intervention. Contemporary theorists of the just war tradition begin with a presumption against the use of force, then specify conditions under which the presumptions can be overridden as a morally justified exception. The exceptions are defined in terms of the criteria of the just war ethic, broadly summarized as *jus ad bellum* (defining conditions under which force can be used) and *jus in bello* (defining how force is to be legitimately employed).[26]

In previous essays, I have sought to adapt this structure of reasoning to the intervention decision.[27] The position laid out elsewhere and summarized here has an implicit premise that should be made more clear than I have in the past—that is, that although war should never be easily justified, it should be even more difficult to justify intervention. This premise seeks to acknowledge the wisdom of the legal tradition's concerns about intensifying interstate conflict as a consequence of legitimating some forms of intervention.

The premise leads to the first step in an ethic of intervention: the presumption of the moral position is noninterventionist. The conclusion of the legal tradition should be in possession. Several reasons support this move: the enormous disparity among states in terms of power, wealth, and influence highlights the need for norms that seek to limit such disparity without any illusions that the playing field of international politics can be leveled; intervention has historically been open to the kind of rationalization by major actors against which the realist tradition constantly warns; finally, a presumption against intervention will strengthen other restraints in the ethic, such as the requirement of last resort. While the foundation of the ethical argument reaffirms the legal tradition, it does so in a way that foreshadows the possibility of change. A presumption is not an absolute rule; by definition it is open to morally justifiable exceptions that reverse the weight of the presumption when it fails to address morally compelling characteristics of a situation.[28]

The legal tradition acknowledged one clearly defensible exception: genocide. As noted earlier, however, it did not include humanitarian intervention in the same category. The basic revision of the legalist tradition proposed here is to expand the first category of the *jus ad bellum*, "just cause," to include a broader range of exceptions than genocide. Once this move is made, a multiplicity of possibilities arise for consideration as justifying causes for humanitarian intervention. Beyond genocide, the recent experience in Bosnia with "ethnic cleansing" highlights its proximity to genocide and its weight as a just cause; similarly, the phenomenon of "failed states," a newly minted term of art that identifies a situation in which sovereignty has collapsed within a country, also qualifies as just cause. The reasoning in both of these cases rests on the nature and extent of human rights violations and killing that have accompanied both ethnic cleansing and failed states.

To illustrate that not every proposed exception should be approved, however, I raise the generic term *human rights*. To some degree, as Damrosch notes, it is the logic of the human rights regime in the U.N. Charter and its supporting texts that provides the foundation for a more interventionist international system. While the charter protects "domestic jurisdiction" in Article 2 (7), it also challenges the notion by legitimating international action on behalf of human rights. Without question, therefore, any form of human rights violations within a state should generate response from the wider international community. In the last twenty years the idea, elements, and strategy of such policies have been a focus of both state action and especially the work of nongovernmental organizations.[29] They are not, ipso facto, however, a cause for military intervention. Although it is true that human rights violations are the core of both genocide and ethnic cleansing, it is also true that the language of human rights is used to identify abridgement of religious freedom, freedom of speech, press and assembly, the right to strike and so forth; in my judgment, the scores of regimes throughout the world that could be properly criticized for these abuses should not be targets of military intervention. The presumption of nonintervention trumps human rights claims when the action is military, but not when it involves political or economic strategies to overcome human rights violations. It is the sad but clear fact of how broadly distributed human rights violators are in the community of states that provides a crucial guideline in this moral calculus. To legitimate military intervention on human rights grounds alone would essentially eliminate the restraint of the nonintervention norm.

One of the strengths of the just war ethic is its systematic character; each of the criteria stands alone, but all must be tested together. It is this dynamic that comes into play when the case is made to expand the reasons for intervention. Among the *jus ad bellum* categories, just cause is closely linked to "proper authority" (i.e., who has the right to undertake the use of force). The purpose of this criterion in the ethic of war is to rule out vigilante activity within states; only a legitimate sovereign state has the right to take up arms. Transposing the authority question to intervention yields a different focus: which sovereign state has the moral and legal right to intervene against another state? In this proposal for an ethic of intervention, the logic at work asserts that expanding the reasons for intervention should be joined with restricting carefully who has the right to intervene. Restraint is achieved by requiring some form of multilateral authorization for any humanitarian intervention to be legitimate. The process of legitimation must be set by the standards of the U.N. Charter, but it would be useful to have several levels of possible authorization lest the United Nations simply be paralyzed by these cases. Precisely because there is such an historical memory of how intervention has been used by Great Powers, there is added value in having regionally based institutions take responsibility for authorizing intervention in their area. Candidates include the Organization of American States (OAS), the Organization of African Unity (OAU), and the Organization for Security and Cooperation in Europe (OSCE). A final distinction that should help the move from normative standards to policy choices is that requiring multilateral authorization for intervention does not lead inexorably to multilateral implementation. The authorizing function is designed to clarify the necessity and purpose of invoking the use of force; it is a hedge against intervention for purposes devoid of normative content. But the institutions that can fulfill this critical function may not be equipped for effective action and may need to designate a state or a coalition of forces to undertake intervention.

The authorization process is in turn tied to two other *jus ad bellum* criteria of the just war ethic that are useful norms for intervention: right intention and last resort. Right intention refers to the inner logic and purpose of policy—as opposed to what might be the *declared purpose* of an action. In a sense, the role of multilateral authorization outlined earlier might be summarized as clarifying the intent of those proposing military intervention. One test of both right intent and the absolute need of using force is the "last resort" criterion, which requires that all reasonable means have been exhausted before military action is mandated. The last resort criterion is a complex element in the policy process. It has an indeterminate quality, less open to evaluation than just cause, since prudential arguments can always be made that "one more" effort short of war is needed. To use Michael Walzer's critique of last resort:

> War as a "last resort" is an endlessly receding possibility invoked mostly by people who would prefer never to resist aggression with force. After all, there is always something else to do, another diplomatic note, another meeting.[30]

Strategically, critics of last resort argue that it deprives enforcers of norms with the element of surprise or tactical advantage, or it can mean that intervention is delayed until its effectiveness in preventing harm is seriously diminished. Finally, the instrument of choice in implementing last resort is usually some form of economic sanctions. These measures do fulfill the role of postponing the use of force, but they also often directly impact the most vulnerable groups in the society being sanctioned; sanctions are seldom able to be targeted so precisely that civilians are protected from their impact. In spite of these empirical and ethical objections to last resort, to omit it as one of the tests of intervention policy is to erode the nonintervention norm by failing to highlight the qualitative significance of passing from political and economic measures of constraint to war as an instrument of policy.

The *jus ad bellum* criteria of the just war ethic establish the moral basis to invoke the use of force; the *jus in bello* criteria set limits to how force can be used even in pursuit of justifiable purposes. The two principles that shape the *jus in bello* are noncombatant immunity and proportionality. The first rules out direct attacks on civilians; the second requires that any tactic in the use of force be assessed by the harm done and the good it seeks to achieve. Together these principles are meant to direct and contain the use of force, so that only those committing crimes are killed or restrained and the consequence of resorting to military means is not to cause more harm than good.

Given the destructive nature of modern technology and the difficulty of protecting civilians in situations that require intervention, the *jus in bello* criteria are essential to any judgment about justified intervention. They too must be related to another criterion in the just war ethic: the possibility of success. This criterion seeks to restrain useless or hopeless military enterprises. It does not require a guarantee of success, but it does demand an assessment of ends and means in both ethical and tactical terms, lest military measures be undertaken that can only succeed at the price of violating proportionality or noncombatant immunity. Two recent cases illustrate the way in which these criteria of ends and means play into policy choices. In the case of Bosnia, many in the policy process were hesitant to commit forces to the Bosnian conflict because of different judgments: either a concern that it would be an endless struggle without effective resolution or that the introduction of sophisticated military technology would enormously increase the suffering involved. In Rwanda, a still pertinent critique of outside powers is that an early use of proportionate force could have prevented genocide, but lack of will prevented this action. In one case fear of failure restrained action; in the other the moral criteria highlight the cost of failing to act when success and proportion seem achievable.

The cases illustrate how the moral principles act as a test of policy, a restraint on policy, and/or a catalyst for policy. The interpretation of the moral principles proposed here would change the political-legal understanding of what constitutes justifiable intervention, but it would not dispense with the norm of nonintervention as a basic standard in international relations.

The Policy of Intervention

If moral principles and values are to have an impact on history, they must be embodied in policy choices. John Courtney Murray, S.J., described policy as "the meeting-place of the world of power and the world of morality, in which there takes place the concrete reconciliation of the duty of success that rests upon the statesman and the duty of justice that rests upon the civilized nation that he serves."[31] The argument advanced in this chapter, that the moral criteria for humanitarian intervention should allow for an expanded doctrine of legitimate intervention, must influence several "publics" if it is to be effective. These include international relations theory, international law, the policies of states, and the mandate for international institutions. It is, therefore, necessary to conclude this essay with a sketch of the policy components that an expanded doctrine of humanitarian intervention would require for effective implementation.

Both the structure and dynamics of the international system today and the experience of the 1990s point to the necessity of a policy framework that includes three kinds of agents: international institutions, states, and nongovernmental organizations (NGOs). Representatives of each category have been significant players in the intervention cases of the 1990s, and the diffusion of power in world politics today, along with the redefinition of interests, points to the need for a policy framework that somehow includes these three types of international actors. What follows may best be described as notes for a coherent policy conception of humanitarian intervention.

The role of states in shaping an effective policy is without question still the key political issue. Although the debate among theoretical perspectives regarding the changing role of the state in world politics is alive and well, no major position disputes the comparative advantage of states over other actors. The potential of states regarding humanitarian intervention can be assessed at two levels: the role of major states ("Great Powers") taken as a group and the specific role of the United States. In a comprehensive essay on the changing nature of "The Politics and Ethics of Military Intervention," Stanley Hoffmann makes two fundamental comments. The first is in the form of a normative assertion: "The concept of the 'national interest,' most often cited by opponents of intervention as ground for inaction, should be widened to incorporate ethical concerns."[32] The second is for Hoffmann an empirical question: "Will the 'top of the hierarchy' " shape up, so to speak, and act as a kind of steering group, of the sort that existed in the days of the European Concert or that was assumed by the drafters of the U.N. Charter?"[33] Both of Hoffmann's comments highlight the difficulty of shaping a coherent policy framework.

Neither the experience of the Bosnian saga nor the abject international failure in Rwanda point in the direction of a broadly conceived national interest among any of the Great Powers. The first case yielded clashing conceptions of how to relate the national interest to a complex, violent disaster in the heart of traditional Great Power diplomacy. The second case illustrated the power of psychic denial and political disengagement that characterizes the policy of major states when it comes to situations of massive human suffering devoid of classical power significance. Both cases illustrate the difficulty of establishing a convergent conception of interests and a coordinated policy among major states. Although this is a general statement, it is particularly evident in the area of intervention. Russian concerns to control policy in the "Near Abroad" where possibilities of internal conflicts are very high combine with the quite rigorously Westphalian conceptions of Chinese policy to make consensus among the Great Powers virtually impossible. But three years of debate among NATO partners on Bosnia illustrated that the former communist giants are not the only obstacle to a consensus on humanitarian intervention.

The United States provides a glimpse into why the Western states are finding humanitarian intervention so difficult. The 1990s have witnessed three distinct moments in U.S. policy making. The first was President Bush's classically Westphalian distinction drawn between the moral-legal imperative to reverse Saddam Hussein's aggression in Kuwait and the argument that his oppression of Kurds was an issue beyond the proper concerns of other states. Only public outcry—domestic and international—produced a reversal of U.S. policy. The second was President Clinton's early endorsement of a multilateral policy as the principal way through which the United States would contribute to specific instances of humanitarian intervention. The third was Clinton's retreat from an activist role in light of domestic reactions to U.S. losses in Somalia.

Beneath the variations of policy lie unresolved elements of U.S. policy. First, clarity is lacking politically about the U.S. role after the collapse of communism; both official policy and broader commentary manifest alterations between unilateralist instincts and sporadic indications of multilateral conceptions of the U.S. role. Second, debate, rooted in the Vietnam era then reshaped by the Gulf War experience, remains unresolved about how military power should be used. A stream of ideas—the Weinberger criteria for U.S. intervention, the Powell Doctrine on the massive use of force, the Christopher guidelines for "exit" policy—have produced a policy construct that makes the use of force for anything short of U.S. vital interests very unlikely. There are many reasons to endorse this reserved attitude on the part of the remaining military superpower, but one troubling aspect is that most instances in which military intervention may be the only way to prevent human slaughter will not be cases threatening a U.S. vital interest. Third, the lack of a domestic consensus on U.S. policy reinforces political uncertainty and strategic reserve. The domestic opinion is not well described as consistently opposed to U.S. involvement in humanitarian interventions; responses to suffering often generate calls for effective U.S. action. But public opinion is volatile; it does not provide a stable point of reference for policy makers. The volatility reflects a less than clear consensus about the costs, complexity, and time frame that play into a decision to intervene in civil conflicts.

These three factors—politics, strategy, public opinion—are thus related to how the U.S. and the other Great Powers understand their relationship to multilateral institutions. Although several organizations fit under this title, the United Nations is the best illustrative example precisely because of its status and because its charter in Article 2 (7) reflects the legal tradition's noninterventionist position. The complexity of the total position of the charter has been noted earlier—namely, that the combination of the human rights norms of the United Nations plus creative use of Chapter VII provides the basis for a range of interventionary activity. The ethical argument made in this chapter presumes the Chapter VII justifications for intervention and seeks to add to them situations internal to a country that might not be a threat to international peace and security, but still require inter-ventionary action. The ethical argument seeks to expand the bound-aries of the legal case made in Chapter VII.

At the policy level, however, the issue of legitimation of an action or a strategy must be joined with its possibilities for effective imple-mentation. The Cold War era severely curtailed the ability of the United Nations to function in accord with its charter. The end of the Cold War and the authorizing role the United Nations played in the Gulf War catalyzed a rising sense of expectations concerning the role of the organization. In retrospect, and with a touch of irony, one could note that both Bill Clinton and Boutros Boutros-Ghali shared an expansive vision for the U.N. role at the beginning of the decade. Part of the experience of the decade since the end of the Cold War has validated these expectations. From Central America to southern Africa to the Middle East, the United Nations has been an effective agent in helping the transition from war to peace in situations that were a combination of internal conflict and Cold War competition.

It is equally true that expectations and assignments given to the United Nations in the 1990s outran its capacity for effective action. The purpose here is not to write a balance sheet for U.N. activity but to return to the question of a framework for an effective policy of humanitarian intervention. Such a policy requires the United Nations to play multiple roles: as an authorizing agency; as a forum in which the debate on intervention can preserve the wisdom of the noninter-vention principle and yet not paralyze the international community when it is confronted by aggression, injustice, and conflict; finally, as a coordinating body in which some division of labor can be worked out that gives the international community a long-term capacity to address humanitarian intervention.

The United Nations can play these multiple roles only if there is a conception of state policy, among the Great Powers and beyond them, that explicitly incorporates at the conceptual and operational level a much expanded sphere of collaboration between states and the United Nations. This is another version of the plea to move beyond a "statecentric" conception of policy and security. It would maintain national command and control but allow for specific measures of joint action, particularly focused on humanitarian intervention. The proposal here is for a process of policy planning and cooperation that is less than a standing U.N. force but more than the *ad hoc* coalition that fought the Gulf War, then had little substance after it.

The final piece of a policy framework is the role of NGOs. Their significance in the politics of the 1990s is rooted in what Samuel Huntington has called "the transnational revolution,"[34] the growth in the last fifty years of transnational actors in world politics. These institutions—based in one place, functioning in several countries with a single guiding philosophy, skilled personnel, and sophisticated communication and management capabilities—have proliferated, flourished, and now exercise a substantial impact on the domain of state politics. The dominant form of transnational activity is either through international institutions or through corporations, but the last twenty years have evidenced the multiplication of institutions committed to issues of human rights and humanitarian concerns. In many ways the International Committee of the Red Cross was a prototype of these more recently founded institutions.

Although many of these agencies grew and developed a network of significant activity during the Cold War, they were by design and purpose nonpolitical in their character and function. They had to find space to work within the context of the superpower competition, often in countries where the big powers used proxies to carry on their conflict. In the post–Cold War setting, the partial disengagement of the Great Powers from conflicts in failed or failing states and the inability of the United Nations to fill the vacuum have drawn the NGOs into a realm of activity of a more political character than their original mandates called for. Sometimes the political dimension is simply that the NGOs have been the voice calling for action by states and international institutions, including, at times, military intervention. Alternatively, the political action may take the form of NGOs being left alone to mediate between warring factions, both in search of goods, services, or support that they believe the NGOs can provide.

It may be that this more recent politically charged involvement of NGOs is a passing phenomenon, dictated by the transitional character of world politics in the 1990s. Even if this is the case, the NGOs have demonstrated their unique capabilities to function across national lines in ways that involve human rights policies, disaster relief and long-term development, education, and health care. They are by all signs here to stay as a permanent part of the international landscape. Consequently, there is a need from their side and from the perspective of states and international institutions to see them as participants in the realm of policy and institutional action. They are not marginal actors, and their role needs to be more clearly recognized and addressed. From the side of the NGOs, maintaining their identity and independence (in fact and in perception) from states and international agencies is crucial. But of growing importance for them is a policy vision that is explicit about selective, strategic engagement with states and others in addressing situations in which the NGOs can play a unique role but need resources that are beyond what they possess. Conversely, just as states need to engage international institutions in a more systematic fashion, they also need to expand more intellectual and operational energy in working through their relationships with NGOs. Once again the specific issue of humanitarian intervention poses unique problems. The NGOs will rightfully be very cautious about any identification with the use of force, but they are often key actors in the very situations when nothing else but force seems capable of restoring order. Finally, the NGOs are today a key catalyst for domestic opinion within countries faced with decisions about humanitarian aid or military intervention. How they play this role and how states react to their advocacy is part of the mix that can determine domestic support, indifference, or opposition to choices made about various forms of intervention.

To summarize the broader argument: The politics of the 1990s have moved humanitarian intervention toward the center of world affairs; the ethics of intervention (drawn from the moral tradition) calls for an expanded range of interventionary action (thereby revising the legal tradition); the policy choices needed to respond to the ethics of intervention should engage states (a different conception of national interest), international institutions (a broader role for them), and NGOs (a more expansive role for them). Systemic change has been one reason that humanitarian military intervention grasps the world's attention; systemic response—moral, legal, and political—is needed to address this question.

Notes

1. Michael Walzer, *Just and Unjust Wars: A Moral Argument with Historical Illustrations* (New York: Basic Books, 1977), 5.

2. Examples of the realist perspective on intervention: Michael Mandelbaum, "Foreign Policy as Social Work," *Foreign Affairs* 75, no. 1 (January–February 1996): 16–32; Stephen J. Stedman, "The New Interventionists," *Foreign Affairs* 72, no. 1 (1992–1993): 1–17.

3. Stanley Hoffmann, "The Crisis of Liberal Internationalism," *Foreign Policy* 98 (Spring 1995): 161–62.

4. Lori Fisler Damrosch, "Changing Conceptions of Intervention in International Law" in *Emerging Norms of Justified Intervention,* ed. Laura W. Reed and Carl Kaysen (Cambridge, Mass.: American Academy of Arts and Sciences, 1993), 96.

5. Whereas the United Nations Charter provides clear support for resisting aggression across international boundaries, it is highly restrictive about intervention: Article 2 (7) protects the realm of domestic jurisdiction of states, and the U.N. system is based on the twin principles of state sovereignty and nonintervention.

6. Marc Trachtenberg, "Intervention in Historical Perspective," in Reed and Kaysen, *Emerging Norms,* 16.

7. J. Bryan Hehir, "The Ethics of Intervention: Two Normative Traditions" in *Human Rights and U.S. Foreign Policy,* ed. Peter G. Brown and Douglas MacLean (Lexington, Mass.: Heath, 1979), 121–39; J. Bryan Hehir, "Intervention: From Theories to Cases," *Ethics and International Affairs* 9 (1995): 1–13.

8. S. Hoffmann, "The Problem of Intervention" in *Intervention in World Politics,* ed. Hedley Bull (Oxford: Clarendon, 1984), 6–28.

9. For the background of this complex period, see James T. Johnson, *Ideology, Reason and the Limitation of War* (Princeton, N.J.: Princeton University Press, 1975); Le Roy B. Walters, Jr., *First Classic Just War Theories: A Study in the Thought of Thomas Aquinas, Vitoria, Suarez, Gentili and Grotius* (Ph.D. diss., Yale University, 1971).

10. John L. Gaddis, "Coping with Victory," *Atlantic Monthly* (May 1990): 49.

11. John Vincent, *Nonintervention and International Order* (Princeton, N.J.: Princeton University Press, 1974), 19–144.

12. A spectrum of positions includes C. Krauthammer, "The Unipolar Moment," *Foreign Affairs* 70, no. 1 (1991): 23–33; Henry A. Kissinger, *Diplomacy* (New York: Simon & Schuster, 1994), 804–35; Joseph S. Nye, "What New World Order?" *Foreign Affairs* 71, no. 1 (1992): 83–96.

13. John L. Gaddis, "Toward the Post–Cold War World," *Foreign Affairs* 70, no. 2 (1991): 102–22.

14. Samuel Huntington, "The Clash of Civilizations?" *Foreign Affairs* 72, no. 3 (Summer 1993): 22–49.

15. Samuel Huntington, "The West and the World," *Foreign Affairs* 75, no. 6 (1996): 41–43.

16. Kissinger, *Diplomacy*, 810–11.

17. Henry A. Kissinger, "Somalia," *Washington Post*, 13 December 1992.

18. Joseph S. Nye, "International Conflicts after the Cold War," in *Managing Conflict in the Post–Cold War World: The Role of Intervention*, Report of the Aspen Institute Conference (Washington, D.C.: Aspen Institute, 1996), 63–76.

19. Nye, "International Conflicts," 74–76.

20. See John L. Gaddis, "The Cold War, the Long Peace and the Future," in *The End of the Cold War: Its Meaning and Implications*, ed. Michael J. Hogan (Cambridge: Cambridge University Press, 1992), 21–38.

21. Michael Walzer, "The Politics of Rescue," *Social Research* 62, no. 1 (Spring 1995): 53–66.

22. Damrosch, "Changing Conceptions," 91.

23. Trachtenberg, "Intervention," 31.

24. Damrosch, "Changing Conceptions," 92.

25. Trachtenberg, "Intervention," 31.

26. For an elaboration of the just war ethic, see James Childress, *Moral Responsibility in Conflicts* (Baton Rouge: Louisiana State University Press, 1982), 63–94.

27. See Hehir, "Intervention," and J. Bryan Hehir, "Expanding Military Intervention: Promise or Peril?" *Social Research* 62, no. 1 (Spring 1995): 41–51.

28. Childress provides an explanation of this mode of reasoning in his use of W. D. Ross's concept of *prima facie* duties; see Childress, *Moral Responsibility*, 67–68.

29. For an assessment of the role of human rights in world politics, see R. J. Vincent, *Human Rights and International Relations* (Cambridge: Cambridge University Press, 1986), 111–52.

30. Michael Walzer, "Perplexed: Moral Ambiguities in the Gulf Crisis," *New Republic* (28 January 1991): 14.

31. John C. Murray, *We Hold These Truths: Catholic Reflections on the American Proposition* (New York: Sheed & Ward, 1960), 272.

32. Stanley Hoffmann, "The Politics and Ethics of Military Intervention," *Survival* 37, no. 4 (Winter 1995–1996): 29.

33. Hoffmann, "The Politics and Ethics," 32.

34. Samuel Huntington, "Transnational Organizations and World Politics," *World Politics* 25, no. 3 (April 1973): 333.

3

Peacekeeping, Military Intervention, and National Sovereignty in Internal Armed Conflict

Kofi A. Annan

The United Nations faces moral dilemmas as a matter of course. In the broadest sense, there is the gap between the ideals set out in the U.N. Charter—which we take as a moral imperative—and the realities of what the organization can actually achieve. With limited resources for the fight to eradicate poverty, we cannot possibly satisfy the needs of all who turn to us for help. Moreover, given the often harsh political facts of member states' interests and relations, the United Nations can respond to only some threats to the peace while other emergencies are left to unfold, untreated by the salve of international action.

If these are the dilemmas of inaction, the United Nations also encounters moral quandaries when it does act, when it does become present on the ground, carrying out its diverse work for peace, development, and human rights. Nowhere is this more true than when the organization is called on to deal with internal armed conflicts. These are often the most intractable of situations, and the United Nations is usually summoned when all other efforts have failed. Moreover, these sorts of conflicts often do not lend themselves to the traditional peacekeeping treatment. They are typically fought between regular armies and irregular forces or among irregular forces. Many involve more than two parties or groups, often accountable to no one. The distinction between combatants and civilians is often blurred, and child soldiers are not uncommon. Nations find themselves facing questions about the cohesion of their societies and even their very ability to endure as functioning states. Civilians are not only caught in the cross fire but are often the targets of violence; denied food, shelter, and dignity; and subject to suffering less likely to occur in more conventional wars between the armies of two states. These circumstances require a coordinated political, military, and humanitarian response. The resultant intertwining of mandates and personnel is not without complications; indeed, the record of the international community in meeting this challenge is mixed.

Recent years have seen United Nations interventions succeed in helping several troubled nations make the difficult transition from conflict to reconciliation, reconstruction, and long-term development. Elsewhere, however, the organization has become embroiled in circumstances that scarred its credibility and moral stature. In an era of loosening restraints—on sovereignty, on military intervention, and most of all on the behavior of armed individuals—the United Nations has drawn many lessons from these experiences. The organization has come a long way in determining what it can and cannot do to save lives and promote peace.

Evolving Notions of Sovereignty

Respect for the fundamental sovereignty, territorial integrity, and political independence of states is a cornerstone of the international system, one of the most important building blocks of global stability, security, and progress. The founders of the United Nations enshrined this principle in Article 2, paragraph 7, of the United Nations Charter, which states, "Nothing contained in the present Charter shall authorize the United Nations to intervene in matters which are essentially within the domestic jurisdiction of any state." That stricture is just as relevant today; violations of sovereignty remain violations of the global order.

However, the understanding of sovereignty is undergoing a significant transformation. Satellite communication, environment degradation, and the globalization of markets are just a few of the contemporary phenomena that are bringing into question the extent of state authority. The starving child on television screens around the world has generated global constituencies and pressure for action that governments cannot ignore. The implications of human rights abuses and refugee and other migratory flows for international peace and security are forcing us to take a fresh look at sovereignty from a different perspective: sovereignty as a matter of responsibility, not just power.

This idea predates the interdependence among nations that characterizes the current era. The United Nations' joint responsibility to member states and to their citizens is reflected in the first words of the preamble of the charter: "We the peoples of the United Nations." In 1948, shortly after the adoption of the Universal Declaration of Human Rights, the United Nations General Assembly debated its right to express concern about the apartheid system in South Africa and reached a historic decision: the principle of international concern for human rights took precedence over the claim of noninterference in internal affairs. In the decades that followed, outside support for the antiapartheid movement within South Africa—in the form of trade sanctions and arms embargoes, global public awareness campaigns, and other measures intended to isolate the apartheid regime—played a crucial role in the eventual triumph over racism and the establishment of democratic rule. It is no exaggeration to say that this effort of moral suasion helped shape the conscience of the international community.

On many issues and in many of the world's disputes and conflicts, governments or other parties are adamantly opposed to any third-party or United Nations intervention, and sovereignty is the first line of defense. But let us also remember that nations routinely accept restrictions on their sovereignty in order to cooperate with others in the pursuit of various common global goods. States that are party to the major international human rights covenants have chosen to make themselves accountable to treaty bodies that monitor adherence to these instruments. Environmental agreements, such as the Montreal Protocol on Substances That Deplete the Ozone Layer (1987), and disarmament texts, such as the Chemical Weapons Convention

(1997) and the Convention on the Prohibition of Antipersonnel Mines (1997), likewise place limits on the actions and autonomy of individual states, constraints that are accepted in view of the larger benefits at stake.

What *is* different today, particularly since the end of the Cold War, is the rapidity with which the balance is shifting: away from indifference, away from acceptance of what might be called the misuses of sovereignty, and toward greater moral engagement, toward an international community based on shared norms and standards and a willingness to uphold those basic values. Each of my immediate predecessors commented on this trend. Javier Pérez de Cuéllar wrote in 1991, "It is now increasingly felt that the principle of non-interference with the essential domestic jurisdiction of States cannot be regarded as a protective barrier behind which human rights could be massively or systematically violated with impunity." Boutros Boutros-Ghali, in *An Agenda for Peace,* his 1992 report on preventive diplomacy, peacekeeping, and postconflict peace building, wrote, "The time of absolute and exclusive sovereignty . . . has passed; its theory was never matched by reality." Today, I say that the sovereignty of states can constitute an essential bulwark against intimidation or coercion, but it must not be allowed to obstruct effective action to address problems that transcend borders or to secure human dignity.

The Changing Face of Military Intervention

The evolution in thinking about sovereignty has been one of the major factors behind the profound changes in United Nations peace operations since the late 1980s. Another, of course, was the end of the Cold War. With the end of ideological and superpower rivalry, the potential for consensus in the Security Council made possible much that had not been possible before and created an impetus for the international community to extend its reach. As a result, military interventions grew dramatically in both number and scope, and our responsibilities became more varied than even the most prophetic among us would have dared predict.

In most of the earliest, "traditional" peacekeeping operations,

United Nations military forces were interposed between belligerent parties, principally to monitor a cease-fire and/or to report on the implementation of the peace agreement that had brought them there. The United Nations still performs these functions successfully in Cyprus and on the Golan Heights. But in recent years the international community has mandated the United Nations to undertake additional assignments, most commonly in the aftermath of internal conflicts, as opposed to wars between sovereign nations. Many of these operations are consent based, in which the U.N. has been asked to monitor and help implement comprehensive peace agreements. The United Nations has performed tasks as varied as organizing elections, demobilizing and reintegrating former combatants, and repatriating and resettling refugees and displaced persons. It has helped rebuild economic and social infrastructures; it has protected the delivery of humanitarian aid; it has monitored respect for human rights.

In these cases, the parties themselves temporarily cede a degree of sovereignty to the United Nations for the life of the peace agreement. The value of such "road maps" for reconciliation and peace is indisputable, as successful operations in Cambodia, El Salvador, Mozambique, and Namibia testify; they provide not only a precise timetable and detailed set of objectives but also a template against which compliance can be measured. In Angola it has proven more difficult to fully implement the peace agreement owing to the recalcitrance of one of the parties involved, but this point should not obscure the considerable progress that has been made thus far.

More difficult have been cases in which the United Nations has been called on to intervene in conflicts without the full and reliable consent of all the relevant parties. Clearly, civil wars and other internal situations arise that are on one level internal but that also have international dimensions: the risk that hostilities will spill across borders, flows of refugees, crimes against humanity, and other violations of international humanitarian law. In response, the Security Council has adopted resolutions and embarked on operations that have set precedents and helped redefine the ideas of sovereignty, military intervention, and humanitarian action. Thus, in April 1991, the Security Council adopted Resolution 688 concerning the situation in Northern Iraq which for the first time recognized that a humanitarian emergency and massive population displacement could constitute a threat to international peace and security. Since then, the United Nations has acted in the following countries.

Somalia

Faced with conflict, famine, obstacles to the distribution of humanitarian assistance, and a complete breakdown of supervening authority, the Security Council (in Resolution 794 of 3 December 1992) authorized member states "to use all necessary means to establish as soon as possible a secure environment for humanitarian relief operations"—a rare use of military force for largely humanitarian goals. With no functioning government to grant consent for such an operation, the council invoked the enforcement provisions of Chapter VII of the U.N. Charter, the first time this was done to deal with a conflict confined within a state's borders. Months later, when a United Nations peacekeeping force took command of the mission from the United States–led multinational Unified Task Force (UNITAF), the mandate set out in Resolution 814 of 26 March 1993 included enforcement powers for disarmament as well as the delivery of humanitarian relief. UNOSOM II also had a mandate to help rebuild the nation, although no one expected this could be done coercively. That it failed to fulfill completely this ambitious mandate highlights the dangers of trying to mix peacekeeping and peace enforcement, especially in the absence of a coherent or solidly supported international policy. The humanitarian goals of the mission were largely accomplished, but the unhappy ending of UNOSOM II has in the eyes of some observers been the main cause of the Security Council's hesitancy to authorize any operation like it since.

Former Yugoslavia

The involvement of the United Nations in the conflicts in the former Yugoslavia began as a classic case of peacemaking and peacekeeping but then became much, much more. For the first time since the Nuremberg and Tokyo tribunals were set up following World War II, the Security Council established a tribunal to investigate and prosecute alleged war crimes. In the former Yugoslav Republic of Macedonia, the organization deployed its first "preventive" force on the borders of that country to help insulate against the spread of fighting from neighboring states. In Croatia, United Nations peacekeepers serving with the U.N. Transnational Administration for Eastern Slavonia, Baranja, and Western Sirmium (UNTAE) were assigned the rarely undertaken task of administering a disputed territory. With the weight of a 5,000-strong mechanized peacekeeping force and the watchful eyes of NATO behind it, the U.N. oversaw—in one of the most successful multifaceted peacekeeping operations in its history—the peaceful restoration of Croatian sovereignty while creating the conditions necessary for the maintenance of the region's multiethnic character. But it was the situation in Bosnia and Herzegovina that posed the greatest, most novel, and most disturbing challenges; these are discussed in greater detail below.

Rwanda

Rwanda is in many respects the intervention that did *not* happen, at least in the crucial early weeks of the crisis. Occurring so soon after the troubled operation in Somalia, the violence was left to unfold, which it did with ferocious speed and intensity, sparing not even children and the elderly and intruding on sanctuaries such as churches and hospitals. I have said on many occasions that a force of even modest size and means could have prevented much of the killing, but the opposite course was taken: a reduction in the size of the United Nations force that was already in place to police an earlier peace agreement. The international community is still coming to terms with that decision, with that failure to mount an adequate response to the genocide that ensued. Eventually, the United Nations became deeply involved in the search for peace in Rwanda and the surrounding region. Unique aspects of the organization's response included efforts to cope with the militarization of refugee camps in what was then eastern Zaire; the decision of the Security Council to authorize a French-led multinational intervention known as Operation Turquoise; the dispatch of a human rights field operation; and the creation by the Security Council of an international war crimes tribunal, only the second such body established since World War II.

If intervention can work, if intervention has become more grand in design and accomplished in its outcomes, it is also true that these new, multidimensional interventions also encounter more obstacles and greater complexities, not to mention the risk of outright failure. A change in quantity, as has been said, produces a change in quality. Add one atom of oxygen to hydrogen oxide, and you have water. Add humanitarian assistance to a military operation, and you change the quality of a mission. Introduce outside players to an internal situation, and you change the quality of a mission. With lives and the integrity of the United Nations at stake, we must be ever vigilant to the dangers involved in such developments.

The U.N. Involvement in Bosnia and Herzegovina

When war erupted in Bosnia and Herzegovina in 1992, United Nations peacekeepers were thrust into a theater of operations where there was no peace to keep; humanitarian personnel were dispatched to a situation in which the denial of humanitarian assistance became an instrument of war and the inhumane practice of "ethnic cleansing" a central aim; and the international community was quickly immersed in a complex debate concerning mandates, political will, impartiality, the use (and nonuse) of force, and other wrenching questions. That debate, fervent throughout the war, has continued even after the signing of the Dayton Peace Agreement and has had significant implications for the ongoing use of one of the organization's most prized assets: its moral authority.

Mandates

The United Nations peacekeeping force dispatched to Bosnia-Herzegovina was not sent to end the war or to intervene on behalf of one side or another. Rather, the Security Council deployed a mission whose mandate was initially limited to delivering humanitarian aid and whose pattern of deployment and style of conduct reflected this aim. Subsequent resolutions asked the same force to contain the conflict through measures such as an arms embargo and a "no-fly zone" and to promote prospects for obtaining an overall settlement, for example, by negotiating local cease-fires. However, because the nature of the conflict, including "ethnic cleansing" and concentration camps, seemed to call for something more ambitious; because the operation's name, the United Nations Protection Force (UNPROFOR), suggested that something more militarily assertive was intended to be done; because of ambiguities and contradictions in the approach settled on by the Security Council; and unavoidably because of the actions of the parties to the conflict in Bosnia and Herzegovina, the force quickly ran into ethical and operational problems that affected its performance and credibility.

One such problem concerned the Security Council's apparently limited objective of alleviating the humanitarian consequences of the conflict. When the council operates in a principally humanitarian mode, it raises concerns that humanitarianism is being used to contain only the most visible ramifications of a crisis or as a substitute for the political and possibly military action and long-term commitment necessary to address the root causes of a crisis. This approach has serious consequences for relief actors and any troops deployed to assist a relief endeavor, as well as for the council itself as a body capable of responding effectively to threats to international peace and security.

A second dilemma arose with the confluence of humanitarian and military personnel and tasks. Some humanitarian organizations fear that military action makes their job more difficult and tarnishes their image as a disinterested party. This problem is especially acute when humanitarian issues become linked in negotiations with political and military issues. However, some of the same groups feel they have the right to take whatever action they deem necessary and that United Nations forces must be available to protect them in the course of doing so. That cannot be. There must be coordination; the military, political, and humanitarian components of an operation must each ensure that none of them takes an initiative that might compromise the others.

A third dilemma involved the U.N.'s response to ethnic cleansing. The Commission on Human Rights held its first-ever emergency session to condemn the practice. The Security Council created the first international criminal tribunal since the Nuremberg and Tokyo war crimes panels were established following World War II. The United Nations High Commissioner for Refugees (UNHCR), however, in fulfilling *its* mandate of protecting refugees and displaced persons by conveying to safety people who otherwise would have been forcibly expelled from their homes and/or murdered, was accused of abetting ethnic cleansing. The response to this charge is clear: saving the lives of people in jeopardy had to take precedence. And, indeed, the UNHCR was criticized for both not doing enough and doing too much to evacuate populations. The conundrum underscores the difficulty of putting relief actors on the front lines, not just physically but politically.

Consent

In addition to a practicable mandate, the consent of the parties is another prerequisite for successful peacekeeping and military intervention. Consent means more than having a government and/or factional leaders agree to the presence of the United Nations peacekeepers and mediators. It is a commitment to the path of negotiation and dialogue, an admission that armed force has failed, that there is no military solution to the prevailing circumstances. Consent can come from exhaustion on the part of combatants and noncombatants or from the calculation that more is to be gained at the negotiating table than on the battlefield. The international community can also nurture consent through the use of positive inducements. In the short term, such inducements might include the provision of medical care or quick-impact projects to rehabilitate local infrastructure; over the longer term, the international community could offer financial and technical assistance for transforming a guerrilla group into a legitimate political party and for facilitating former combatants' reintegration into society. But the will to reconciliation and peace cannot be imposed. Absent a genuine interest by the parties themselves in a settlement, there are limits to what outsiders can accomplish. There is no doubting the international community's patience—witness long-standing involvements in Cyprus, Jerusalem, Kashmir, and the Golan Heights. But one can also ask whether it is ethically sound for the international community to expend resources and political will coaxing recalcitrant parties into negotiations, or becoming involved prematurely on the ground, where there is little chance of compliance and prospects for success somewhere else are not as daunting.

In Bosnia and Herzegovina the consent of the parties, when it came, tended to be hard-won and short-lived. Cease-fires were agreed to and immediately breached. Humanitarian aid convoys were blocked despite guarantees of safe passage. Such difficulties occurred largely because consent, particularly on the part of the Bosnian Serb side, would pose a hindrance to war aims. With the imposition of United Nations sanctions against the Bosnian Serb party, the question of consent became even more troublesome. And when the Security Council declared it would protect six "safe areas"—cities under siege by the Bosnian Serbs—UNPROFOR was obliged to cooperate and negotiate daily with a party on whom it was also expected to call air strikes in certain circumstances. The result was that Bosnian Serb leaders largely withdrew their consent and cooperation from UNPROFOR, declaring that they were applying their own "sanctions" to the United Nations in response to United Nations sanctions on them. UNPROFOR thus found itself obstructed, targeted by all sides, denied resupply, restricted in its movements, and subjected to constant criticism.

Impartiality

The impartiality of the United Nations enables it to enter war zones and other conflict areas and be accepted by the parties as good-faith interlocutor, as a presence for humanitarian objectives and peace. In conventional or internal conflicts, this principle is fundamental; the U.N. cannot afford to become part of the problem. In Bosnia and Herzegovina, that stance was tested to the extreme. One side suffered the overwhelming majority of casualties and atrocities and was often outraged by the decisions of the international community. One side was a recognized member state of the United Nations, which expected the organization to defend its interests. One side was the principal aggressor and therefore the primary target of sanctions and military force used by the international community. Peacekeepers, representing the will of the international community, were themselves scorned, taken hostage, attacked, and killed. Unfortunately, impartiality in the execution of the mandate was sometimes misconstrued as unthinking, or even amoral, neutrality between the warring parties.

In the face of illegal behavior (including violations of international humanitarian law), the Security Council is capable of granting a mandate that addresses the problem—and is therefore not impartial—and deploying an operation with the means to achieve this mandate. At the same time, the mandate must be implemented impartially and fairly, "without fear or favor." If the U.N. has both the assets and the political backing to do the job, this will make it part of the solution rather than part of the problem. The lesson of Somalia, Bosnia, and Rwanda is that the U.N. must be clear about the problems facing it in discharging a mandate; the lengths to which we are prepared to go to overcome them; the means required; and the risks, costs, and moral dilemmas that will inevitably accompany any course of action or inaction in such difficult situations.

The Use, or Threat of Use, of Force

Can the international community spill blood to save lives and itself remain spotless? Can humanitarian objectives be fulfilled at the point of a gun? Can they be fulfilled at all if the guns are instead pointed at the humanitarians? These are not easy questions, but they arose repeatedly in Bosnia and Herzegovina.

Confronted with a lack of consent from all sides in the conflict but particularly by the Bosnian Serb party, UNPROFOR's mandate was gradually enlarged to include elements of enforcement. But peacekeeping derives from one set of assumptions and objectives and peace enforcement from another; mixing the two creates an untenable position for the force sent out to square the circle. UNPROFOR's resort to force, for example, caused it to be seen as a party to the conflict, thereby jeopardizing the cooperation necessary for it to fulfill its primary objective: to deliver emergency aid. Others criticized the force for *not* pursuing a war, for what was regarded as a woeful reluctance to use the enforcement powers granted to it.

Quite apart from whether UNPROFOR was a peace enforcement operation is the question of credibility in the use, and threat of use, of force. When the Security Council designated the safe areas, the secretary general offered options ranging from 7,600 to 34,000 troops to deter attacks against them. Member states chose the minimum option, and even then they only provided troops to reach the required level after more than a year. The gap between intent and action, between rhetoric and reality, was especially pronounced and contributed to the debacle that ensued when Srebrenica was overrun. The fall of Srebrenica—the inability of the United Nations to keep a designated safe area safe and to avert a human rights tragedy—has stained the record of the United Nations and will make it difficult for the international community to act in the future as a moral force. However, it must not be forgotten that the Security Council resolutions proclaiming the safe areas never asked the United Nations to either "protect" or "defend" them, merely to "deter attacks" by its presence. When the presence of the troops proved inadequate to deter attacks, they did not have the means to protect or defend the areas.

Effectiveness in the use of force is not only a matter of numbers; legitimacy is credibility's necessary counterpart. A military intervention with legitimacy—for example, in the form of a United Nations mandate representing the universal will of the international community—can win broad-based political support but without credibility may be unable to achieve its objectives. A credible force might get short-term results but without legitimacy may be unable to sustain long-term support. Together, credibility and legitimacy are mutually reinforcing, as was demonstrated when NATO played a lead role in monitoring implementation of the Dayton Peace Agreement.

Should the United Nations have used greater force in Bosnia and Herzegovina? A massive military intervention early in the conflict may have curbed or even prevented fighting not only in Bosnia and Herzegovina but elsewhere in the former Yugoslavia. It is likewise possible that no intervention at all might have allowed the parties to exhaust themselves sooner, also sparing the region prolonged bloodletting and destruction. Either of these courses of action might have had the opposite effect—namely, more violence, not less, and other unforeseen and possibly bloody consequences. Between these poles lies the intervention that did happen, which for all its shortcomings and difficulties succeeded in feeding and housing millions of people,

assisting with the country's reconstruction, and laying the groundwork for peace negotiations.

Ultimately, member states must decide whether they want to give
the U.N. the capacity for limited peace enforcement, as proved effective in the case of UNTAES. Whereas some believe such operations
are better delegated to regional organizations and non-U.N. coalitions, these alternatives are not always available, and the United Nations pays a price in terms of moral authority and influence if it consistently declines to mount such operations itself.

Selectivity

The involvement of the United Nations in the former Yugoslavia
dominated the organization's agenda in the peace and security field
and distorted its peacemaking and peacekeeping efforts at the expense
of other parts of the world. At the time of peak deployment in August
1995, the former Yugoslavia accounted for nearly 70 percent of
peacekeepers worldwide and more than two-thirds of peacekeeping
costs. Many member states and others expressed concern that other
conflicts and trouble spots failed to receive a commitment of action
and resources commensurate with the unfolding tragedy. For each
member of the Security Council, this is a matter of national interest
and political will, of course, and also of media selectivity. But it is
also a moral issue in that it prompts the world public to question the
organization's universality. The United Nations cannot be every-
where, but it must be willing and able to respond to fair claims—large
and small, within and beyond its leading members' spheres of interest—for its involvement.

The Vital Role of the Third Party
amid Conflict and Suffering

The founders of the United Nations included a wealth of activist language in the charter: "to save succeeding generations from the
scourge of war . . . to unite our strength . . . to employ international
machinery . . . to take effective collective measures." These words

constitute a rejection of indifference. They send a message of engagement, of international solidarity, of action instead of apathy in the face of hatred, bloodshed, and deprivation. They reflect a belief in the constructive, corrective power of human agency—the power of light over darkness.

The philosopher Edmund Burke once wrote, "The only thing necessary for the triumph of evil is for good men to do nothing." In heeding Burke's words, in trying to do our utmost for the common good, moral dilemmas have been and will continue to be a prominent part of the landscape. As we have seen in Bosnia and Herzegovina and elsewhere, of all United Nations activities, military interventions in internal armed conflicts are particularly fraught with vexing choices and questions. But as we also saw in Rwanda in 1994, where a modest intervention at the right moment could have saved many lives and a larger one could perhaps even have prevented the genocide, inaction has grave perils of its own. Aggressors and tyrants thrive on passivity, a culture of impunity prevails, and the moral standing of the international community (a dubious concept to some but not to me) suffers grave damage. It seems to me far better to accept the risk of error or failure than to remain on the sidelines; there is no purity in the abstract, and only disgrace and worse in retreat toward some imaginary safe harbor.

I entered office as secretary general stressing not only the United Nations' political and diplomatic considerations, not only its legal obligations, not only its fiscal limitations, but above all the moral dimension of its work. At its best the United Nations can be a courageous third party that brings hope to victims and succor to the needy and that rouses the collective conscience of humankind. For all its shortcomings and constraints, the organization has compiled a solid record of achievement in this regard. We must nurture and sustain the moral vision that has made this possible.

4

The End of Innocence

Rwanda 1994

Romeo A. Dallaire

With the experience of being the United Nations Assistance Mission in Rwanda (UNAMIR) force commander from its inception until 19 August 1994, I believe that Rwanda provides a seminal example of several issues vital to future international interventions:

1. The necessity for accelerated evolution of cooperation already growing between U.N. military personnel and U.N. agencies and nongovernment organizations (NGOs);
2. The rapidly growing influence on the governments of troop-contributing nations that NGOs have had and continue to have;
3. The moral necessity for the international community to avoid falling into ill-conceived and ill-planned interventions.

This is not an easy undertaking, as the following pages will demonstrate. However, the essence of the last few years of U.N. experience in the field has unequivocally proven the vital importance of interlocking and *interdependent* solutions to complex humanitarian crises, which must include careful moral calculations.

We must remember that aid cannot be given in naive and arrogant disdain of the sociopolitical realities of the affected area. Purely military missions cannot impose simplistic criteria, autocratic parameters, and domineering black-and-white solutions. As in Somalia and regrettably Rwanda, conducting such missions in haughty isolation from the political and humanitarian organizations that pursue their duties in the theater of operations will result in bloody failure. The rapprochement between military and humanitarian agencies is all for naught if the lead element—the political component—arrives on the scene too late, losing the advantage of the goodwill of the belligerents and thus failing to gain the initiative in the peace process. In Rwanda, this was often exacerbated by a sterile procrastination in efforts to gain the initiative because of a lack of conscientious political foresight and diplomatic statesmanship. Thus, if the political component is walking blind and has not articulated an overall strategic plan, soldiers will become casualties, and, as in the case of the refugee camps in Goma, eastern Zaire, NGOs will waste precious resources fueling a charade of political conscience cleansing by the developed states in deference to the media and their constituencies.

It is still an unfortunate rule of international relations that nations get involved in crises in a substantive way only when they perceive that their self-interests are at stake. This mercantile assessment by the developed world regarding the suffering and slaughter of millions of less privileged human beings in seemingly far-off lands (in situations that are often the result of the power states' original colonial and Cold War involvement) cannot continue with impunity. Yet, instead of blaming powerful states, we should be pressuring them to rise above a narrow interest to a broader interest in the global state of humanity. Although altruistic and perhaps naive, such concern is in the direct political and economic interest of all states.

It does not appear that the international community ever conceived that its commitment to peacekeeping could reach a point of total fatigue. Yet, the increasing tempo of international peace support missions since 1989 has taxed the resolve of the wealthier states, which bear most of the burden. It also introduced a new dimension to the equation: the arrival of new peacekeeping players in a previously select group of troop-contributing nations, whose overall effectiveness in the field is in itself a subject that requires close scrutiny. This fatigue set the stage for the ill-advised U.N. Security Council's classification of the peace process in Rwanda as a low priority. Compared with the then-recent disappointment of Somalia and the ongoing misery in the Balkans, it certainly seemed so.

The U.N. mission and those Rwandans it was supposed to help nevertheless fell victim to an inflated optimism that created expectations that UNAMIR was incapable of fulfilling. It was not through lack of effort or dedication and zeal that the mission was never able to achieve an effective state of operations or gain the initiative from the belligerents in order to advance the peace process. More than 70 percent of my and my principal staff's time was dedicated to an administrative battle with the U.N.'s somewhat constipated logistic and administrative structure, a structure on which the mission and the force was totally dependent. It is a wonder that we were able to conduct any operational activities on the ground even six months after the mandate approval. Add to this the low priority of the mission, the contingents (from poor nations, with the exception of Belgium) deploying without the minimum required equipment and maintenance resources, and being in a land-locked country with next to no infrastructure or stocks, it is small wonder that we were assessed by both sides of the conflict as being of marginal relevance.

United Nations Assistance Mission in Rwanda (UNAMIR)

From its establishment as a result of Security Council Resolution 872 of 5 October 1993, UNAMIR suffered severe shortcomings in equipment, personnel, training, and intelligence gathering, as well as weak political, humanitarian, and military planning. This was one consequence of the mission's low-priority status. Another was that the specialized civilian legal affairs, human rights, and humanitarian activities' coordination staffs were still not deployed a full six months after the publication of the mission mandate. Moreover, the personnel available were inexperienced in dealing with massive humanitarian crises. For example, the U.N. Development Program's (UNDP) permanent representative wore three hats: as coordinator for humanitarian affairs, representative for the reintegration of the future demobilized soldiers, as well as representative for national reconstruction.

Although he had three years' experience in the country, neither he nor his staff had the skills and resources necessary to be fully effective. In addition, there were tensions among the U.N. civilian hierarchy in Rwanda, the major funding agencies and countries, and some NGOs. This limited the mission's ability to implement a multidisciplinary (political, humanitarian, and military) plan to assist the Rwandans in achieving success with their hard-fought Peace Accords, signed in Arusha, Tanzania, on 4 August 1993. As a result, we were not as proactive as we should have been, and we failed to gain or sustain either the initiative or the confidence of the parties involved. This situation compromised UNAMIR's overall credibility and may have contributed to the horrendous scale of the killings and forced movement of millions of Rwandans. Yet, a central moral question still remains unanswered: did the ineffectiveness of the U.N. mission in grasping the situation and poor handling of the political, humanitarian, and military response in extremis abet the genocide? I believe it did.

As of early 1994, the humanitarian problems were escalating exponentially with 300,000 Burundian refugees in the south of the country, another 600,000 Rwandan displaced persons, mostly Hutu, south of the demilitarized zone (DMZ) in the north, a crop failure in the nation's farming region of the southwest, and the Rwandan population receiving scant medical and subsistence support from the Arusha-imposed coalition government in Kigali. In addition, since that government's mandate had run out on 1 January 1994, all these problems were being variously handled by many separate NGOs and U.N. agencies. All of this placed enormous stress on the few resources being allocated, fund-raising, and any possibility of equitable distribution of aid to all groups. The Rwandan nationals, Rwandan displaced persons, Rwandan refugees from Uganda, and the Burundian refugees were all the worse for this migration.

The situation became even more dramatic—indeed, outright explosive—when two separate chains of events occurred. First, the Rwandan Government Forces (RGF) and some extremist elements began recruiting in the Burundian refugee camps. United Nations observers sent into the southern region were being regularly called into the camps by the NGOs to assist in disarming individuals. Because of large numbers of disaffected youth, the extremists recruited many who were prepared to fight, seducing them with the possibility of being able to return to Burundi in force.

Second, the Rwandan Tutsi refugees of the 1959-1962 era began to return by the thousands from southern Uganda. Mostly made up of men and boys of military age accompanied by large cattle herds, they moved directly into the Rwandan Patriotic Front (RPF) zone, taking over the lands of Hutus who had fled the RPF in 1990 and were sitting in displaced persons camps south of the DMZ. The RPF explained this migration as the desire of the refugees to return home now that a U.N. force was in place to ensure the secure environment necessary to implement the Arusha accords. The RPF stated categorically that it could not stop the spontaneous movement, yet it did its best to assist them on the journey with food and other humanitarian gestures. The U.N. High Commissioner for Refugees (UNHCR) regional representative advised us not to assist these returning refugees in any way, because it would encourage an even greater flood south. The RPF, however, could not support the needs of the refugees, who then attracted strong NGO "independent" support with substantial resources.

In concert with this newer problem, the RPF, through its radio broadcasts, also invited all Rwandan displaced persons south of the DMZ to enter the RPF zone. This act caused more ethnic friction, by reinforcing the Hutu displaced persons' suspicion that their lands were being stolen by the Tutsi refugees. Add the new, but to be repeated, complication of the RGF's formal complaints that the RPF was recruiting many of these displaced people to their ranks. Tensions between the opposing forces along the DMZ escalated to cease-fire violations when in three separate incidents more than a dozen RGF soldiers were killed. The RGF authorities complained openly to me that they had information that Ugandan battalions were crossing into Rwanda as RPF reinforcements, although my UNOMUR mission operating on the border between these two countries never reported such troop movements.

This complicated scenario of escalating pressures in and around the DMZ, where my forces never achieved a fully operationally capable state before the start of the war, is an excellent example of NGOs and

U.N. aid agencies getting caught up in a very duplicitous game in which refugees were pawns. Add to this the political dimension of our monitoring role of burgomaster elections in the DMZ, and you have all the makings of a volatile situation. Because of the several unmarked minefields existing north of the DMZ, my troops were unable to effectively monitor the movement of refugees and arms from the Ugandan-Rwandan border. The threat of mines also allowed the RPF to funnel the returning refugees through the DMZ into its zone. Finally, the war started before we had fully grasped the nature of these events.

In the midst of this complexity and confusion, international indifference to the Rwandan crisis, combined with the U.N.'s chronic limitation to raise, equip, and sustain military forces, produced disastrous results. Half-battalions from Belgium and Bangladesh created an inefficient command, control, and support system with few troops available for operations. The Ghanaians were deployed ahead of time because of the urgent need for troops on the ground and with the grudging acceptance that their equipment would follow later. They were in theater for over two months before any substantive equipment arrived. Because of increasing political pressures, I was forced to deploy the 800-man Ghanaian battalion into the DMZ with all the equipment we could spare: twenty-one U.N. Jeep-type trucks and fifty Motorola nonsecure radios. The Bangladesh transport company had only fifteen light-duty trucks to supply the entire force throughout the country. Its engineer company was also deployed into the DMZ but was used as foot infantry, as it had less than a third of the equipment needed to carry out vital duties such as mine clearance and road repair. Its troops had absolutely no self-sustaining capacity whatsoever—not even a kitchen. The Bangladesh half-battalion could transport neither their own infantry companies nor the attached Tunisian company to conduct their operations. Finally, only five of the eight Bangladesh armored personnel carriers (APCs), out of twenty originally promised for the rapid reaction company group, could be counted on at any given time. We had no spare parts, manuals, or mechanics to maintain these essential vehicles, nor had the crews ever fired their main weapon. Finally, United Nations military observers (UNMOs) were employed throughout the country in their monitoring tasks with next to no communications capability. Even those deployed within the Kigali Weapons Secure Zone (the most secure area in the country) at the various RGF camps had little communications equipment. None of the mission's communications were secure.

In my opinion, no individual state would have permitted its troops and its operations to be put into such a predicament, one that would surely lead to disaster in the face of altercations or violence between the belligerents. The situation persisted even when we requested a review of the capabilities available on the ground when the growing pressures from the NGOs, displaced persons, belligerents, political stagnation, and civil unrest in the capital all demanded that a more effective mission be deployed quickly. Requests by those of us in the field, and by the staff at the Department of Peacekeeping Operations at U.N. headquarters (UNHQ) in New York, went without any tangible results. This gap between the intensely complex and desperately critical situation and the inadequacy of the resources provided to deal with it raises a profound question of moral pragmatism: If the intervention comes to a point where it has little to no chance of being effective, should it have been withdrawn (or some might say undertaken) in the first place?

The Civil War

The 6 April 1994 assassination of President Habyarimana of Rwanda triggered an escalation of violence culminating in the extermination of nearly one million of his people, with another two million either displaced or as refugees in surrounding states. The slaughter began with the Presidential Guard responding to the death of their president by carrying out a series of reprisal killings of Tutsis and Hutu moderates, political leaders, and other people perceived as a threat by the Hutu extremist factions in their campaign for total power. These killings were initiated by local members of two Hutu militias known as the *Interahamwe* and the *Impuzamugbmi,* as well as elements of the RGF and gendarmerie.

A state of lawlessness, violence, and mass murder spread throughout the country, raging unchecked for weeks. Local populations turned on each other as Hutu extremists were spurred on by their radio station RTLM, spewing racist propaganda, exciting Hutus to kill all Tutsis as well as elements of UNAMIR. Roadblocks at fifty- to hundred-meter intervals were erected supposedly to prevent RPF infiltration and were manned by intoxicated youths and extremists, including military personnel. They killed on the spot anyone physically resembling or identified as a Tutsi or a sympathizer. Many people turned on neighbors and friends to avoid being killed themselves. This was our *Krystalnacht,* the Night of the Long Knives, and the Holocaust merged into several weeks of mass murder.

At this point I must mention that in mid-January 1994 I had requested permission from UNHQ in New York to raid and disarm militia groups in the Kigali region. Information from an informant indicated that some Hutu cells were preparing for a massacre if a suitable opportunity arose. I indicated this in a coded cable to the U.N. Permission was denied on the grounds that such a raid could only be viewed as hostile by the Rwandan government. Unfortunately, our fears were realized a few months later. Mass hysteria ran unchecked, and UNAMIR was only able to protect a few isolated sites while assisting individuals to escape. During this mayhem, several UNAMIR detachments were detained, and ten Belgian paratroopers were slaughtered within twenty-four hours of the start of the killings. As the commander of UNAMIR and therefore of the Belgian contingent, I bear full responsibility for their deaths. As a human, I am disgusted that UNAMIR was so marginalized as to permit such an occurrence both to peacekeepers and to the millions of Rwandans destroyed through genocide and civil war.

The Darkest Hour

The subsequent withdrawal of the Belgians emasculated the force available to stem the flood of violence surrounding us. The fact that nearly 1,500 highly capable troops from France, Italy, and Belgium landed in Kigali within days, with several hundred U.S. marines standing by in Burundi, to evacuate the expatriates and a few hundred selected Rwandans, and then left in the face of the unfolding tragedy and with full knowledge of the danger confronting the emasculated U.N. force, *is inexcusable by any human criteria.* UNAMIR was abandoned by all, including most of our civilian staff (by order), and we were left to fend for ourselves for weeks. That we were left in this state with neither mandate nor supplies—defensive stores, ammunition, medical supplies, or water, with only survival rations that were rotten and inedible—is a description of inexcusable apathy by the sovereign states that made up the U.N. that is completely beyond comprehension and moral acceptability.

Throughout most of the ensuing carnage, UNAMIR's hands remained tied. The U.N., having no power akin to a sovereign state, is only able to act on the expressed wishes of member states through the Security Council, which floundered in the face of mounting heaps of bodies growing daily and televised by the world media in the country. As long as these states procrastinated, bickered, and cynically pursued their own selfish foreign policies, the U.N. and UNAMIR could do little to stop the killing, let alone offer help or hope to those moderates hiding and trying to survive, or even contemplate counteracting the extremists.

The Belgian pullout was not the only factor that prevented UNAMIR from taking a more proactive role in halting the violence in the first days. In many cases, the various contingents did not have the mandates from their national capitals to use force to intervene, nor did they possess the means to do so. Some contingents received orders to limit their activities and wait for the violence to blow over. Others were ordered not to expose soldiers to the possibility of becoming casualties. Others still were simply ordered to get out of the country as quickly as possible and by whatever means. It took me more than two weeks to find out where all my troops were or gain access to them. The rump of UNAMIR was finally consolidated into a few reasonably defendable sites and opened its doors to those seeking protection who could reach these sites. Ultimately, over 30,000 Rwandans from both sides and behind both belligerent lines were protected in this way. Many died while under our protection as we lacked basic resources and on too many occasions received incoming fire from both sides. We continued to negotiate cease-fires and truces, and ultimately we kept an international community presence throughout the crisis so that the Rwandans would not feel completely abandoned to their fate. I made sure that the media was fully supported in *all* aspects, even at the risk of my personnel, in order to ensure that they could get their gruesome stories out every day. We had to try to shame the international community into action.

I first recommended, then ordered, the reduction of the force to about 450 personnel in the face of the carnage because UNAMIR had almost no ammunition, only a few days' worth of rations, and no medical stores. The only supplies available were those flown in sporadically by a lone Canadian CC-130 Hercules. I cannot praise highly enough the courage and determination of those crews, often landing and unloading under mortar and small-arms fire; they saved the mission from being completely pulled out. However, under these conditions, no major reinforcement or resupply was possible inside Rwanda. The steadfastness of the Ghanaian, Senegalese, Uruguayan, Congolese, and Tunisian governments in particular in leaving their contingents throughout the war are sterling examples to the rest of the world. My only reinforcement for the first three months of the war and genocide were twelve staff officers and sector operations staff Canada sent within days of the start of the war to replace the Belgians.

A complete withdrawal from Rwanda was out of the question, since such an action would have been seen by the belligerents as a sign that the world did not care *at all* and that genocide was an acceptable solution to Rwanda's problems. On the other hand, the possibility of having to fight our way out of the country was a very real and very desperate option that was prepared for and nearly executed on at least two occasions. The threat to the mission became even more severe when the French-led Franco-African coalition force called *Operation Turquoise* was launched and our own Franco-African elements were targeted by the RPF, which resulted in their urgent evacuation under threats to their lives.

Operation Turquoise was approved by the U.N. Security Council under a Chapter VII authority, which authorized the use of force. Established to provide a humanitarian security zone in the southwest of Rwanda, it had the mandate to coordinate humanitarian relief efforts for the large displaced population (over 1.5 million Rwandans) in an environment of security in that zone. The relief effort started very slowly with the extraction of some white expatriates and Rwandans as an initial priority, coupled with the potential of or indirectly stopping the RPF advance. The French military had been a belligerent to the RPF in previous encounters by providing weapons and training to the RGF while also occasionally engaging in direct combat with the RPF. This put UNAMIR at immediate risk because, with UNAMIR and *Turquoise* having the same boss in the U.N., and with Franco-Africans serving in both forces, the RPF reacted as expected to the *Turquoise* deployment—with violence against my force. All this at a time when we were entirely deployed behind RPF lines.

Why France did not equip and help deploy the volunteer Franco-African nations that were on record as standing ready to provide UNAMIR with the necessary troops is still beyond me. Following on the heels of the Belgian withdrawal, and at a time when I was desperately trying to build up support for my new mandate, the immediate evacuation of the *whole* UNAMIR force was only stopped at the last minute when we successfully accomplished the withdrawal of UNAMIR's Franco-African elements from Rwanda. The lack of coordination between *Turquoise* and UNAMIR has been the subject of considerable discussion. For U.N.-sanctioned Chapter VI and Chapter VII operations to be deployed to the same theater at the same time, for basically the same reason reflects, in my mind, the absence of responsible integrated planning and, most important, evidence of individual states running roughshod over the Secretariat and even the Security Council.

UNAMIR was constantly being asked to do more to help expatriates, missionaries, and Rwandans who were caught in dangerous locations and who had been forgotten or missed by the foreign troops at the start of the war. My force was standing knee-deep in mutilated bodies, surrounded by the guttural moans of dying people, looking into the eyes of children bleeding to death with their wounds burning in the sun and being invaded by maggots and flies. I found myself walking through villages where the only sign of life was a goat, or a chicken, or songbird, as all the people were dead, their bodies being eaten by voracious packs of wild dogs. During those first seven to eight weeks of the war, with little mandate, no reinforcements in sight, and only one phone line to the outside world (which a mortar round knocked out for nineteen hours), I felt the ghost of Gordon of Khartoum watching over me. Dying in Rwanda without sign or sight of relief was a reality that we faced on a daily basis.

The Humanitarian Effort

Unlike most international organizations and foreign nationals, the small U.N. civilian humanitarian cell and the magnificent International Committee of the Red Cross (ICRC), supported by *Médecins sans Frontières*, stayed in Rwanda. The U.N. also set up the Rwanda Emergency Office (UNREO) in Nairobi, but the result was that the humanitarian coordinating staffs were too far away and generally too weak and inexperienced to be able to coalesce all NGOs and U.N. agencies into a coherent strategy. They valiantly attempted to deal with both the crisis in Rwanda and the problems that would arise once the civil war and genocide stopped, but their efforts were also often trampled by aggressive, unilateral actions taken by some agencies and NGOs.

The NGOs resisted cooperation with the U.N. leadership in central Africa, often claiming to have had enough experience operating in dangerous environments as not to need the help, protection, and coordination of the U.N. mission and its troops. In a number of cases, NGOs flatly refused to follow UNAMIR/UNREO procedures and plans of action intended not only to ensure their own protection but, most important, to maximize the delivery of humanitarian relief in the Great Lakes region. Some even refused to allow UNAMIR forces to support their efforts or to deliver the supplies to Rwandan civilians. In some cases, this meant that the supplies were delivered directly to the belligerents, who would take all of the credit with the suffering people for distributing some of the food supplies and material while hoarding the rest, including fuel and medical supplies, for their own military campaigns. At one point, substantial amounts of aid were being distributed to the RPF, while nothing was reaching behind RGF lines where the slaughtering and large-scale displacements were occurring.

This inequitable relief effort, and the significant security risks, heightened the tensions between the belligerents and UNAMIR, making negotiations for even limited truces difficult at best. In fact, UNAMIR was accused of supporting the RPF war effort through this lopsided and undisciplined humanitarian effort, thus discrediting further the already battered reputation the mission had earned because of the pullout and exacerbating the stagnating cease-fire negotiations.

Providing aid to those in need cannot and *must* not be done in blissful, naive isolation from the political and security considerations in the crisis or mission area. It became painfully apparent to me in Rwanda that an ad hoc emergency provision of aid to those in need without situating it in the political and security context ultimately not only puts at risk those currently receiving aid but, more important, increases the prospect of not being able to help an even larger number of people at a later date.

Needless to say, the humanitarian efforts in Rwanda were of a much more reactive and haphazard nature than the product of effective planning and coordination. This is not to suggest that help was not provided to Rwandan refugees, as distinct from displaced persons inside Rwanda. Indeed, those refugees that ended up in Tanzania in the first months of the war were as well taken care of as those in eastern Zaire in July and August 1994. Yet, no mandate or effort was made to establish real security in these camps. RGF troops and militiamen were mixed in with the general civilian population, and as a result, an underground command element took control of the camps and put at risk not only Rwandan civilians but all the relief personnel as well. At the same time, there was an inability to address the larger problem of encouraging the Rwandans to return home, which could have been advanced by increasing humanitarian assistance and security inside the country. On the contrary, the flood of aid reaching areas outside Rwanda was encouraging thousands to spill over the borders.

UNAMIR's mandate was limited to Rwanda, while in areas outside the state, nearly two million Rwandans were starving, sick, or being held hostage or executed. In this environment the special representative of the secretary-general (SRSG), designated by the secretary-general as the overall authority for humanitarian efforts for Rwandans *in the region,* was severely restricted in his ability to coordinate the overall effort. As late as July 1994, disagreement continued between UNAMIR and the UNHCR concerning the Goma "overaid" effort and bickering about whether UNAMIR's increased troop capabilities could cross the borders and enter the refugee camps to try to separate genocide suspects from innocent civilians. The broader interpretations of Security Council Resolution 925 of 8 June would have permitted UNAMIR to assist the refugees held hostage by RGF forces and militias in remote border regions to return to Rwanda, where they could be better fed and protected, and to assist in the overall stabilization of the situation. This mandate specifically authorized UNAMIR to come to the aid of those refugees and displaced persons while pursuing cease-fire negotiations.

The presence of the armed gangs in the camps jeopardized the relief effort and the protection of human rights. Open conflicts of opinion and methods among UNAMIR, the U.N. agencies, and NGOs on how to handle the former government forces and their families created much confusion. The restricting of UNAMIR's role played into the hands of the same extremists who had participated in the slaughter of hundreds of thousands of Tutsi and Hutu moderates, as the gangs were now in a position to rebuild their forces, particularly in eastern Zaire. Thus shielded from accountability for the use of humanitarian aid and from the human rights investigators and international legal agencies, they were able to prepare for their return to Rwanda and potentially to oust the RPF within the months or years to come, ensuring a continued destabilization of the region and a waste of hundreds of millions of dollars of aid resources that filtered through their black-marketing hands. In my opinion, it was morally and tactically wrong to sterilize the refugees in the peripheral camps under the control of the extremists. No doubt the humanitarian agencies, particularly the UNHCR, faced incredibly intense moral, legal, and operational dilemmas of their own and also received mixed signals and direction from various authorities and national elements. Here again the lack of compatibility between the humanitarian assistance agencies on the ground and the overall U.N. mission hampered plans to deal with Rwanda's refugees, even after both U.N. military strength and aid began to arrive in larger amounts *inside* Rwanda by late August 1994.

While the UNAMIR force and others were attempting to balance moral concerns with practical considerations, the international community finally began to respond more adequately to the crisis. U.N. Security Council Resolution 928 in mid-June 1994 (two months into the genocide) enabled a more proactive humanitarian protection and support mandate, backed up by authorizing the size of the force to grow to 5,500 personnel. The mandate included the establishment of secure humanitarian sites for refugees and displaced persons, the provision of support and security for the distribution of humanitarian relief supplies, human rights surveillance, and the establishment of an arms embargo against Rwanda.

Conclusion

A strong debate on the use of military force in such complicated and high-risk humanitarian efforts was pervasive in my small force then, and it is still ongoing. Is risking a soldier's life worse than risking a civilian NGO worker's? What criteria do the major powers use when determining that soldiers should avoid risks of casualties while civilians face it head-on? As an example, the U.S. involvement in and around Rwanda presents a paradox that does not suit a global power. In my mind, it remains evident that even though U.S. soldiers and field commanders were more than willing to do much more, they were ordered to stay out, avoid casualties, and smile for the cameras. Of course domestic politics have a direct influence on foreign policy, but when spin doctors slow and enfeeble relief efforts of the big powers well below the minimum of support required to stop the enormous suffering at hand, I believe we should look more closely at what middle and third world nations, which also had to balance moral assessments of support against risks of casualties, can ultimately do. Canada, Australia, the United Kingdom, Ghana, India, Ethiopia, and Tunisia all put their efforts *inside* Rwanda in earnest support of the SRSG's overall regional humanitarian support efforts, staying out of the media limelight but right in the front line where they were needed most. These nations, some desperately poor, shamed the world by doing the right thing. So, do we pursue these middle powers to deploy up front and keep the world's first powers in reserve, in support of the operations? I believe this option merits serious study and review.

A successful U.N. operation or mission must increase the level of consultation and coordination among national governments, grass-roots organizations, U.N. agencies, and front-line NGOs. This will occur only through the competence of a new generation of political, military, and humanitarian officials who are well schooled in the multidisciplinary skills of all elements of a mission structure and fully integrated planning. In the start-up phase, at a negotiating impasse, or certainly if a crisis erupts, only well-educated and trained political, military, and humanitarian officials, and ultimately troops and civilian police will be able to grasp the initiative and build a sustainable, integrated, and effective implementation of the complex mandates of this new generation of peacekeeping operations. The Canadian proposal tabled in September 1995 at the U.N. General Assembly for a Rapid Reaction Capability with an integral vanguard force would be a helpful approach. In the not so distant future, I foresee an even greater level of harmonization between U.N. operations and NGOs in spite of the shortcomings mentioned here. But our Rwanda experience also tells us that there are more fundamental requirements if the United Nations is to undertake interventions that can do more humanitarian good than harm. Such success will never be achieved by merely deploying U.N. troops in a classic fashion with unduly restrictive mandates that are simply too late and too limited. Clearly, peacekeeping cannot be an end in itself—it merely buys time. In its goals and its design, it must always be part of the larger continuum of peacemaking: conflict avoidance and resolution, relief and rehabilitation, development and hope. For this to come true, the U.N.'s most influential actors must collectively commit to viable strategies and back them up, instead of living by indulgent rhetoric and superficial action doomed to fail and by definition morally flawed. Then we can hopefully prevent the fourth genocide in this century, or the first genocide of the next.

Note

I acknowledge with gratitude the assistance of Lieutenant (Naval) Hugh A. Culliton and Captain James R. McKay in the preparation of this chapter.

5

Mixed Intervention in Somalia and the Great Lakes

Culture, Neutrality, and the Military

Mohamed Sahnoun

S ince the Cold War, the environment for humanitarian intervention has radically changed. The new challenge to humanitarian organizations leads them to a larger reassessment of their traditional methods of action, as they must now deal with new combinations and cope with a complex legacy. In a sense, history had been put in a freezer during the Cold War, given the central obsession of East-West confrontation. All the other ethical, political, and economic issues would have to wait until the world was saved from communism and atheism, so to speak. At the end of the Cold War, the freezer was opened and history exploded in our face. Pent-up frustration and animosity burst out, human rights abuses were revealed, and violence erupted in several theaters at once. In 1995 over thirty complex emergencies arose around the world. These conflicts were met with often confused and hastily organized responses from an ill-prepared but deeply concerned international community, reflecting, however, different kinds of priorities and interests. The international community, though stressing the desire to alleviate human suffering and searching for the best ways to bring about stability and order, is often paralyzed by these conflicting interests, while drawing suspicion about foreign intervention on the part of the recipient populations.

Four paradigms of humanitarian intervention are useful to examine, in an effort to better understand these new realities and how to deal with them. They are the interactions with a sensitive population, the recipients of aid; with often suspicious government officials and political actors, including belligerents and warlords; with international entities, both political and military; and with the issue of human rights, including protection of victims of humanitarian tragedies. Working with these paradigms in the context of Somalia and the Great Lakes, largely from the viewpoint of the humanitarian agencies, this chapter focuses on respect for the local culture, neutrality and coordination in humanitarian aid, and the impact of the military element.

Working with the Local Population and Respect for the Local Culture

Somalia's Siad Barre government collapsed in early 1991. For more than a year there was a collapsed state with no kind of economy or politics and where people were literally starving. No humanitarian intervention occurred in Somalia until early 1992. The International Committee of the Red Cross (ICRC) and a few nongovernmental organizations (NGOs) were the only ones in the country, and when the U.N. Children's Fund (UNICEF) and the World Food Programme (WFP) arrived, the Somalis, out of their terrible frustration asked, Why didn't you come to help us earlier? Late intervention created an atmosphere of suspicion in the country, and this was the first impact on the local population: the erosion of trust. *Quick response* is a major factor as a way of creating both better conditions for a political solution and also a friendly environment.

Effective relations with the indigenous peoples of a country depend on *understanding,* ideally starting with a better analysis of the political and social dimensions of conflicts. A clear awareness of the historical and cultural background of the country can enable the managers and operators of humanitarian programs to see things relatively. For instance, it is important to know how Somalis are divided into tribal groups as a way of understanding how they make decisions. The divisions, the clans, the groupings, are less determined by ethnicity, language, or anthropology than by economic and ecological conditions. The scarcity of water and pastoral land shaped a tribal system made up of clans defending what they perceived as vital interests. This led to a built-in need to consort and consult thoroughly within the clans and subclans, along with a very strong resentment toward people coming from outside and trying to impose solutions on them. We were able to make progress in Somalia only through our understanding of the clan system and our ability to work with the elders. As we sat on the floor with the main elders in each area and sought their views and advice, they returned this respect, moved by the fact that we had taken the time to visit them. One of the reasons that the U.N. lost ground in Somalia was that we undermined the traditional system by antagonizing the elders and a number of relays within the civil society, including grassroots institutions. The point is that help from the outside will not be effective without an understanding of the traditional consultation and decision-making process.

Showing a motivation and an ability to work with indigenous human resources is therefore a necessary element for effective relationships with local populations. Except for the ICRC and a few others, most international humanitarian institutions clearly failed to identify with local NGOs in Somalia or in the Great Lakes region or to make a serious effort to engage them in humanitarian and rehabilitation activities. Too often the various engagements of outside parties in Somalia failed to make use of local networks, good channels for assistance, which led to a top-down process rather than a grassroots approach and was symptomatic generally of a low priority placed on local participation.

There is no greater example when advocating the value of working with and mobilizing local people and capacity than the case of women. In Africa, especially, women are potential messengers of peace and dialogue. They are really in charge of a number of sectors in economic and social life. They are the ones who very largely control the markets. They are extremely efficient and regarded as ethically correct because they will not divert goods and become a vector of corruption. Tending to present themselves as sisters, mothers, and wives, they can be very persuasive. Even warlords are vulnerable to their advocacy. Women can organize spontaneously and quickly if they are given the means to do so, such as mimeograph machines to issue newsletters and other documents, tape recorders, etc. When a serious confrontation was cooking up in Mogadishu, between the warlords across the north-south line, I called on the Somali women to ask for their help. The next morning a large demonstration of women took place, and representations made by them to the warlords had a major effect on that specific danger.

Of course, the gender issue has to be approached very carefully, in some cultures more than others, and interlopers must take care not to violate or create animosity with local norms when pursuing a given policy course even in those instances when it can be characterized as highly motivated, idealistic, or efficient. Yet, addressing the needs of women and working with them as much as possible—having women-led NGOs, for instance—should be an integral principle for humanitarian intervention, carefully thought through and respectfully engaged.

What happens when the essential principles that must govern the assistance providers come into conflict with local practices and norms? The answer to this moral quandary is found in the attempt to respect both sides in the application of humanitarian programs. If no workable reconciliation can be practically achieved, then it would be incumbent on the intervenors to withdraw rather than sacrifice their basic precepts. But this should not be done summarily or arrogantly, and a lot can be achieved by patient, mutual effort. In whatever country, the humanitarian agencies must not abandon their commitment to the equal treatment of women in the face of an extreme fundamentalist, dogmatic stand. This is not a matter of respecting local culture but of dealing with an ideology imposed by outside forces and elaborated largely as a reaction to the period during the Cold War when Afghanistan was under a Marxist occupation and as a way to cope with social and economic inequities in other countries.

Nevertheless, the manner in which humanitarian authorities and agencies design, negotiate, and implement their programs may avoid an open confrontation. This goal is not easy, but I believe that sometimes it can be attained by applying the approach of minimum assistance: that is, determining what humanitarian aid is absolutely crucial for the survival of the community, for the survival of people, and channeling this aid in the least objectionable way; concentrate on this basic priority, and go about it with some proportion and sensitivity. It is important here not to be cowed by the dogma of others but also not to respond to it in a dogmatic manner yourself.

Respect for and the ability to work closely and effectively with the people of an aid-receiving country clearly lie at the moral core of humanitarian intervention. Intervention cannot be morally justified without demonstrating devotion to this principle while attempting to resolve the inherent complexities that will inevitably be involved. Here lie the complexity and difficulty of the challenge.

Interaction with Government and Political Leaders

Decisions to be made regarding proper political relationships by a multiple international presence—humanitarian, economic, political, and military—in a crisis-ridden country are critical to its success as a purely operational matter. But setting the standards for and conducting these relations with the various parties in a complicated, confused local scene also involve important moral calculations. And the central question here is the principle of neutrality, impartiality, and choices as to how to interpret and apply it, which is absolutely central to working efficiently, coping with the political environment, and establishing good working relations with the given officials.

Different schools of thought, or models, about neutrality have emerged over the past few years. I see some great disadvantages in recommending that humanitarian agencies work very closely with the political-military operational elements. Although some coordination should be sought, a very close association would be harmful to the humanitarian agencies that would then be identified as instruments of the broader political-military strategy. This view would clearly lead to suspicion and mistrust toward the institutions whose objective is to help the local population and, therefore, need to be trusted. I prefer the way the ICRC operates, which implies that of course there should be coordination among humanitarian organizations and with the military and political institutions, but their operational activities should remain totally separate. This model reflects the discipline and integrity necessary to combine principle, pluralism, and operational efficiency, to strive for an arrangement that sacrifices neither principle nor pragmatism.

The credibility of the work of the humanitarian agencies depends on its efficiency and ability to assist as many people as possible. It also requires full acceptance by the various influential political forces. To achieve these objectives, humanitarian agencies will need to maintain a high degree of impartiality. It is necessary for them to reduce the danger of being exploited, co-opted, or even blackmailed by other priorities in their own alliance. Humanitarian agencies will have to be aware of the tendency of some donor countries to get away from their responsibilities by substituting humanitarian assistance for meaningful political and economic action. Humanitarian agencies must thus be as totally open as they can be in explaining to the donor countries the need to sustain their neutrality and state firmly that no pressure from them or their political constituencies will change their agenda or abdicate their impartiality.

Efforts to reconcile the interdependent but often quarrelsome imperatives of assistance and protection offer a vivid example of the need to guard neutrality, apply a principle, respect local views, and invent new policy formulas to deal with unprecedented challenges. The classic contemporary example of this dilemma can be found in the Rwandan refugee camps of eastern Zaire, where the U.N. High Commissioner for Refugees (UNHCR) faced the problem of separating combatants from aid recipients. This problem was never satisfactorily resolved. The UNHCR was effectively rebuffed by both the host government and the Security Council when, feeling it did not have the power to accomplish this task itself, it requested security help, which it never got. There will probably not be an end to confrontations between emergency assistance and human rights protection, and except for attempting to measure the practical exigencies with real moral deliberation, there is no calculus that can be counted on to work in different circumstances. Help the people and not the combatants, protect the principles of human rights and humanitarian law—yes. Honor the need for neutrality and separateness, and stick with principle in the face of local political or cultural intransigence—yes.

But there must also be the capability both to make the judgment and to act on it. In the event that the situation is so impacted and international efforts are sufficiently unable to deal with complex realities on the ground and more harm than good results, then the best course is to stop, withdraw, and seek other means to address the crisis.

One contemporary development at New York headquarters discussed in some quarters as an outgrowth of the 1997 U.N. reform exercise is the designation of the Department of Political Affairs (DPA) in the U.N. secretariat as the "focal point" for nation building. The consequence of this development is difficult to interpret, and we will have to wait to see how it actually plays out. But on the face of it, a U.N. staff unit with the political affairs mandate being assigned overall responsibility for rehabilitation and development activity (which the term *nation building* encompasses) raises the danger of the loss of impartiality of U.N. agencies in the field. Nation building certainly requires coordination in many sensitive areas—the setting of priorities for governance, for instance, and issues such as corruption and reconciliation. But my experience leads me to believe that if the political branch is dealing with this issue, there will be a propensity to see a hidden agenda and efforts at control to arise that will interfere with alliance building between the humanitarian and developmental agencies and the local authorities. The way the U.N. organizes itself also should not run the risk of trying to be the trustee of the process when it should be assisting the process and ultimately preserving its role as political mediator. The junction between humanitarian and development work—rehabilitation—requires delicate dovetailing, coordination, and collaboration, which is not happening yet. But putting in charge a headquarters agency that in effect knows very little—and is neither responsible nor rewarded for knowing—about the substance of this work and can in no effective way be held accountable for it is not the way to encourage nation building.

For humanitarian agencies to interact effectively with local political leaders and to avoid hopeless operational confusion, there must be serious coordination among themselves and between them and the other intervenors. This precept, like so many others set forth to help illuminate our subject, is much easier said than done. It also reminds us again of the central argument that to approach humanitarian inter-

vention morally, one must start with a willingness to struggle with
the vagaries, conflicts, and obstacles involved without submitting to
illusion or fantasy. *Coordination* has even become a pejorative term,
often used as the scapegoat for the lack of real authority or the excuse
for unilateral behavior. But its difficulty or misuse does not call into
question its importance.

Coordination in the field requires the headquarters of the various
agencies not only to act so that cooperation in field programs is encouraged but also to make clear that this goal is what their representatives in the recipient countries are expected to bring about. These
agencies have different mandates and talents, constituencies and
funding sources, but their diversity and individuality must not be allowed to create chaos. Better sharing of information and stronger
continuing consultation among them are necessary. In my opinion, it
would be useful for a code of conduct among the different agencies
to be established to reduce competition and overbidding for office or
storage space and payment for local employment and services. There
should also be more unity on policies and practices relating to the
provision and conditions of security and criteria for withdrawal of
personnel and cessation of programs. In addition, both clarity and
stability of the mandates of U.N. entities, at least, would be helpful
toward achieving greater coherence and better output; nothing is
more disruptive than fuzzy responsibilities and shifting activity, and
both of these tendencies were prominent in both Somalia and the
Great Lakes region. Humanitarian and development agencies must be
ready and willing to cooperate with, get help from, and follow the
guidance of the U.N.'s political and military authorities when appropriate, particularly with respect to protection, but this can be done
without sacrificing their institutional integrity and their neutrality.
The coordination imperative must be honored along with its requirement for operational separation, the latter being no excuse for behav-
ing blindly and disrespectfully toward other groups of intervenors
with their own roles and contributions.

Good coordination necessitates some entity to have the coordinating responsibility as part of its duly constituted mandate. For that
responsibility to be carried out effectively requires qualities of persuasion, the talent of catalyzing cooperation, rather than command—

which simply will not work in the case of experienced, overstretched agencies with a long history of autonomy. A coordinating entity that thinks of itself as the supreme court can lead to serious misunderstandings. Consider, for example, the Department of Humanitarian Affairs (DHA), headquartered in the U.N. secretariat in New York and named the coordinator of humanitarian programs in Somalia starting in 1992. This unit seemed to interpret its role to mean that it was the chief orchestra. This created problems. Wanting to demonstrate that it was in charge of coordination, it would hold meeting after meeting to this end. But representatives of the operational agencies would after a while either not come to the meetings or just sit there and not participate. I tried to emphasize that coordination meant to be of service, to understand what the needs are and try to get them answered. I told them I needed a DHA representative at the airport in Mogadishu, for instance, to be an intermediary with local officials and resolve problems for the humanitarian agencies. Then I would go and they were not there, and I would find them back at the office briefing media people.

It is important in the coordinating role to avoid going in just to show that you are coordinating and by so doing actually frustrate getting the job done. Also, whatever coordination structure or process exists must not be so dominating as to undermine local efforts but rather include them in its facilitating role.

The Effects of Military Intervention

Relations between humanitarian efforts and the military role are going to be inherently difficult in any crisis area. Once again, there is the lurking concern, if not danger, of humanitarian assistance becoming an instrument in political strategy for military objectives. When the military intervention began in Somalia, it was for the purpose of protecting the delivery of humanitarian assistance, but it soon became something else—an intervention to organize a political process for reconciliation. When the imposition of this agenda on the humanitarian programs was resisted, the environment became less congenial and more suspicious. And later, when the military intervention went

further and began to hunt down an individual leader, the relations
with his particular camp were severely jeopardized, and the overall
environment became nonviable both within the collaborative intervention and with the Somalis. Integrating security with assistance and
rehabilitation programs is intensely challenging in the best situations,
but I believe that specific decisions were taken that were wrong in this
case and that, from a moral perspective, were likely to undermine the
overall mission undertaken by the U.N. and its partners.

To go back to the beginning, if the political and humanitarian intervention had been made earlier, then the military option would have
presented itself in a different fashion. The banditry and chaos and
warlordship had built up too far. This situation, in turn, led to a
disproportional emphasis on security and too many troops. The size
of the military intervention in Somalia could have been much more
limited than it was, which would have been better, because such a
large number can result in ambitions and objectives that will lead
beyond the stated mandate. You cannot move 30,000 soldiers and
then say, "We are only here to protect humanitarian assistance." You
may think, "Why not use this military intervention to solve the whole
political problem?" Such a mind-set takes on a life of its own, and
the chance for balance and equilibrium is lost. Of the $2 billion in-
vestment in the intervention in Somalia, a very small amount, less
than 10 percent, went toward assisting the Somalis in institution
building and social and economic reconstruction; everything was
really spent on the military operation.

To cite a specific issue, I had felt that small military units should be
posted in specific areas, where the security was needed and with the
agreement of the local authorities, principally ports and airports, to
support unloading and dispatching prior to delivery of humanitarian
assistance. Among them were four ports: Mogadishu, Kismayu, Bos-
saso, and Berbera, key entry points in covering the four important
regions of Somalia that had been hard-hit with starvation and misery.
With Security Council approval, a technical team was to assess how
many soldiers were needed under this approach for each location.
The team, with my participation and guidance, had to consult carefully with the Somali leaders of each region and work out a good
mutual understanding and gain their acceptance before we could pro-

ceed. But when this process had just begun, we heard over the BBC that Secretary-General Boutros Boutros-Ghali had announced the figure of 3,000 troops. The Somalis turned to me and said, "What is this nonsense? How can you send 3,000 people here without telling us about it?" Here is, to my way of thinking, an example of the military mentality overemphasizing size at the expense of a sensibly focused— constrained as to location and function—deployment of forces and at the expense of viable relations with the local political environment.

Humanitarian organizations must also achieve enough solidarity among themselves so that they are able to resist the imposition—for instance, by the deployment of security assets—of political-military priorities in the delivery of humanitarian goods and services that do not conform with their own best humanitarian criteria. This kind of concentration of aid in certain areas can increase tension and misunderstanding. Another danger of humanitarian principles being undermined that must be guarded against relates to the local worry and suspicion of arms being trafficked by intervenors to this or that warlord. The case actually occurred that U.N.-marked planes that were run during the day by the WFP or UNICEF were also transporting military equipment into Somalia by night for one of the two main factions. Great care must be applied regarding any move that can be perceived by the local environment as being partial, especially in the case of military activity.

To avoid some of the problems discussed here, when the Security Council is drafting resolutions affecting intervention and considering specific actions in a conflict area, the expertise and views of humanitarian organizations should be included in the process. At the time of the conception of a political and military intervention, not just during its implementation, the humanitarian perspective can thus be made available, and the risk of humanitarian agencies being committed to things that are compromising or dangerous is lessened.

I am not opposed to the principle of a military presence; I think that sometimes it is absolutely justified. Such a presence, however, must be capable of being absorbed by the local environment: tolerance for it must be measured first, then acceptance gradually developed. There might have been moral legitimacy for some kind of military presence in Somalia. Those who first argued in favor of a military presence there felt that the situation during October, November, and December 1992 deteriorated so abruptly that the humanitarian organizations themselves could not operate, and some were asking for help. Until my departure in October, I and the people who were there then did not see such a pressing need for a military presence. We were able to move around and do our work; most organizations had hired some guards for some time. Had the situation dramatically changed after I left, then probably some kind of limited presence was needed, but I doubt that it required a very large one, and here we come back to the question of size.

Eventually, the U.N., which is supposed to make peace, found itself killing people, hunting people, and bombing a meeting of elders under the mistaken impression that General Aideed was among them. In terms of human ethics, this was not a happy page of history for the U.N. If the basic objective and criteria become military, then everything has to respect the military logic. A distortion, an imbalance, a disproportionality is introduced—morally and operationally. Once you introduce into such a fragile and complex situation such a huge number of soldiers, that reality is likely to dominate the agenda, and everything must align itself to that. The political moves, as well as some of the humanitarian and developmental moves, are conditioned accordingly, and local norms and people may be overrun. Forces have been set in motion that are likely to get out of control, and such consequences need to be considered with greater insight and wisdom when the intervention is first contemplated.

6

Military-Humanitarian
Ambiguities in Haiti

Colin Granderson

On 30 September 1991, the government of Jean-Bertrand Aristide was overthrown in a military coup. This was the time-honored way of resolving political conflict in Haiti, aptly summarized in the Haitian Creole adage that "constitutions are made of paper and bayonets of steel." The old ruling elite, whose long-standing interests and privileges had been threatened by the fundamental social, political, and economic changes that the Aristide government had sought to bring about, applauded warmly this brusque return to the old status quo. They were smugly confident that, as in the past, the rhetorical storm of critical statements, declarations, and resolutions whipped up by the international community would abate swiftly. However, as the immediate future would show, they had misjudged the very real changes that had taken place both locally and in the international arena and that would bring about an unexpected and unprecedented reaction.

The presidential and parliamentary elections of December 1990, the culmination of long-held popular desires and bitter and sometimes bloody struggle, represented in many ways a clean break with Haitian electoral practice. With the assistance of the international community, the Provisional Electoral Council was able to organize what were widely hailed as the first free and fair popular elections in

Haitian history. The Haitian people voted overwhelmingly for the candidate who best symbolized their aspirations. Consequently, the overthrow of President Aristide was not merely the destitution of a president but also the reversal of popular will and the negation of eagerly awaited expectations and necessary social change.

In the international arena, the collapse of the Soviet empire and communism and the end of the Cold War were altering some of the basic tenets of international relations. Respect for human rights and fundamental freedoms, good governance, and strengthening democracy were now being given far higher priority by both the Organization of American States (OAS) and the United Nations. In this new environment, the U.N. began to play a more active role in conflict resolution. Nowhere was this more noticeable than in the area of peacekeeping, where the number of operations increased and their character changed. Today's second-generation operations are multifaceted, involving military, political, and humanitarian aspects. As U.N. Secretary-General Boutros Boutros-Ghali pointed out in "An Agenda for Peace," "increasingly peace-keeping requires that civilians, political officers, human rights monitors, electoral officials, refugee and humanitarian aid specialists and police play as central a role as the military."[1] The phenomenon of Haitian "boat people" also added an international dimension to what had been a purely internal problem. A controversial issue injected into American politics would ensure that over and beyond its hemispheric role, the United States would have a direct interest in finding a solution to the Haitian political crisis.

The crisis in Haiti involved both civilian and military actors, first separately, and then together within a "second-generation" peacekeeping effort. In addition to dealing with the problems inherent in their respective mandates and areas of responsibilities, some of these civilian actors had to operate in ambivalent emergency situations in which contradictions, difficult choices, dilemmas, and moral tensions would be the order of the day, even before the military intervention took place.

The Dilemmas of International Civilian Action

Immediately after the coup d'état, diplomatic efforts to resolve the political crisis were initiated. They continued for three years, first by the OAS and later by the U.N., punctuated by ephemeral break-throughs and negotiated agreements that were thwarted ultimately by the intransigence of the Haitian military. Diplomatic efforts were bolstered by two mechanisms, a regional and, later, an international economic embargo, as well as by the fielding of a human rights observation mission.

The international community and its organizations have few powerful means of dissuasion at their disposal in dealing with regimes that trample international law or inflict systematic abuse on their people. Not surprisingly, there has been frequent recourse to the embargo over the years. However, its effectiveness and morality have always been a matter of dispute. To the extent that an embargo relies on attrition to produce the desired result, it more often than not extends over long periods of time and has a significant negative impact on the most vulnerable groups of the targeted country. This outcome was indeed the case in Haiti. An embargo can also make the functioning of developmental agencies virtually impossible.

The Specialized Agencies

As the poorest and least developed country in the Western Hemisphere, and having endured very long periods of notoriously repressive authoritarian rule, Haiti has attracted the ministrations of a multitude of international agencies and organizations, governmental and nongovernmental, in the areas of development, humanitarian relief, human rights, and proselytization. All these international actors were affected, to a greater or lesser extent, by the constraints of the political and economic crisis that resulted from the 1991 coup d'état. However, the civilian international actors linked to the regional and international governmental bodies (the OAS and U.N.) found themselves particularly constrained by the political decisions of their supervisory organizations, which refused to recognize the de facto government and implemented economic sanctions.

Consequently, humanitarian relief took precedence as development and aid programs were brought to a halt. Distinguishing between what was developmental and what was humanitarian became an agonizing exercise for the specialized agencies. This dilemma was particularly striking in November 1992 when the OAS and the U.N. jointly undertook to draft an emergency relief program for Haiti. Was providing seed, fertilizers, and seedlings to planters who might otherwise starve humanitarian or developmental? What about family planning and assistance to children and women? Should condoms be placed on the WHO/PAHO (World Health and Pan American Health Organizations) list of essential medical items and drugs? When did meeting a basic need cease to be humanitarian and become developmental? The answers were not always clear, leading to differences of opinion among the representatives of the different agencies. The situation was rendered even more difficult by the scarcely veiled hostility of the local representatives of the constitutional government to the humanitarian assistance programs, which were seen as strengthening the hand of the de facto regime and as a way for the international community to give itself a clear conscience with regard to the embargo's effects.

Tensions between pragmatism and principle were constant. When in mid-1993 fuel ceased to be available in gas stations, the only source of supply for organizations involved in humanitarian relief was the black market, controlled by the military and its allies. This remained the case until January 1994 when PAHO initiated a humanitarian fuel project. The human rights observation mission thought it politically wiser not to apply lest the hostility its operations elicited from the military become an obstacle to the smooth functioning of a critical humanitarian mechanism.

Another dilemma stemmed from the existence of a constitutional government in exile and the consequent need to avoid contact with the de facto authorities so as not to convey legitimacy. To the extent that certain formalities (e.g., importation of essential drugs and relief supplies) could not be circumvented, some minimal contact was unavoidable. This problem became even more acute in mid-1994, when the last de facto regime actually sought to impose contact in exchange for permitting the continuing importation of relief supplies and the rotation of personnel. A number of expedients and ingenious administrative procedures were conjured up in response to this predicament.

The OAS/UN International Civilian Mission in Haiti

The joint OAS/U.N. International Civilian Mission in Haiti (MICI-VIH) was deployed in February 1993 at the request of President Aristide and in response to a situation characterized by systematic and grave human rights abuses. The continuing efforts of the de facto authorities to derive some sort of legitimacy from their contacts with the OAS and U.N. led to the unprecedented and ambivalent situation of MICIVIH having two separate terms of reference, one *de jure*, agreed with the constitutional government, and one de facto, accepted by the illegal regime. The latter did, however, grant MICIVIH broad powers, particularly with respect to gathering information, gaining access to places where human rights violations had been reported, and reporting publicly on violations.

The human rights observation mission was also viewed as an instrument to facilitate a political solution. In addition to its initial task "of verifying compliance with Haiti's international human rights obligations," the mission was also called on "to assist in the establishment of a climate of freedom and tolerance propitious to the re-establishment of democracy in Haiti."[2] Indeed, the agreement of the de facto authorities on the deployment of the mission was perceived as a first and significant step in a comprehensive strategy leading to a political resolution of the crisis.

Linking the monitoring mission to the political efforts to resolve the crisis peacefully could have led to contradictions and tensions between the political imperatives of the negotiating strategy and the human rights remit of the mission, which would have jeopardized the effectiveness of the latter. As the Lawyers Committee for Human Rights points out in its study of MICIVIH, "according to UN officials, a deliberate decision was made to distinguish clearly between the process of political negotiations and the work of the MICIVIH. This was supposedly done to safeguard the impartiality and objectivity of the Mission."[3] Such a distinction proved difficult to apply, however, and although the dual mandate resulted in unprecedented autonomy for the monitoring mission, it did have negative consequences. Human rights information documented by the monitoring mission as an indicator of the wider political situation was not fully utilized. As a result, warning signals of political deterioration were not always immediately heeded, as was the case in the post–Governor's Island Agreement period. Second, the Governor's Island Accord made no mention of the need for the military to improve the human rights situation. This omission was partially rectified in a letter addressed to

President Aristide by the special envoy in which the latter stated that respect for human rights would be one of the criteria used to measure the military's adhesion to the accord. Unfortunately, the head of the Haitian army was not a party to this side letter. Third, MICIVIH's absence from the Governor's Island negotiations arguably weakened the moral authority of the monitoring mission vis-à-vis the military and the de facto authorities. This political marginalization of the mission and human rights undoubtedly reinforced the military in its belief that human rights were not a priority for the international community.

The issue of amnesty for the perpetrators of human rights abuse highlighted the differences between the political goals of the diplomatic negotiator and the human rights objectives of the observation mission. On the one hand, the mission was doing its utmost to document and report on egregious human rights violations with a view to putting an end to the traditional impunity of wrongdoers. On the other hand, the amnesty to be granted by the president and broadened by parliament became an important carrot to win political concessions from the military, thereby further entrenching impunity.

In addition to these political ambiguities, the mission also had to wrestle with the moral practicalities of impartiality, neutrality, and objectivity in working out its operating strategies. As far as the military and de facto authorities were concerned, the mission by definition could not be impartial. It had been deployed by the OAS and U.N. at the request of the overthrown president, following a number of scathing reports directly attributing to them the responsibility for the gravity of the human rights situation. To what extent could the mission overcome this inbuilt bias by being seen to be impartial in order to establish a working relationship without which it could not successfully try to mitigate the human rights situation? The mission had no enforcement mechanisms available to it and could therefore rely only on moral suasion and the pressure of public opinion. Did the military and the mission have the same understanding of impartiality? To the extent that the military denied forcefully that its men were committing human rights violations, impartiality meant for it the mission remaining silent. This would have been tantamount to being complicit. In any event, could a human rights–monitoring mission morally remain neutral between a human rights victim and the perpetrator of the abusive act? As far as the local human rights organizations and like-minded associations were concerned, there could be no quibbling with regard to the moral practicalities of impartiality and neutrality. The mission was seen as having been sent by the international community to protect its members from the all-pervasive repression and the trampling of their fundamental rights.

The mission's response to these considerations was facilitated by the unrelenting reluctance of the military leaders to be forthcoming. A strategy of forceful public reporting on the human rights situation was therefore adopted in order to bring public pressure and the weight of international opinion to bear on the military. In the context in which it found itself, MICIVIH could clearly not be a neutral player. Its forceful stance on denouncing human rights violations was crucial in establishing its credibility, though this irritated the military.

To an even greater extent than the humanitarian relief agencies, the human rights–monitoring mission was confronted by the dilemma of contact with the de facto authorities and the attendant tensions between principle and pragmatism. According to the mission's terms of reference, "the authorities" were responsible for ensuring the safety of members of the mission. They were also requested to supply any information that the mission required and to refrain from obstructing its work. Despite the deliberate ambiguity, the document was clearly referring to those very authorities who were not recognized by the international community. In addition, the security forces (the Armed Forces of Haiti) were both the power behind the de facto government and the perpetrators of systematic human rights abuse. The mission could choose between simply observing, documenting, and reporting what was taking place and intervening with the authorities to alleviate the plight of victims or even to preempt certain occurrences by being proactive. The mission adopted the latter course, embarking on a strategy it called "active observation." Initial criticism of this contact with the military by prodemocracy organizations soon disappeared when it became evident that the mission's interventions on behalf of victims met with some success.

However, contact and dialogue with the Haitian military came to an end when the mission returned to Haiti in January 1994 from evacuation after the October 1993 withdrawal of the U.S.S. *Harlan County*. The military refused to recognize the legitimacy of the mission's presence. It also impeded its freedom of movement by delivering threats and harassment and by physically preventing observers on occasion from entering provincial towns.

As the repression intensified and the human rights situation deteriorated, MICIVIH found itself confronted with a number of difficult policy choices while adapting its tactics to the changing reality. Information collected indicated some disturbing new patterns. The repression had become more selective and appeared to be seeking to decapitate the most active popular organizations. Programs put in place by the U.S. authorities to accelerate the political asylum process for this category of human rights victim were being castigated by the prodemocracy popular sector as an effort to weaken them politically by expatriating their leaders. The U.S. authorities had requested the assistance of the MICIVIH in helping sift *bona fide* applicants from those simply trying to take advantage of a narrow window of opportunity.

The mission did not wish to jeopardize its hard-won credibility by appearing to be supportive of a controversial program. At the same time it could not idly stand by as these leaders were hunted down. The decision was therefore taken to help on a case-by-case basis and to provide information when requested by the applicants who had made previous complaints of human rights violations to the mission. In a small number of critical cases, the mission made representation to the U.S. authorities in support of the applicants or to expedite their departure procedures.

Military International Actors

United Nations Mission in Haiti (UNMIH), 1993

In accordance with the Governor's Island Agreement, by its resolution of 23 September 1993 (S/RES/867) the Security Council decided to establish the United Nations Mission in Haiti (UNMIH). The mission was to entail 567 U.N. police observers and an engineering unit of approximately 700 men, of which 60 were to be military instructors. Their responsibilities included helping establish a separate civilian police force, modernizing and improving the professionalism of the military, and carrying out civil construction projects.

On 11 October 1993, the U.S.S. *Harlan County*, carrying some 200 U.S. and Canadian trainers and construction engineers as well as their equipment, arrived in the Port-au-Prince harbor. It was prevented from docking by the port authorities and an unruly mob of FRAPH (Revolutionary Front for the Advancement and Progress of Haiti) paramilitary members acting with the complicity of the Haitian army. The U.S. authorities took the decision to withdraw the *Harlan County*. However, the question as to whether narrow, short-term security and domestic political considerations outweighed broader, long-term political consequences in reaching this decision was inevitable. Clearly the Clinton administration could not risk the political backlash of U.S. military casualties in Haiti so soon after the Somalian trauma. But did such a risk really exist? Emmanuel Constant, the FRAPH paramilitary leader, confided to an interviewer that he had experienced great difficulty in keeping his demonstrators on the docks and that they would have fled at the merest sign of hostile intent. Would not the withdrawal of the *Harlan County* send the wrong political and military message to Haiti, and elsewhere, and raise questions about U.S. political capacity to use its military might overseas? This was precisely the lesson the Haitian military drew from the ship's departure. Two days later the Haitian minister of justice, Guy Malary, was assassinated in broad daylight. He had been formerly a legal adviser to the U.S. Embassy in Port-au-Prince, and his portfolio included as a priority issue the constitutionally required separation of the police from the army. In this rapidly deteriorating security situation, the advance UNMIH parties of U.S. military and Canadian civilian police already in the country was withdrawn. The Governor's Island Agreement had started to unravel.

The insertion and abrupt withdrawal of the first UNMIH military elements also had an immediate, deleterious impact on the presence and activities of the agencies working in the humanitarian and human rights field. In the eyes of the U.N. security experts, the personnel of these agencies were no longer protected from the Haitian security forces by the possibility that attacks against these personnel could trigger a forceful response from the international community. Perceived as being much more vulnerable to an increasingly defiant Haitian military, the civilian personnel were instructed to leave the country. The U.N. agencies argued successfully that because of the embargo, continued humanitarian relief work was a priority, and they evacuated only the members of staff deemed to be nonessential, as well as dependents.

Considered to be more of a security risk because of the political nature of their work, the human rights observers of MICIVIH were evacuated following a joint decision of both organizations. The mission's management argued that evacuation would be an abdication of moral responsibility. The victims and informants who had, at great personal risk, displayed confidence in the mission would now be left exposed to the reprisals of the military and its thugs. The same was also true of the local staff members. In addition, the question of whether the mission's withdrawal would do more harm than the good done by its presence was also raised. The mission director argued that there were no direct threats against mission members, or indeed any information to that effect, and that the mission staff had safely weathered earlier difficult security situations and was capable of doing so once again. These arguments were to no avail. Moral considerations had to yield to security imperatives. The observers also viewed their evacuation as a betrayal of trust on their part and responded with great outrage and even hostility. In many respects the evacuation was a deeply traumatic experience for the mission members—all the more so as the human rights situation worsened sharply during the three-month evacuation period. The first fleeting experience of mixed military-humanitarian intervention in Haiti was therefore not an auspicious one. It indicated that the civilians and the military had widely divergent views as to what constituted a security threat to the civilian actors. The second experience would bring to the fore very different problems.

The Multinational Force

The collapse of the Governor's Island Agreement in October 1993, the inability to craft a new diplomatic initiative to give new life to it, the expulsion of the MICIVIH in July 1994, the increasing exodus of Haitian boat people, and a steadily deteriorating political and human rights situation led inexorably to external military intervention. On 19 September 1994, the U.N.-authorized and U.S-dominated Multinational Force (MNF) entered Haiti. Thanks to a last-minute agreement hammered out by the Jimmy Carter delegation, the use of force took the form of a "permissive intervention" that averted the loss of lives and destruction an outright military invasion would have brought. The goals of this force, as set out in Security Council Resolution 940 of 31 July 1994, were to ensure the departure of the military regime, restore to office Haiti's constitutional authorities, and establish a secure and stable environment to facilitate the reinforcement of institutions and the rebuilding of the country.

Because of the Carter Agreement, the MNF found itself with a radically altered mandate. It was now to cooperate with the Haitian troops that it had been initially sent to dislodge, a situation that the U.S. soldiers and the ordinary Haitians had difficulty comprehending at the outset. The ambiguity of the situation was deepened by the fact that the Haitian military and their civilian thugs continued to ill treat and abuse Haitian citizens in full view of U.S. troops. This situation eventually led to a deterioration in relationships and to a more assertive and aggressive U.S. military stance vis-à-vis the Haitian security forces.

Two other policy positions of the MNF seemed contradictory and incomprehensible to many Haitians and outside observers. First, FRAPH, the paramilitary group created by the Haitian Armed Forces in August 1993, was initially treated as a legitimate political opposition group despite its well-known record of terror and large-scale human rights abuses as proxies of the Haitian military during the last year of the coup d'état period. Second, the MNF refused to undertake an aggressive and widespread disarmament campaign that many Haitians thought was critical in view of the large number of weapons in the hands of the paramilitary groups and also distributed to civilians during the weeks before the intervention. Instead, after seizing the heavy weapons of the Haitian Armed Forces, the MNF relied on a buy-back program, roadblocks, and searches following tips. This low-keyed approach was in part the consequence of the Somalia syndrome and the policy of "force protection" that sought to limit the exposure of the U.S. military to potentially dangerous situations.

Inevitably, these policy positions raised questions about Washington's political agenda and intentions. They also reinforced the doubts and cynicism of the many Haitians who were viscerally suspicious of Washington's plans and motives. The conclusion could, however, be drawn that after having taken a side militarily in the Haitian crisis in favor of the restoration of the constitutional government, the U.S. policy on the ground continued to be guided by the traditional principle that holds that intervention in civil conflict should be both limited and impartial in order to retain legitimacy and effectiveness.

As we saw earlier, the issue of impartiality had also arisen for the international civilian actors. However, in the highly polarized atmosphere of the postintervention period, U.S. impartiality was perceived as favoring one set of actors. This perception was reinforced when U.S. Embassy officials and the U.S. military facilitated the holding of a press conference by one of the leaders of the FRAPH paramilitary group.

For MICIVIH, which had repeatedly and publicly denounced the active participation of FRAPH in the repression of the coup d'état period, there were clearly fundamental differences in approach with regard to dealing with the paramilitary group. On the ground, the emerging pattern of cooperation and complicity between U.S. troops and FRAPH members, especially in the provincial capitals and towns, caused tensions and frictions with prodemocracy grassroots groups and popular organizations. In their routine meetings with U.S. military officers and units, MICIVIH officials and observers sought to explain the idiosyncrasies of local politics and to express their concerns over the damage being done to the political credibility and image of the international community by U.S. military contacts with well-known FRAPH elements.

Another potential source of conflict with the MNF was its involvement in cases of illegal arrests, detention, and searches of homes without warrants. Though the number of these incidents was relatively low, bearing in mind that the MNF was acting under the authority of the U.N. Security Council, their occurrence did point to the need for the integration of human rights concerns and mechanisms into the planning and implementation of peacekeeping-type activities.

Though monitoring the MNF respect for human rights was not part of MICIVIH's mandate, it could not simply turn a blind eye to these incidents. The quandary was deepened by the fact that in Port-au-Prince many of the persons arrested and detained by the MNF on security grounds were suspected by the mission of having been involved in serious human rights violations. These detainees included FADH (Armed Forces of Haiti) officers, notorious and dangerous *attachés* (thugs), and members of General Cedras's[4] bodyguard drawn from well-known merchant families, one of whom had frequently harassed MICIVIH staff, on one occasion confiscating radios and weapons of U.N. security agents. They were not prisoners of war but persons arrested by soldiers carrying out what were essentially civilian law enforcement and police tasks. Neither Haitian nor American due process requirements had been respected. Faced by a moral dilemma, the mission did what it thought best in the circumstances. It did not raise the matter of these due process violations officially with the MNF authorities but made known its concerns in the course of regular meetings with officers of the judge advocate's office of the MNF. The mission also kept itself informed of the situation of these detainees through its informal contacts with the representatives of the International Red Cross Committee who visited them regularly. Some of the detainees were subsequently released by the MNF as local security conditions improved. Others were handed over at the end of the MNF mandate to the Haitian authorities, who in turn released them because they lacked legal grounds for detaining them. With regard to the persons arrested by the MNF and handed over to Haitian police and judicial authorities, MICIVIH dealt with these cases locally, availing itself of Haitian legal and constitutional recourses.

On one occasion MICIVIH felt itself compelled to bring to the attention of the MNF commanding officers an incident that, because of the victims' official status, could have become politically embarrassing for the MNF itself and, ultimately, for the forthcoming U.N. peacekeeping mission. Some local officials and the director of a state company had attended a meeting at the invitation of the MNF Special Forces to discuss improving the supply of electricity. To encourage greater efficiency, these officials were briefly locked up and intimidated. To their credit, a senior MNF officer made a public apology for the behavior of his troops in the town where the incident had occurred, and disciplinary action was taken against the offending soldiers.

Nothing better illustrated the ambiguities and contradictions of the military–human rights mission coexistence than the brief arrest by the MNF of two MICIVIH human rights observers visiting a Port-au-Prince police station to investigate the arrest of a notorious *"attaché."* Despite identifying themselves and showing their U.N.-issued identity passes, they were detained because the MNF sergeant did not know who they were and had become suspicious of their inquiries. To avoid this type of situation, MICIVIH had briefed the MNF commanding officers on the mandate and responsibilities of the human rights observers. However, most MNF members never fully understood the observers' role and were constantly surprised to find them, without military escort, in the most isolated places. The U.S. Special Forces that remained with UNMIH after 31 March 1995 grew to better understand MICIVIH's activities with the passage of time and eventually collaborated and exchanged information with the observers, particularly with respect to the initial deployment of the first Haitian National Police contingents.

The MNF confiscation of the archives of the Haitian armed forces and documents belonging to FRAPH created a recurring problem for MICIVIH. The mission and the U.N. were repeatedly criticized by the regional branch of a local human rights organization for not ensuring the return of these documents, which they believed could have played a useful role in the investigation of human rights abuses of the coup d'état period.

In the final stages of the MNF presence, cooperation and coordination between MICIVIH and MNF were facilitated by the designation of an MNF liaison officer. In addition, the two missions found common ground in their collaborative attempts to improve the insalubrious conditions of detention in Haitian prisons, as well as to address the issue of prolonged pretrial detention that led to prison overpopulation. The MNF interest in prisons was a late development that came about after a change in commanding officers. It represented a complete about-face compared with its earlier avoidance of the question and its attendant problems. Indeed, a midlevel MNF officer was court-martialed in 1995 for visiting the National Penitentiary without permission after his superiors had turned down his repeated requests to do so on humanitarian grounds.

Despite differences in goals, perceptions, policy, and culture, the MICIVIH-MNF experience showed that with goodwill and cooperation it was possible to develop a working partnership in a situation of mixed military-humanitarian intervention and to contain conflict between the civilian and military elements. This initial experience would help prepare the ground for MICIVIH-UNMIH (U.N. peace-keeping mission) relations.

United Nations Mission in Haiti (UNMIH)

The United Nations Mission in Haiti (UNMIH), which was first authorized in September 1993, was finally deployed on 31 March 1995, taking over from the MNF. Security Council Resolution 940 of 31 July 1994 establishing the MNF also revised UNMIH's mandate, authorizing it to sustain the stable environment established by MNF and to assist Haiti in creating a new police force and professionalizing its army. This latter aspect of the mission's mandate became moot as the Haitian army was dismantled before the deployment of UNMIH. The mandate of the mission was extended on several occasions after it first expired on 29 February 1996 and came to an end on 30 November 1997. The mission's designation was changed to United Nations Support Mission (UNSMIH) in November 1996 and to United Nations Transitions Mission (UNTMIH) in July 1997. At its peak the mission had a total of 6,106 troops and 874 civilian police (CIVPOL). In its last phase (UNTMIH), it contained 1,300 troops and 250 CIVPOL.

Though separate missions with distinct mandates, MICIVIH and UNMIH had in common one overriding objective: building and reinforcing the institutions that underpinned democracy and the rule of law. In addition, they complemented each other in a number of ways. Whereas UNMIH placed emphasis on the structural, operational, and logistical aspects of the new police force, MICIVIH focused on its respect for human rights and international standards for law enforcement officers. To the extent that monitoring and mentoring the new police were essential aspects of the activities of the U.N. civilian police, they also played a key role with respect to the human rights conduct of the police in support of the efforts of MICIVIH. Joint training activities were carried out in the field in the areas of community policing (with MICIVIH emphasizing conflict resolution techniques), interrogation techniques (with MICIVIH focusing on the need to respect the physical integrity of detainees), respect for human rights in police operations, report writing, and the upkeep of police custody records (jointly devised by MICIVIH and CIVPOL).

In addition to their complementary mandates and activities, coordination between MICIVIH and UNMIH was facilitated by a number of factors: the presence of a special representative of the secretary-general of the U.N. (SRSG) who oversaw both missions and facilitated the harmonization of policies; coordination mechanisms such as the regular executive meetings chaired by the SRSG and attended by the force commander, the CIVPOL commissioner, the chief administrative officer, and the executive director of MICIVIH; the separate mandates of MICIVIH and UNMIH that permitted clarity of focus and prevented confusion over roles, purposes, and limitations; and excellent working relationships between the unit heads. An initial and key contributing factor of a more general nature was the Joint Staff Training orientation course on peace building for headquarters and field officers that took place in March 1995 before UNMIH was deployed and in which MICIVIH participated. The course facilitated wider understanding of the respective mandates, rules of engagement/terms of reference, and areas of overlap of UNMIH and MICIVIH, although the initial benefits of this course were lost subsequently with the successive rotations of officers, troops, and CIVPOL agents.

However, other factors intervened to offset the benefits of these initiatives and to introduce areas of misunderstanding and ambiguity. The unique nature of MICIVIH as a joint OAS/U.N. mission caused confusion in the minds of the military and police agents of UNMIH. The orientation course for UNMIH also permitted the SRSG to introduce a novel and, for some, unsettling notion that MICIVIH would monitor the conduct of both the CIVPOL and the military as a way of ensuring the highest standard of behavior from all UNMIH personnel. This idea colored the perception of MICIVIH held by the U.N. military and police and created a scintilla of distrust that never completely dissipated over time. On one particular occasion when the military police cracked down on the members of one contingent in an isolated post for breach of regulations, they were convinced that it was MICIVIH observers who had given them away. On another occasion, U.N. peacekeepers were accused of human rights violations during an incident in which they fired shots to disperse a crowd surrounding a house in which armed persons were at bay. The investigation into the incident carried out by the U.N. military and civilian police was inconclusive, as the responsibility for the shooting of the victims was never established. MICIVIH's efforts to inform itself of the events and its support for an inquiry to clear the air on the incident did cause some temporary unease within the upper spheres of the peacekeeping mission. The unresolved incident also exposed MICIVIH to criticisms of closing its eyes to U.N. peacekeeping abuses.

With MICIVIH's exclusively civilian composition and its immediate past experience of antagonistic and sometimes hostile relationships with the Haitian military and police, initial relations between the observers and the U.N. military and police were awkward and wary and lacking in mutual confidence. This was not facilitated by the very real differences of culture and perspective that divide civilians and military in an operational setting. As a result, the mission cultivated its separate identity and independence from UNMIH. The knowledge that the ordinary Haitian distrusted reflexively the military and police also contributed to this distancing from the uniformed components in order to better retain the links of trust and confidence MICIVIH had developed over time with local communities. The gruff, no-nonsense manner in which the military dismantled roadblocks put up by citizens protesting government inaction kindled strong sentiments among many human rights observers who witnessed such operations. So did what appeared to be disproportionate shows of force and even hostile intent in seemingly innocuous situations, a by-product of "force protection" policies, in itself a concept not fully grasped initially by the civilian observers.

Another early source of skepticism was the assumption that to the extent that the Haitian police and CIVPOL belonged to the same profession, that because of bonding the latter would somehow be more tolerant and understanding of Haitian police misconduct. The reverse was perhaps also true that the human rights observers did not always factor in extenuating circumstances and that their approach could sometimes appear to be self-righteous. In some localities these uneasy early relationships were exacerbated by the disparaging attitude of a few U.N. civilian police to the notion of human rights and very real differences of opinion over what constituted police misconduct. However, with the passage of time greater mutual understanding developed, and the quality of professional and institutional relationships between MICIVIH and UNMIH improved considerably.

One possible source of disagreement between MICIVIH and UNMIH that never did arise was the potential clash between objectivity, the need to take positions and report publicly on human rights violations, and neutrality, seen as a political tool to further peace building and maintain good working relations with the constitutional authorities. The dilemma of whether human rights criteria should take precedence over political priorities, or vice versa, was averted in great part because of the political will displayed by the Haitian authorities with regard to enforcing accountability and rejecting impunity. In this cooperative environment, the public reporting and advocacy of MICIVIH on human rights issues were perceived by the Haitian oversight authorities as supportive of their own efforts. In many respects, this was a uniquely refreshing attitude displayed by a sovereign government to human rights reports on the behavior of its security agents and judicial officials. In addition, MICIVIH was successful in pursuing a strategy that combined public reporting and behind-the-scenes advocacy and that allied human rights verification with institution building and practical recommendations. A third factor was in general the understanding that the special representatives displayed of the importance of the human rights dimension in the larger equation of institution building and reinforcing democratic processes and the rule of law.

This having been said, MICIVIH did at times encounter tough choices of a different nature. For example, faced with a serious incident of human rights abuse, would it be best tactically to resort to quiet advocacy, or would it be more effective to bring it to public attention? Should the mission run the risk of undermining its relations with the authorities by denouncing the suspicious death of a notorious criminal at the hands of the police and for which the latter were praised by the public, or should it wait for a more propitious moment to make the point about excessive use of force? Would MICIVIH be equivocating on its moral responsibilities and human rights principles? On occasion when the morally right course of action conflicted with nonmoral considerations, the latter won out.

Conclusion

The humanitarian problems confronted by the Haitians and the international community resulted in great part from the disruptions caused by the coup d'état. They also sprang from the coercive measures put in place by the international community, through its representative organizations, to counter the overthrow of the legitimate government and restore democracy. The most acute dilemmas and conflicts faced by the international agencies on the ground stemmed precisely from the inherent contradiction of seeking to mitigate the effects on the local population of the coercive measures put in place to help it. The international actors had to respond to these quandaries in an ambiguous, complex situation for which there were few precedents and no guidelines. The innate sense of what was right and what was wrong, as well as sensitivity to the politics of the situation, were the only moral and political compasses in which decision makers in the field could confide.

In Haiti, the response to the humanitarian emergency situation was limited to civilian actors. The military intervention, whose objective was the restoration of the democratic process, created the conditions in which the embargo could be lifted and the transition from humanitarian emergency support to development assistance could be effected. During the MNF interlude, differences in priorities and perception between the civilian and the military were more prominent. But when there were shared lines of authority and commonality of purpose, a willingness to be flexible and make compromises, to confront imperfect choices and difficult trade-offs, the differences in mandate could be overcome. In this way complementarity, cooperation, and clarity of focus between the peacekeeping force and the human rights observation mission was achieved, alleviating tensions and minimizing the dilemmas and ambiguities inherent in the situation. The Haitian experience does show on balance that despite differences of culture and approach, civilians can work harmoniously with military and police when common goals and objectives and a premium on cooperation have been clearly established.

For most of their history, Haitians have lived under authoritarian regimes. The civilian and military recourses used by the international community to reverse the coup d'état and end the ensuing crisis have once again created an opportunity for Haitians to put in place the key building blocks of the democratic process: elected representatives, a new civilian and professional police force, a revamped judiciary, and social and economic development programs to address poverty and deprivation. In this sense the costs, mistakes, and liabilities of the mixed international intervention in Haiti are far outweighed by its benefits, successes, and potentialities, in this way reconciling moral considerations with the pragmatism of international politics.

Notes

1. Report of Secretary-General Boutros Boutros-Ghali, *An Agenda for Peace*, 2d ed. (1995), 59.

2. U.N. General Assembly Resolution A/Res/47/20B, 20 April 1993.

3. Lawyers Committee for Human Rights, *Haiti, Learning the Hard Way: The UN/OAS Human Rights Operation in Haiti 1992–1994*, 1995, 97.

4. General Cedras was the commander in chief of the Armed Forces of Haiti (FADH) and one of the leaders of the coup d'état that overthrew President Aristide on 30 September 1991.

7

Weaving a New Society in Cambodia
The Story of Monath

Mu Sochua

Background

C ambodia's emergence as a constitutional monarchy in 1993 resulted after more than twenty years of civil strife and social dislocation. A peace agreement signed in Paris in October 1991 by the major political factions and supported by the five permanent members of the U.N. Security Council allowed for a United Nations–regulated democratic election and the constitution of a new government. For eighteen months during the 1991–1993 transitional period, the United Nations Transitional Authority in Cambodia (UNTAC)—composed of 15,000 peacekeeping troops and police and 7,000 civil administrators and U.N. personnel—working with the Cambodian Supreme National Council (SNC) was responsible for helping Cambodians throughout the country organize national elections for May 1993.

UNTAC was one of the largest operations ever to be conducted by the United Nations, costing close to $2 billion. Its mandate took the following phases: (1) repatriation and reintegration of Cambodian refugees; (2) general elections; and (3) economic, social, and political reconstruction and consolidation.

The repatriation phase was claimed by the U.N. and the international community as a commendable success. Within the designated time frame, 360,000 refugees were repatriated, and no significant incidents occurred. But no major report has been made of the failure to reintegrate large numbers of returnees, including the most vulnerable, who became homeless or experienced extreme physical and economic privation.

The 1993 elections supervised by UNTAC were more or less peaceful and fair. However, UNTAC failed to disarm the four factions that had signed the October 1991 peace accords, and the Khmer Rouge refused to participate in the electoral process. The 1993 elections, nevertheless, allowed for the formation of an elected coalition government to guide the nation.

Although the political situation stabilized during the first two years following the elections, the Royal Government of Cambodia continued to face constant conflicts as power sharing remained unresolved between the FUNCINPEC Party, winner of the elections, and the Cambodian People's Party (CPP), which refused to relinquish the power it had held since 1980. Khmer Rouge dissidents continued to remain a threat to national security. After a military coup d'état on 5 July 1997 led by the second prime minister, who was also vice president of CPP, the first prime minister and president of FUNCINPEC was forced into exile, and a number of FUNCINPEC supporters were executed, fled the country, or went underground. The coup resulted in withdrawal of assistance to the government from major donors such as the United States, Japan, and Germany.

The personal story of this chapter recounts the real life of a middle-aged Muslim woman from Cambodia, although Monath is not her real name and some details of her life have been varied to fit the circumstances. Monath is a member of the Cambodian Muslim community that was decimated by the Khmer Rouge, which ruled the country from April 1975 to December 1979 and was responsible for hunger, malnutrition, starvation, and genocide in Cambodia, taking the lives of more than one million men, women, and children. Those who were strong enough, including Monath, escaped across the border to Thailand, looking for a miracle: transiting to a third country or finding temporary refuge in the refugee camps along the border. Monath's story begins with her escape to a refugee camp in Thailand.

Assisting the Refugee Population: The Border Operation

In early 1980, Monath finally escaped through the heavily mined Cambodian forest with her two young sons and her eight-month-old daughter before reaching Camp 007, one of the largest refugee camps in Thailand. During the escape, Monath was separated from her husband, but she held out hope of his reaching the camp. She found refuge with a widow in one of the quarters the camp had designated for women. The hut, constructed with bamboo and thatch received from the U.N., was barely big enough to provide shelter for her family.

During the first days she stayed in the quarter, Monath was almost paralyzed by fear. Evenings and nights were the worst moments as all foreigners and expatriate volunteers were out of the camp. Soldiers, Cambodians and Thais, roamed the different quarters looking for prey. The women's quarters were the most vulnerable. The second day, as dusk approached, Monath was bathing her children when soldiers came and demanded to see her husband. Her friend shouted from the hut, "You have no right to bother her. You know where all our husbands are, and we know exactly what you want." The soldiers returned the following night and dragged Monath out of her bed, almost stripping her, looking for gold and other valuable things women refugees usually hid on their bodies. A few nights later, another group of soldiers appeared and took Monath to the military quarters in the back of the camp.

Monath heard voices from the other cells and realized that they were all women. She was struck by terror when the cry of one of them was heard that night. The thought of being raped strangely made Monath stronger. It was then she realized she had to survive for her children. She was still breastfeeding her last child, and she could feel her milk dripping inside her blouse. The warmth of her milk bonded her even stronger to her baby girl.

During the following three months, Monath escaped from camp to camp with her three children. The trick was to come up with a new story in order to justify her movements. After three months she became strangely accustomed to the refugee life, waking up every morning ready to face the system. It became a game, and beating the system meant getting more food or a little more basic goods for her children. Rice distribution day became a day Monath learned to look forward to as she could stop worrying about finding extra food to feed her children, who were starting to eat more. The day was physically tiring as thousands of refugee women and their young children would try to be first in line or first to get in the shade under the big tree or behind the hospital building, and Monath would have to carry the ten kilograms of rice and canned fish on her head back home. But it was also a day of joy as Monath would meet other women and chat and receive the latest news from the neighboring camps and, if she listened closely enough, even news from Cambodia.

Besides getting more rations from the U.N., Monath was preoccupied by other means to earn some cash in order to purchase kerosene, clothes, and medicine or to pay for her oldest boy to attend English class. Monath began saving her weekly rice ration and from her neighbor learned to make rice noodles and various types of cakes that she could sell at the market set up illegally at the back of the camp. Trading inside the camp meant learning to bargain with the Thai villagers who controlled the market and being ready to run when the authorities decided to sweep the market. Monath learned to cope, and trading was her only way to find the financial means to meet her basic physical needs.

The camp population invented many other creative means to earn income. Some of these even included setting up the transfer of refugees to a transit camp further inside Thailand. Refugee families had to pay a tremendous sum to cross the border at night at the risk of losing their lives or being caught and put in the camp jail and, for women, the possibility of being gang-raped.

The refugees, Cambodian civilians and military officials, and the U.N. and agency staffs were aware of the various activities that took place. Interventions from the International Committee of the Red Cross (ICRC), the U.N., and the medical staffs of different agencies helped bring some protection and save some lives, but many cases of violence and human rights abuse were unreported, or interventions were too late or faced with denials by the camp authorities.

The silence of the night no longer terrified Monath. Nighttime became the most peaceful moment for her. She rested her soul at night *when her children were sound asleep. Her mind would wander back to her town, to the close and distant relatives whom she had left in Cambodia and terribly missed. She prayed and she kept her hope alive: one day she would return home and perhaps find her husband.*

The quarter and a half million Cambodian refugees who found shelter and survived in Thailand for more than a decade demonstrated that they had extraordinary survival skills, not only physically but also psychologically. The border camps not only provided physical refuge for the camp population but also served as resistance bases for the different Cambodian military factions. Although the U.N. and international organizations did not officially recognize the military authorities of these camps, the lives of the refugees were controlled by the military, especially in the initial stage of setting up the camps, during periods of shelling or attacks by forces inside Cambodia.

The United Nations Border Relief Operation (UNBRO) was organized in late 1982 with the mandate to assist the primary needs of Cambodian displaced persons seeking refuge in more than eighteen camps along the 800-kilometer border between Cambodia and Thailand. UNBRO's own operation was responsible for food distribution, infrastructure, camp security, primary education, social services, and human rights. Other services including primary health care, nutrition, and assistance to landmine victims were contracted to international nongovernmental organizations (NGOs), and UNBRO cooperated closely with the ICRC for the protection of civilian prisoners.

In situations of armed conflict abuses, violence, and denials of human rights are inevitable, but the counterforces that usually rest untapped are the participation and the collective pressure of the refugee populations when such abuses occur. Too often, U.N. and international organizations assume roles as negotiators, protectors, and advocates for refugees without allowing the recognized representation of the refugees themselves. U.N. and international interventions should not separate physical survival of the refugees from their spiritual survival mechanisms, which depend strongly on the refugees' ability to function as active players in seeking immediate or long-term solutions to the dangers. Building the human capacity of the refugees through training programs, using the participatory approach for all interventions, preparing refugees to represent themselves, and providing moral support should be essential components of the intervention package.

Refugees are human beings who should be protected but not underestimated. Limiting their capabilities to care for themselves, their families, and their community places too much faith in outside interventions. Refugees will survive because of their role in rebuilding their lives, families, communities, and nation.

Repatriation: Fulfilling the Refugee Dream

Monath wanted to return to her native village in the province of Kompong Cham along the Mekong River in the center of Cambodia, home to the majority of Khmer of Muslim origin. Through a woman who attended the same mosque while they were in the camp, Monath was able to learn that her uncle, her mother's second brother, had survived the Khmer Rouge regime and had remained in their native village. With great difficulties, Monath had found a way to get letters out to her uncle, and the uncle and niece exchanged news of each other. Monath had written to her uncle to request his permission to live with him and his family.

When Monath's family was finally among those to be called for repatriation, she was full of joy. Monath had two weeks to gather the belongings she had accumulated in the past ten years. Looking at the few bundles of clothes, pots and pans, her children's school books, and a few other essential household items, Monath could not hold back her tears. A large part of her was represented merely by these bundles. In the past ten years, Monath had long become used to being a widow. She felt that she had been able to maintain this status with pride because of Islam. Her religious belief seemed to have given her more strength. Many other widows she knew in the camp whose husbands never made it during the escape through the land-mined jungle had remarried, as Buddhism had fewer restrictions on women.

Monath did not know who to blame for so much human suffering, so many horrors and complexities she had lived through. Many children had not lived long enough to have the chance to return home to where their souls could have rested in peace. She was only thankful that the U.N. was now calling her family number to get on the bus for the return home.

When Bus 35 finally went through the camp gate, the passengers let out a big sigh of relief. The passengers looked back and saw the fence that for ten years had kept them in captivity. Many of these people had never ridden a bus before. As it passed kilometers of rice fields, the landscape began to look familiar and the air got cooler. Emotions on the bus were high as the passengers became certain that they were approaching Cambodia. Its passengers began to listen to the murmuring of the elderly man who was building up his hope of relocating the family he had left ten years ago and repossessing the land and cattle he had given up when he crossed the border to the refugee camp. The sobbing and tears in the bus seemed to have been silenced by more passengers joining silently in the dream of the elderly man.

When the bus turned into a lot where other buses were parked, Monath took hold of her youngest child, although she was ten years old now. Outside the bus, a sea of people was rushing back and forth. Monath was struck by a deep feeling of emotion and apprehension. She now became uncertain about being back. Would her relatives welcome her back? How many of them had survived the war?

Monath and the other returnees were requested to clear the lot as more buses were entering and more returnees had to be unloaded. Once again, the U.N. seemed to have worked out its plan and system. The newcomers were no longer refugees but returnees. This was no longer a border operation but a repatriation program. One difference this time was the fact that there were no more Thai soldiers to push and control the Cambodians.

Monath and her children got off the bus, but they did not see her uncle in the crowd of people waiting to welcome their relatives back home. Maybe he was too old to travel the hundred or so kilometers to meet them. Maybe he was just late. Monath watched the lucky families who were reunited and were starting to leave the lot on ox-carts, motorcycles, or bicycles. She brought her children to a shaded area to wait a while longer and to chat with those who were also waiting to find their relatives. It was reassuring to know that she was not the only one deserted. It slowly became real to her that a new life had just begun. She felt much older now, stronger to face this new beginning, yet overcome by the thought of tomorrow.

Monath remained in the transit camp for two days before word came that her uncle had arrived from Kompong Cham. The journey from the village was difficult for a man of seventy-three. He had traveled by boat out of the village to reach the district that was two hours away and then by motor taxi found his way to the provincial town. There, he had to spend a night at the bus station before reaching the transit camp where the returnees were off-loaded. He was obviously tired when she saw him slowly crossing the courtyard of the camp. The reunion was what Monath had been dreaming about—joyful and emotional. The first hours were spent with accounts of both their lives, although Monath let her elderly uncle do most of the talking. Monath kept a few details about the camps to herself. Why sadden this very dear uncle who had also gone through so much? Her uncle described the night the Khmer Rouge took away his five children, only one of whom survived. His wife had died slowly of starvation. The family land had also been taken away, but the new plot he and his youngest son received from the new government was big enough to plant rice for his family. And that was the new home Monath and her children would be taken back to.

Monath received a sum of cash and the few household items each returnee family was entitled to according to the U.N. system. The small house her uncle shared with his son and the son's family was obviously too small for her and her children. Monath spent about $50 purchasing some bamboo and thatch and with the help of the men built a small hut a few meters from her uncle's house. Monath considered herself very fortunate as she had heard of many widows or families without the help of able male relatives who had to be resettled on new land provided by the government, but the land was covered with mines laid first by the Khmer Rouge and later by the government soldiers to keep away the Khmer Rouge and other resistance groups. Monath had heard much about land mines. A few men, even women and children, in the village were victims of them. Land mines in the fields were the first thing her uncle had warned her children about.

For the first few weeks Monath enjoyed her freedom and was optimistic about building a new life for her children. Her oldest son, now a young man of twenty-two, had easily found employment as a translator with one of the international organizations in charge of resettling the returnees. Monath's son had been a diligent student in the border camp's school, and his language skills made it much less difficult to find employment. His salary was welcome, and Monath happily shared it with her uncle. She would have been proud to send her daughter, now reaching her eleventh birthday, to continue her education that she had left after sixth grade, but the family could only afford to pay for the oldest son's education, and, as a girl, her daughter was expected to be close to home and help her mother.

Monath herself put her business skills to use by opening up a small grocery store under the house. She would travel to town once a month and come back with the goods she knew were needed in the village. It was a very small business because the community was poor. The harvest season was approaching, and the farmers did not have much rice left. The village had few wells, and the village pond was almost dry as the rain was late this year. It was uncertain that the farmers could plow the land, which had gone dry in the past three months. With the lack of irrigation, the land in most of the villages sat unused until the next rainy season. Rain had not been sufficient in the previous years, and rice production in the village had suffered from it. Another bad season would be devastating for the families.

Listening to the worries of the families in the village made Monath realize how easy life had been in the camps. The refugees had no complaints about the weather as all food supplies were provided by UNBRO. In the camps, the U.N. even had a system to distribute water. Monath kept these details from her new friends and neighbors for fear of jealousy. Nevertheless, some families resented Monath and her children who seemed to have more means. They had heard of the cash Monath and other returnees received as part of their repatriation package. Most of all, the young men envied her sons, who had had the chance to attend the secondary school in the refugee camps while boys of their ages who had stayed inside the country had had to stop school because their village was too far away from the provincial town.

When rain finally came, the villagers hurried into their rice fields and began turning the soil. Monath closed her store in the daytime to help her uncle and his son in the fields. She had forgotten how hard it was to work in the hot sun. Even young children had to pitch in. Not a single person could sit idle, not even amputees. There was work to be done from dawn to dusk. Monath felt physically exhausted by the end of each day, but she was emotionally rewarded, and she loved the land. From small seedlings, the rice stalks slowly began to grow, and later the fields turned bright green. Soon the harvest season would be here. Monath had longed for this moment as she knew that the entire village would be blessed and the villagers would celebrate.

The repatriation of the refugees and the displaced was directed by UNHCR and coordinated with the Cambodian Red Cross and local authorities to ensure safe physical repatriation. The UNHCR offered three main options to the returnees: (1) cash of $50 per person, (2) reunification with relatives with basic supplies of thatch and bamboo to build a new house, or (3) land allocation. As the availability of mine-free land and the willingness of the authorities to allocate land was limited and returnees were eager to quickly resettle, over 90 percent opted for cash or reunification with relatives. Among those who opted for land allocation, only a small percentage remained on the allocated land due to poor infrastructure, lack of long-term assistance, and intimidation from local police and military over land titles.

The repatriation program sponsored by UNHCR took care of the logistical aspects of the returnees' lives back in their homeland and not much more. For many thousands of widows, orphans, the elderly, amputees, and the mentally ill, there was an inefficient social safety net to welcome them home. The repatriation program also dismissed the fact that, for many of the returnees, the native village and the once close relatives had completely changed or were too deprived to care for them. Many of these people soon began to eulogize life in the refugee camps, where needs were met by the U.N. or other international agencies. Even now, it is not known how many returnee families remain unsettled.

Giving People a Choice: Elections

During a trip to the provincial town to purchase goods for her store, Monath had heard of foreign troops coming to the province. She was struck by a familiar feeling of fear. Was Cambodia being invaded again? Had the communists returned? What foreign troops, Monath shyly asked the people at the market. French? Americans? Vietnamese? The local merchants could not really tell but were reassured by the fact that these new troops did not carry arms and smiled to people. Even more noticeable, there seemed to be more than one nationality. They had even seen black or Indian soldiers. Monath was still not reassured but felt happy that she and her family lived in a small and forgotten village. Maybe these new troops from different nations would never find them.

After traveling more than an hour toward her village, Monath felt more insecure. She decided that she would turn back to town to find her eldest son. He would surely know about the new development or at least could talk to these new troops and, if it was not too late, the family could escape back to the border. Yet as she approached her son's office, she realized her return home, although for only less than a year, had made her even more attached to Cambodia. Safe in the refugee camp, she had always felt uprooted and dependent on outsiders, almost trapped at times as she always had to be prepared to run or be moved whenever the camp was shelled or attacked by soldiers. Since her return, Monath felt the responsibility of helping rebuild her homeland. She was attached to the land, the barn was full of newly cut rice stalks, and the family cow had just produced a strong calf. Whatever happened now, she would not leave Cambodia again.

Monath's son comforted his mother and even teased her for not being aware of the latest development. The state radio had announced the coming of the U.N. troops to assist Cambodia in preparing for the general elections, to be in the country to ensure that the elections would be free and fair and that no violence would occur. Soon the U.N. would begin the registration process to allow each Cambodian, eighteen years old and above, to vote. Voters' registration would be even available for the prisoners and the people living along the river, for the poor as well as the rich. Monath's son expressed pride when he described how a local police officer who had unlawfully used his power had been arrested by one of these U.N. troops.

Monath thought the U.N. was only responsible for food distribution and caring for refugees. Was the U.N. that important, and could it have that much power? What about the Cambodians? What would the police and the military do? She had heard that beloved Prince Sihanouk was inside the country. Would he control the U.N.? All these questions were slowly answered for Monath as months went by and more U.N. troops became visible in the province. Monath followed the news more often, and she and the women in the village listened to a special program on the radio.

Monath and the village women became interested in gaining information on how to vote. A program was repeated many times during the day on how to keep the vote secret. What secret could they have? How could they not discuss their choices among each other? The village chief was supposed to be told every detail of every family. Monath had always made decisions for the family, but the vote was about Cambodia, the nation. What if her choice should bring back war? What if the U.N. soldiers had to stay much longer?

Rumors went throughout the village about the wealth of the new troops, which did not loot the villages as other Cambodian and foreign troops had done during other times of conflict. The chief of the district had just rented out his wooden house to them for $500. It would take Monath and her uncle two years of hard work to make that much money. How could one be so rich? Rumors also spread that a particular UNTAC soldier shared his house with a local woman he had brought back from the city. She was not the maid as he had more than one maid. What a lucky woman she was! She rode in his car, wore nice clothes and jewelry, and could follow him to the provincial town every day and even all the way to the capital city whenever he went. Each day these rumors came and either amazed or shocked the villagers.

The villagers held lengthy debates about the presence of UNTAC soldiers, which reflected a sense of hope as the people could see the importance of the troops in keeping the level of violence down and reducing the incidents of armed conflicts between the Khmer Rouge, which had maintained a presence in some areas, and the government soldiers. As much as she was impressed by this, Monath was perturbed by the changes that had occurred in such a short time. She was upset to learn that some parts of her own province and the capital city were reserved for the UNTAC troops and how women and young girls entertained them. The debates would always start with who the people would vote for and end up with the wealth and the behavior of the UNTAC troops.

The day of the election was approaching. The villagers noticed how the village chief was asking openly of the future voters as to what their choice would be. The people who had gained self-confidence through the UNTAC voters' education program about the secrecy and importance of the votes did not feel obliged to answer. The district chief also visited Monath's village more often as election day was closer. His trips became more frequent, and his personal choice of the candidate was not a secret to anyone. But his candidate was not the villagers' choice, and it was always the line of his party that he passed on to the people.

Monath, like many other people, somehow felt reassured by the message put out by UNTAC radio. They felt protected, although not completely safe. There were rumors of violence and deaths. The debates were focused on the parties and their candidates. For some the choices were obvious, but others remained silent not because of uncertainty but because of fear. A sense emerged of apprehension about peace. Cambodia had known so much war. Could UNTAC convince the leaders to agree to sign a contract for peace? To Monath and the villagers, peace seemed such an easy and reachable reality. All that the villagers wanted and needed was a healthy crop each year, a school for their children, and time to pray and enjoy the traditions. Was peace that complex?

The day had arrived to go to the polling stations. The women woke up earlier than usual to tend to children and prepare lunch, as voting was expected to take the entire day. The men had to feed the cattle quickly, and oxcarts had to be ready as the villagers would all go together to facilitate transport. As always, the village chief led the way. Before Monath's oxcart had reached the polling station, the line was already very long and the sun was hot. It was obvious that precautions were being taken, and UNTAC soldiers were present. The night before, Monath and her uncle and a few neighbors had gone over the logo of the party, its color and place on the list, because some of the men and women could not read or write. They had all practiced to tick the box in front of the party of their choice. It all seemed rather simple. But this morning, Monath was feeling apprehensive.

Was it joy? Fear? Was it just physical fatigue from the trip and the hot sun? How could this little tick make a difference for Cambodia? How could she make herself believe it? Monath made her choice for herself, for her children, for her village, and for a new Cambodia. By the time all the people had been gathered to return to their village, the sun had begun to slowly set. As for generations, it was the coolest and most peaceful time.

The elections prepared by UNTAC ended two decades of armed conflicts and allowed the Cambodian people to express their self-determination. However, they were flawed from the beginning because UNTAC was not able to successfully engage the Khmer Rouge, which boycotted the elections at the very end, and because UNTAC failed to neutralize the army and police. But for UNTAC to have fully controlled and completed the disarmament process would have meant confrontations with some of the political parties that had their own armies and to change its mandate from peacekeeping to peacemaking.

UNTAC had a specific mandate—to serve as a transitional authority while preparing for the elections—and that mandate had a specific time frame—eighteen months. Once again, the reality of the people and the internal politics of the country were second to that time frame. The disarmament issue was a strong moral issue for a country such as Cambodia whose civil population had long been controlled by guns and the power of warlords, the total rule of the Khmer Rouge, and the strong presence of the reformed communist party, the CPP. This unfinished task had grave consequences to the peace process in Cambodia as the power of guns continued to rule, and it prevented the people from free expression, free speech, and free political association. The U.N. nonetheless declared the 1993 elections in Cambodia the most successful operation in the history of the U.N.

Conclusion

Subsequent to the elections, Monath's son was an active member of a local prodemocracy students' association openly opposing the use of violence of the private militia. During the first day of the July 1997 coup, Monath's son got caught up in the violence and, fearing for his family's life, convinced Monath to find an escape route to the border. After hiding in a mosque outside Phnom Penh, the family escaped up the Mekong River and then overland back to where she had started, in a refugee camp inside Thailand. Emerging from Monath's seventeen-year story are some challenging moral questions about the efficiency of relief, human rights advancement, the meaning of peacekeeping, and the viability of short-term U.N. interventions, which, because not immediately answerable, demand further and more urgent attention.

Because Cambodia and its people had suffered great atrocities, the international community was very supportive of the plight of the Cambodians who fled genocide, famine, and land mines to seek refuge in Thailand, their neighboring country. Assistance to Cambodians in refugee camps lasted over ten years. However, the resources and authority allowed each U.N. organization limit its efforts and the roles of its staff and representatives even when human rights are openly violated. The U.N. protection mandate is applied more to providing basic needs and much less to saving lives from torture, genocide, rape, and political killings. The U.N. security role in the case of Cambodia has not been preventive and has only been partially curative.

The percentage of the U.N. budget used for logistics, infrastructure, personnel, and programs for quick results is extremely high, whereas the remaining budget for programs to address social issues and support the democratization process is very limited. For people and factions caught in prolonged and bloody conflicts, quick results are not significant and often can add to the conflict and put more pressures on the people. The process of recovery, conflict resolution, and healing demands time.

Although the significant and visible U.N. and international presence can make emergency, repatriation, and reconciliation operations more efficient, it can also be counterproductive when the local people are not fully engaged in decision making, planning, and monitoring. The U.N. cannot take the blame for the indigenous population not doing its part; it cannot do it all or stay forever. But the United Nations not pursuing opportunities for the people to have a voice in their own reconstruction as one of the highest priorities of the U.N. intervention is only a cause for the return to man-made emergencies and crises.

Local leaders as well as world leaders should share moral commitments and responsibilities in seeking durable solutions based on policies that reflect the overall needs of the victims of conflicts. The peace process is not complete without this identity and dignity. In contrast, the Cambodian intervention was incomplete not so much because of the failures of the policies or unsuccessful implementation of what was attempted; it was more the insufficient importance given to the depth of human suffering and incapacitation, to the empowerment and healing process.

UNTAC support for human rights during the 1993 elections followed by the establishment of the U.N. Center for Human Rights headed by a special representative of the U.N. secretary-general have helped local human rights and prodemocracy activists continue their roles in keeping the voice of the civil society heard. However, the U.N. mandate, which calls for the respect for people's fundamental rights, can be frustrated when its policies are split by the internal politics of a country. The July 1997 coup has threatened the democratic process in Cambodia, and the preparations for the 1998 elections are tainted by internal politics controlled by both politicians and military leaders. The U.N. role in the 1998 elections will be limited to coordinating international observers to ensure free and fair elections, despite widespread intimidation, threats, and killing of the members of the opposition. In a culture of violence, the fundamental base for democracy is the respect for human rights, and the international community's policies must be based on them.

In Cambodia, the U.N. made the right difficult choice to have kept its intervention as peacekeeping and not peacemaking, despite the threats made by the Khmer Rouge and the level of violence during the general elections in 1993. The Cambodian people would have totally lost their self-confidence if the UNTAC peacekeepers had intervened with force at each situation of violence. Their restrained use actually preserved their continuing value in maintaining enough security to allow stability and recovery. But UNTAC peacekeeping forces and its entire administration pulled out shortly after the elections, in the summer of 1993.

Eighteen months was not long enough. The world community cannot afford to act only to attend to a major influx of refugees. If it is serious, its resources must be further applied for protection, promotion of human rights, good governance, and long-term development.

.

8

"You Save My Life Today, But for What Tomorrow?"

Some Moral Dilemmas of Humanitarian Aid

Mary B. Anderson

There can be little doubt that humanitarian assistance is under challenge. Time after time, aid that was meant as simple, neutral, and pure "act of mercy" becomes tainted by subsequent negative ramifications in the complex settings of today's war-induced crises. We have lost our innocence about the impacts of aid. We know that, even as it saves lives and reduces human suffering, humanitarian assistance can also lead to dependency on the part of those who receive it. We know that aid provided in conflict settings can feed into and exacerbate the conflicts that cause the suffering it is meant to alleviate. And we know that aid too often does nothing to alter—and very often reinforces—the fundamental circumstances that produced the needs it temporarily meets.

Faced with strong evidence that emergency aid has negative side effects and too little systemic positive effect, and faced with the moral conundrum that these realities entail, aid providers have several responses.

Some affirm their commitment to "the primacy of the humanitarian imperative" and conclude that, despite aid's negative consequences, it is imperative to respond to others' urgent needs as a matter of conscience. They feel that if they can save a life and do not do so, they do wrong. They are concerned that accepting responsibility for potential side effects of their actions may immobilize them entirely. These providers of aid accept the negative side effects of aid but believe that the good they succeed in doing still outweighs the harm they unintentionally do.

A second response to the negative effects of aid comes as direct criticism. After each major outpouring of assistance in response to a crisis, another book or television special appears that reports on the multiple problems caused by aid. The critics tell true stories. They assemble evidence familiar to every field-based worker.

They conclude that no aid would be preferable to the aid that does such harm. This position, however, entails a logical and moral fallacy. Demonstrating that aid does harm is not the same as demonstrating that no aid would do no harm. Nor does the conclusion that aid does harm justify the additional conclusion that providing no aid would result in good. If there is moral ambiguity in providing aid, there is also moral ambiguity in providing no aid.

Are providers of humanitarian assistance morally trapped between giving aid with its bad outcomes or not giving aid with other probable negative effects? I will argue here that the answer is no. Citing field experience of aid workers who have found ways to avoid the most commonly accepted negative outcomes of aid, I argue that this evidence suggests that it is possible for all aid workers to do so if they learn and employ the lessons of experience.

This point does not mean that providers of emergency assistance can altogether escape moral uncertainty. The same experience that suggests it is possible to avoid aid's negative impacts that have been considered virtually inevitable also suggests that other areas are emerging in which aid raises new moral challenges.

I first discuss two areas in which most observers locate the moral *problematique* presented by the negative impacts of emergency humanitarian assistance: (1) the tendency for humanitarian aid to result in long-term dependency of recipients on donors and (2) the tendency for humanitarian aid that is provided in conflict settings to feed into, worsen, and prolong wars that cause the suffering it is intended to alleviate. I shall also consider how these tendencies are linked to the failure of emergency aid to address the fundamental problems that underlie and cause emergencies.

Having considered these dilemmas, I shall then cite evidence that shows them to be more apparent than real. As aid workers incorporate the lessons learned from experience in many settings, they can avoid repeating these past wrongs. These two dilemmas, often considered inevitable, can be averted.

I then discuss what I believe are the real moral dilemmas of humanitarian assistance. These involve the complications that arise from the perpetuation of inequality in today's world and the corresponding unequal and problematic relationships embodied in giving and receiving humanitarian aid. They highlight the moral imperative for aid providers—even those who undertake brief, urgent, emergency interventions—to come to terms with the causes of the emergencies they seek to ameliorate.

I turn first to the two areas in which aid providers and critics have traditionally thought the difficult moral challenges lie.

The Tendency for Aid to Result in Long-Term Dependency of Recipients on Donors

When humanitarian aid workers rush into a crisis to save lives and reduce human suffering, they do so with bravery and goodwill. They very often achieve significant success. However, they also often adopt a mode of operation that assumes that victims of crises can do little or nothing for themselves.

Aid providers adopt what they believe to be efficient delivery systems. To provide food, shelter, sanitation, and/or medical services, assistance agencies import or rent fleets of trucks and other equipment, they hire drivers and experts (also often imported), and they set up warehousing facilities and communications systems. They set up large-scale, centrally managed delivery systems focused on getting a product from donors to recipients, usually managed by expatriate staff. Aid is focused on meeting the needs of the "poorest of the poor." Learning from past experience that crisis victims received goods they could not use or did not need or that aid had been received by advantaged rather than disadvantaged people, aid providers now begin interventions with "needs assessments." These concentrate on physical lacks that are easily enumerated. Donors know how to respond to requests for a given tonnage of food or for specific quantities of housing materials or medical supplies.

The criteria for effectiveness of centrally managed, materials-focused aid systems include speed, accountability to outside donors, and, of course, receipt by individuals and groups deemed to be most needy.

The role for local people—those seen as "victims"—to manage any aspects of this aid system is minimal or nonexistent. Concentration on the delivery of things *to* these people, rather than on problem solving *with* them, places the beneficiaries of aid in a passive, accepting role.

Experience shows that such aid, by failing to recognize and connect with existing decision-making, management, distributional, or other productive and psychological capacities of the people affected by crises, undermines and weakens these capacities. More and more, recipients of aid accept what is given from outside as their due, their right. The experience of having needs met by outsiders produces a belief that outside aid is necessary for survival. Not only does aid thus disrupt existing decision-making and marketing systems that represented strengths in recipient economies, it also undermines networks and relationships on which the social order rests and any sense of efficacy that individuals had prior to their crisis.[1]

In addition, emergency aid usually ignores the causes of the emergency that prompted it. Often, responders focus on "getting things back to normal." However, it is the conditions of "normalcy" that gave rise to the emergency in the first place. That is, the disastrous impacts of emergencies (whether initiated by a natural event such as a flood, cyclone, or earthquake or by a political event such as a riot or war) fall on different groups of people with varying weight. Who suffers and who does not suffer reflect differences in economic, social, and political status. The vulnerability of people to disasters varies.

Emergency aid too often fails to address the circumstances that cause people to be vulnerable to the disasters from which they suffer. When aid is provided only to address the symptoms of crises, it leaves in place the causative factors of the crises. Thus, aid may reinforce vulnerabilities and even lead to new areas of vulnerability through creating privileged groups, undercutting coping systems, or encouraging unwarranted expectations about the availability of outside resources.

Aid does not have to be given in this way. Field-based experience from many sites shows that it is possible to avoid creating dependency among aid recipients and to provide even short-term emergency aid in ways that address the underlying root causes of an emergency. I shall return to this point later after examining the ways in which aid provided in war settings worsens conflict.

The Tendency for Aid Provided in Conflict Settings to Exacerbate the Conflict

A second area in which experience shows that well-intentioned assistance often has negative consequences is in relation to conflict. When aid is provided in war settings, even when it is effective in saving lives and alleviating human suffering, it very often, at the same time, inadvertently feeds into, worsens, and prolongs the conflict that prompted the need for aid. Again, many observers have written about these effects.[2]

The most obvious way that aid feeds conflict is through the direct misappropriation of aid goods by warring parties. Aid workers frequently report that the goods they deliver are routinely "taxed" as they pass through military checkpoints to reach intended beneficiaries. Aid goods are often stolen, diverted, and manipulated to serve the interests of those at war. Warriors also use aid in indirect ways. By controlling the locations where aid may be delivered, commanders manipulate population movements. By negotiating with aid agencies for the safe delivery of goods, commanders gain legitimacy in the eyes of those who depend on aid for survival and, sometimes, in the eyes of the international community.

When aid agencies assume the responsibility for supporting civilian survival during wars, fighters can use available internal resources for the purposes of battle. This approach also allows the warring leaders to define their responsibilities solely in military terms. Local so-called leaders are able to abdicate their responsibility for civilian life because it is adequately handled by the international aid community.

Aid goods represent both an economic resource and a source of power and control for people at war. It is neither surprising nor mysterious that aid, provided in a context of conflict, becomes an active part of that context.

Avoiding the Moral Dilemmas of Creating Dependency and Exacerbating Conflict

Concerned about the negative impacts of humanitarian aid, donors and aid providers have undertaken concerted efforts to understand, analyze, and find ways to avoid them. From examination of field-based experience, lessons have been learned about how to provide aid in ways that reinforce its positive impacts rather than lead to negative outcomes.[3]

The lessons learned point to a central principal of non-dependency-creating aid: providers should always start from the recognition that "victims" have capacities and that they are already coping with their own crisis before aid arrives.[4] Even very poor people have materials, social systems, attitudes, and beliefs that enable them to survive and on which their future lives and livelihoods must be based. When aid providers begin from a recognition of local capacities and supply aid in ways that support these, they help people both survive immediate life-threatening circumstances and strengthen and build a foundation on which their future independent development can occur.

Rather than doing "needs assessments" as the basis for designing interventions, aid providers should (and some do) focus on assessing capacities. A capacities assessment communicates respect for people's competence, their skills in life management, and their minds and spirits. It also lessens the need for imported supplies and management so that it costs less than outsider-managed aid and can be more easily withdrawn when internal recovery becomes possible.

In addition, aid providers should recognize that the needs they address are only manifestations of deeper circumstances that cause people to be vulnerable. It is important that they analyze the circumstances that underlie the crisis and identify the ways that their aid either reinforces and worsens these circumstances or reduces or overcomes them.

Many illustrations show that this approach can work. For example, during a postvolcano relief effort in the Philippines, one nongovernmental organization (NGO) placed community development workers in emergency shelters to live with displaced disaster victims. These NGO workers not only supplied food, blankets, and other things needed for survival but also helped the disaster sufferers plan future community projects to be undertaken when they returned to their villages. During the long days and nights during which they had nowhere to go and nothing else to do, the disaster victims got to know each other, organized committees, and laid the groundwork for community enterprises that they launched later when they returned to their homes.

Recognizing the "capacities" of idle time and an opportunity for daily community interaction and planning, aid workers helped local people use these to good advantage. They assisted these people to assess the underlying circumstances that kept them in poverty, and they supported their development of new systems for organizing to address these circumstances. These aid workers recognized and strengthened the victims' capacities and helped them reduce their long-term vulnerabilities.[5]

In Ethiopia, during the major famine of 1983–1984, many international NGOs helped feed the thousands of people at risk of starvation. Most set up feeding camps along the roadsides where hungry people gathered. They shipped food into these settings and established systems for ensuring that those in the greatest need were fed first. The result was that many people received food who needed it.

At the same time, disease was a constant threat (and reality) in the overcrowded camps, and aid recipients had nothing to do but wait for food to be delivered, measured, and meted out to them. Because some people became weakened by hunger earlier than others, families were often separated by aid workers who determined that only those in greatest need could enter the feeding centers. The concentration of food in camps enticed people to gather around them, waiting until their need was great enough to justify their admission. Vulnerability to disease and dependency increased. When the famine ended, people in feeding camps were often far from their homes and thus not able to take advantage of rains in time to plant a new crop. Their vulnerability and dependence on others was thus extended for another season.

Another NGO, in the same crisis, gave people gathered at roadsides sufficient rations to survive and told them to return home. This agency promised to deliver food "as close as possible" to villages. The people who were still sufficiently healthy organized crews to build roads to reach remote villages. The NGO provided an engineer to advise them on road grades, and the people used their own tools and the abundant stones scattered across the countryside for building. Others organized donkey trains to carry food to even more remote villages. Some organized warehousing in community buildings. Everyone was able to stay at home, families and communities remained together, and, when the rains began, people were on their fields and ready to plant. Recovery was quickly possible. Idle time, stones, tools, community structures, and donkeys all represented indigenous capacities that, when coupled with outside food, allowed people to survive the emergency and to be ready for recovery and development.[6]

In Central America after an earthquake destroyed many homes, an NGO sent a representative to the area to survey the needs. This man arrived in a village that was particularly badly hit and was met by villagers asking how much aid he planned to give them. He responded that, before he could decide, he needed to see what had happened, and he invited people to take him on a walking tour of the town. As they walked (and larger and larger crowds of people joined the entourage), the aid provider asked the community to explain "why this building is still standing" and "why that building fell down." By the time the tour was finished, he told the community that they had answered his questions with great knowledge. He pointed out that they knew what made a building earthquake-resistant and why some structures were vulnerable. He then offered to provide just enough aid to assist them in rebuilding their homes, using their own knowledge and local materials to ensure greater security against future earth tremors. Local knowledge and local building materials provided capacities that, when coupled with minimal external aid, allowed a large number of people in this community to rebuild stronger, less vulnerable houses. They also recognized that their knowledge of the area was superior to that of any outsider.[7]

These illustrations of how aid may build on and support capacities and address vulnerabilities are from areas in which the crisis was based on a natural event—volcano, drought, and earthquake. When aid is delivered in a context of war, former close associates, friends, neighbors, and coworkers are in conflict, and commanders rule over contiguous and conflicting regions. Experience shows that in such a context, identification of legitimate local capacities and the design of aid to address deep-seated causes of the crisis are more difficult.

For example, in 1994, as refugees poured from Rwanda into eastern Zaire and the humanitarian assistance community wished to preserve life in this unhealthy setting, international aid workers report that the circumstances seemed to be "an aid provider's dream."[8] Whole villages arrived together with leadership structures intact so that early decisions about how to allocate and distribute food seemed easy. Relying on apparent local capacities in order to avoid dependency, aid providers accepted these leaders as the appropriate conduit for food distributions. It is now well known that the camp "leadership" was the Hutu militia who had committed the genocide in Rwanda. They were able to use the resources provided by international humanitarian aid to control civilian populations and to rearm and prepare for a return battle in Rwanda.

As this example shows, reliance on local capacities in war settings can reinforce existing power structures that are a part of the conflict. From experience, we are now learning that avoiding the negative impacts on conflict while giving aid in conflict settings requires two distinct levels of analysis and planning.[9]

On the one hand, aid providers must recognize that some indigenous capacities in war settings are capacities for war. They need to analyze the ways that warriors may misappropriate aid resources and develop strategies for avoiding these. On the other hand, aid providers need also to develop skills for identifying—and supporting—local capacities that are, genuinely, capacities for peace.

Though experience is still being assembled, evidence indicates that negative impacts can be avoided and positive peace-supporting activities can be linked to the provision of life-saving humanitarian aid in war situations.

For example, to avoid theft or misappropriation of aid goods by warring commanders, aid providers have been inventive in adopting different, locally effective strategies. In some areas, they have relied on broad publicity of scheduled delivery times and quantities to enable local people to control the aid resources and hold potential thieves accountable if losses occur. In other places, aid agencies have relied on secrecy, delivering goods without prior announcement of times or locations to avoid theft. Dispersal techniques have proven effective in some places. For example, a cargo plane landing in Siem Riep, Cambodia, loaded with bags of cash to pay local aid staff, was met on the runway by a series of small vehicles. A few bags of cash were loaded into the trunk of a car, and it sped away. Another bag went in the back of a truck, and it left. Others went into carts, Jeeps, and a variety of vehicles. As aid providers explained, each of these transports took a different route to the aid office. It would hardly be worth the effort of thieves to stop any one of them because each carried an insignificant amount of money.[10]

To avoid caring for civilian needs in ways that allow commanders to abdicate their responsibilities for civilian survival, aid agencies have also tried a variety of approaches. Some establish a pattern of regular, "friendly" meetings with a local commander to discuss civilian needs and activities and encourage the commander to recognize the interests of his people. Oddly, sometimes a commander has been completely unaware of this aspect of leadership and has appreciated being helped to gauge public opinion on civilian affairs as well as on military issues.[11] In Sudan, aid workers report that the military personnel assigned to work in the humanitarian wings of the Southern Movements indicate that they value the opportunity to be something other than fighters. They feel that circumstances have trapped them into constant warfare; they need and want space to act in non-war ways.[12]

Experience shows that, in every civil war situation, no matter how violent and divisive, certain systems, structures, attitudes, and actions that connect people continue to exist. It is these "connectors" that we call capacities for peace because they represent the base (albeit inadequate!) on which past peace rested and on which future peace must, in part, be reconstructed. Warriors are good at identifying connectors and intentionally destroying them in pursuit of victory. For example, communications systems that allow people to keep in touch and share information across factional lines are often targeted by fighters who control media as a weapon. In spite of this problem, people find ways to maintain systems for staying in touch throughout wars. For example, in Tusla, Bosnia and Herzegovina, one local group maintained E-mail contact with colleagues in Serbia when all other contact was severed. In many war zones, people report that they rely on the BBC for impartial information rather than only on the information beamed to them by war propagandists. In some areas, drivers of aid truck convoys state that they keep radio contact with drivers "on the other side" to share information about areas of danger and safety in a kind of "underground fraternity."

In war zones, many people continue to trade with designated "enemies." This enterprise may occur on the riverbank one afternoon a week, or it may involve formal contracts and bank accounts. When markets are seen to be effective in binding people in mutual interdependence, they may become targets of warriors intent on destroying mutuality. However, more often people on different sides of wars continue to trade with each other in spite of fighting.

Aid workers who enter a war context to provide emergency assistance very often fail to see such continuing connectors. Because they have come in response to war, and because they are themselves in danger from the prevalent violence, they are dramatically aware of societal divisions. Experience shows that they therefore deliver assistance in relation to obvious divisions rather than in relation to (and support of) connectors. The question arises, If humanitarian assistance were channeled to reinforce the things that connect people rather than divide them, could it not only meet immediate needs but also help buttress and enlarge the "connecting space" and "voice" for people to disengage from war?

Isolated Good Luck or Generalizable Experiences?

Some might argue that the stories told here are no more than isolated examples or just good luck. They might feel that, in the face of the complexities of today's war-rent societies, such examples are puerile, insignificant, and misleading.

I would argue that easy dismissal of inventive field approaches that have avoided what were considered "inevitable" negative impacts of aid is misleading. The challenge posed by the stories told here (and they are only a small sampling of a much larger collection of positive and promising experiences) is that options for the delivery of aid without negative outcomes are available.[13] Business-as-usual that accepts aid's negative impacts as justified by positive outcomes is no longer acceptable because experience shows that negative impacts are not inevitable.

So, although moral ambiguity is not yet entirely vanquished in the areas of dependency and conflict, there is hope. More careful analysis and more concerted learning from experience that builds on the progress that has been made can free us from entrapment in these particular moral webs.

New Moral Challenges

As changes occur in the systems and contexts of humanitarian aid, new moral ambiguities emerge. Some of these are dealt with in other chapters of this book (e.g., the role of the military in humanitarian response), but two deserve special attention here. The first has to do with the relationship of inequality that persists between aid givers and aid receivers and the separation that this imbalance produces between them. The second has to do with the tendency for humanitarian assistance to address only the urgent manifestations of a crisis rather than the fundamental and systemic issues that may underlie or reinforce the crisis.

The Relationship of Inequality

The humanitarian assistance relationship that is meant to embody deep generosity, the expression of human commonality, and a dignified gratitude is very often strained by mutual suspicion. Giving and receiving become tainted by manipulation and penalty.

How does it occur that good-hearted individuals who sacrifice comfort and security to enter conflict zones as aid workers develop a palpable mistrust and disrespect for the recipients they came to help? How is it that individuals who, having suffered a calamity, openly recognize the generosity of aid providers, come to resent these givers, and spend time and effort developing ways to manipulate aid for personal gain? Are there factors intrinsic to philanthropy that make this inevitable, or do the arrangements and systems of international humanitarian aid cause this unwanted transformation?

Several changes are occurring in the organization and delivery of aid that, together, may help explain some of the increasing tension between givers and receivers. In addition, characteristics of today's crises also feed into and reinforce the atmosphere of mistrust and antagonism.

Within the organization and delivery of aid, two trends seem to increase separation and reinforce an antagonistic relationship between aid providers and aid recipients. The first is the rapid and dramatic increase in both the quantity and value of emergency aid. The second is the professionalization of aid processes and personnel.

Others have written about the growth in aid resources focused on emergency responses (rather than development), and I have noted earlier that aid resources may be misappropriated by warriors and thereby feed conflicts.[14] The problem I am raising here with regard to the quantity and value of aid, however, lies in the message these convey of inequality and separation between those who *can* give and those who *must* receive.

As noted earlier, the procurement and distribution systems used by most aid agencies working in war zones rely on external sources and involve imported goods. Massive aid delivered by multiple, well-staffed, external agencies signal recipients that aid workers possess and control significant quantities of valuable things. Donor systems that require accountability to distant governments place control of these assets in the hands of outside aid givers rather than local people, but exclusion of recipients from these systems conveys a message that they (the recipients) are perceived as untrustworthy. Such aid agency operations and procedures make visible the inequality and separation between those who have access to and control over aid and those whose survival rests on the decisions of others about providing aid to them.

A message of inequality is further conveyed through a recent tendency for aid workers and systems to become increasingly "professional." How does this occur?

Recent professionalization of emergency aid results from a recognition of past problems in aid delivery. To correct past mistakes, courses have been developed to train people in professional emergency management, and donor agencies have established departments of emergency response staffed by specialized personnel to ensure more professional aid delivery.

But these improvements in the capabilities of aid personnel and agencies have involved other changes that accentuate the inequality between givers and receivers. Professional aid workers tend to be older than the young, inexperienced volunteers of the past. They have family and financial responsibilities and therefore require security. They live in certain kinds of locations (compounds with guards and walls), they need safe vehicles (bulletproof and reliable) and constantly available communications equipment, and they expect to be evacuated if a situation becomes too dangerous.[15]

Guarded compounds, fancy vehicles, and advanced communications systems are highly visible. In war zones, they have become symbols of power, wealth, and superiority. They separate aid providers from aid recipients in terms of wealth and options.

Evacuation plans and operations compound the separation and inequality between the groups. Most aid agencies are committed to evacuating expatriate staff and their families but do not make the same commitment to local people whom they hire.[16] Aid providers always have an option that most "common people" in a conflict zone do not have—namely, the choice (and means) to leave.

Changes in war environments of recent years further reinforce the separation between aid providers and aid recipients. The conditions of many of today's wars involve widespread availability of small arms, multiple localized commanders with troops in their command, generalized lawlessness and roving gangs, shifting loyalties and shifting battlelines. These conditions increase the real danger faced by aid workers. They also feed into their sense of insecurity and corresponding concern that their agencies take steps to ensure their safety.

Together, massive aid under the control of aid workers, measures taken to ensure the personal security of aid workers, and contexts of generalized lawlessness result in visible daily reminders of the differences between providers and receivers.

Many conscientious aid workers are aware of this division, citing their discomfort with their visible advantage. This moral dilemma was captured poignantly in an essay by a young man just returned from working in a war crisis in which he explored the impact on his soul and psyche of eating a meal in front of hungry people.[17] He recognized the importance of maintaining his health and energy if he were to do his work effectively, but he agonized over the experience of putting food into his own mouth as hungry people stood around and watched him do so.

Inequality between aid providers and recipients lessens their ability to identify with each other. Add to these psychological pressures the physical exhaustion overworked aid providers face, and it is understandable why a different ethos begins to emerge among them. As they sit around talking in an evening, conversation frequently involves stories of dangers encountered, local people outsmarted, would-be thieves caught. Tales are told of weaknesses, failures, and shortcomings of local people and local systems that have to be dealt with by the superior knowledge/intelligence/wisdom of outside agencies or personnel.

Most aid workers do not intend to assume this ethos. They begin their missions with genuine compassion and concern. The conditions of daily work, including the overwealthy and security-conscious nature of these conditions, exact changes in their perceptions of the roles they play. Most believe that they fall into such attitudes as a result of overwork and too little support. I would hypothesize that the process of distancing as an "outsider" from "victim insiders" very often represents a way of dealing with painful awareness of inequality. The process by which good-hearted aid providers become antagonistic toward the people to whom they provide aid represents one continuing moral dilemma of humanitarian aid.[18]

Causes That Lie behind the Symptoms of Crises

The failure of aid to go beyond symptoms and to support processes through which systemic issues are addressed constitutes the second critical moral dilemma for humanitarian aid today. As noted earlier, humanitarian assistance rarely addresses the fundamental circumstances that underlie crises. In fact, by feeding dependence and divisions and by undermining existing capacities (and in the case of war, peace capacities), it very often worsens these circumstances.

What is required of aid to address this dilemma? Designing aid programs so that they do not undermine and weaken existing capacities is straightforward. It is more complicated to identify "root causes" of problems and to direct humanitarian aid to address these. The nature of most of today's wars adds to this difficulty.

Although poverty and injustice exist in today's warring societies, they are not the explicit root causes of today's wars.[19] Wars are not started by poor people seeking to change an unjust economic system or marginalized people seeking to obtain a rightful political representation.[20] Rather, the common feature of today's civilian-based civil wars is a shift in previous power relationships followed by a power struggle between would-be leaders who, instead of appealing for support on the basis of a set of ideas that represent a coherent political ideology, excite people on the basis of subnational identities (clan, ethnicity, religion, language) in opposition to other subgroups. They then convince their "constituency" that they must either rule or be ruled, dominate or be dominated. They create a world in which power sharing is impossible.

These putative leaders cite historical "wrongs" as if they are "root causes" of war. However, citizens of many war zones speak openly about their disgust with their "leaders" who manipulate emotions and actions only to enlarge their own power and wealth and not to improve the lives of the people. I have heard people from war zones (Afghanistan, Tajikistan, Somalia, Rwanda, Chechnya, Sri Lanka, Bosnia, and others) say that the wars in which they are engaged are not about anything "real." They note that real injustices exist in their societies and that these need attention. But they also assert that the wars in which they are engaged are "not about these problems" and, in fact, are making them worse. Many citizens of today's war zones do not perceive the war they fight as an effective instrument through which to achieve desired ideological goals.[21] They fight because they become convinced that they must win to survive, and their conviction is reinforced by the experience of civil war in which former neighbors now are labeled, and act as, enemies.

These civil wars further exacerbate injustice in society and create new "root causes" of future wars. They increase the numbers of people in poverty. They accentuate differences between those who suffer most and those who suffer least. Face-to-face fighting with former friends creates divisions between subgroups that are difficult to reconcile. Aid workers need to understand that recently invented or exacerbated injustices are as important to continuing warfare as are root causes, and they must design their programs in ways that do not worsen these divisions but help people overcome them.

Though deep existing societal injustices may not represent the true causes of many of today's wars, a postwar peace will be firmer and more likely to last if such problems are soon addressed in the aftermath of war. History provides examples of postwar circumstances in which, once a victory has been secured, the victorious group turned its attention and resources toward reconstruction of the defeated society. The Marshall Plan at the end of World War II is such a case. In civil wars that result in widespread destruction, however, even a "victor" has few resources to help rebuild the lives and property of the vanquished. Perhaps more than ever in the postwar circumstances of today's wars, the role of the international aid community is to help people reknit common vested interests through joint enterprises, interlinked markets, and social systems.

Conclusion

The dilemmas facing humanitarian assistance today have practical and moral dimensions. If current aid systems separate giver from receiver in ways that taint the humanitarian act, then these must be changed. This practical task, when achieved, will have moral implications. Furthermore, refocusing aid so that it addresses immediate suffering and root issues and does not worsen divisions requires both practical and moral adjustments. Without changes in these areas, humanitarian aid, even as it saves lives and reduces suffering, will also daily demonstrate that inequality between peoples is permissible. With change, humanitarian aid can overcome antagonisms between givers and receivers and reenable them both.

Notes

The quotation in the title of this chapter comes from a personal communication by a man from Sierra Leone where international aid was being delivered by many nongovernment organizations at the time, fall 1996.

1. These tendencies are reported in many analyses of aid. Several of the earliest documentation of these impacts are found in Fred Cuny, *Disasters and Development* (Oxford: Oxford University Press, 1983); Gunner Hagman (with Henrik Beer, Marten Bend, and Anders Wijkman), *Prevention Better Than Cure: Report on Human and Environmental Disasters in the Third World* (Stockholm: Swedish Red Cross, 1984); and Barbara E. Harrell-Bond, *Imposing Aid: Emergency Assistance to Refugees* (Oxford: Oxford University Press, 1986). The International Relief/Development Project also documented and classified the negative effects of relief aid on development, published in Mary B. Anderson and Peter J. Woodrow, *Rising from the Ashes: Development Strategies at Times of Disaster* (Boulder, Colo. and Paris: Westview and UNESCO Presses, 1989).

2. See, for example, Robert Miller, ed., *Aid as Peacemaker: Canadian Development Assistance and Third World Conflict* (Ottawa: Charlatan University Press, 1992); Mary B. Anderson, "International Assistance and Conflict: An Exploration of Negative Impacts" (Cambridge, Mass.: Local Capacities for Peace Project, Collaborative for Development Action, 1994); and John Prendergast, *Frontline Diplomacy: Humanitarian Aid and Conflict in Africa* (Boulder, Colo.: Lynne Rienner, 1996).

3. In the pages that follow, I cite examples found through two projects that I have directed that were aimed, specifically, at collecting from field experience lessons learned on how to avoid negative impacts of aid. These are (1) the International Relief/Development Project (IR/DP), which Peter Woodrow and I codirected at Harvard University between 1987 and 1989 and which resulted in the publication of *Rising from the Ashes* cited earlier; and (2) the Local Capacities for Peace Project, run from the Collaborative for Development Action, Inc., in Cambridge, Massachusetts, which involves a number of donor governments and multilateral agencies, NGOs, and individuals involved in aid delivery in conflict settings.

4. Again, the IR/DP assembled this evidence and put forward a Capacities and Vulnerabilities Analytical Framework for the use of aid workers in planning and running aid projects in ways that avoid long-term dependency. See Anderson and Woodrow, *Rising from the Ashes.* Further, the Canadian Council for International Cooperation has published a series of studies using the framework of the IR/DP to assess and plan aid interventions.

5. Local Resource Management Project, Santo Domingo, Albay, Bicol Region, Philippines, reported in Anderson and Woodrow, *Rising from the Ashes,* 241–58.

6. Ethiopia Emergency Program, Yifat na Timuga, Ethiopia, reported in Anderson and Woodrow, *Rising from the Ashes,* 135–56.

7. Reported from his own experience by Ronald J. Parker in personal communication.

8. Personal communication from an aid worker who requested anonymity. However, I since asked others who were present who concurred with this individual's judgment that it appeared that the circumstances were ideal in terms of relying on local capacities.

9. Finding of the Local Capacities for Peace Project, reported in Mary B. Anderson, *Do No Harm: Supporting Local Capacities for Peace through Aid* (Cambridge, Mass.: Collaborative for Development Action, 1996).

10. Reported in Anderson, *Do No Harm,* 22–23.

11. Personal communication from a staff member of CARE/Canada who had worked in parts of Liberia.

12. From discussions at a Local Capacities for Peace Feedback Workshop held in Nairobi, Kenya, January 1997, for aid agency personnel working in southern Sudan.

13. One person who has examined how to avoid negative impacts of aid on conflict *and* the potential for aid to lead toward peace building is John Prendergast; see his *Frontline Diplomacy.*

14. See, for example, the very able coverage of these issues in Larry Minear and Thomas G. Weiss, *Mercy under Fire: War and the Global Humanitarian Community,* especially chaps. 1 and 4. Although it is almost impossible to keep abreast of actual dollar amounts of aid being provided through NGOs from crisis to crisis, Minear and Weiss report that one agency, CARE, spent over $438 million in 1993 alone. They also note that, in some cases, the NGO resources in a crisis setting are greater than those of bilateral and United Nations agencies combined. (Of course, many of the U.N. and bilateral monies are, in these cases, being channeled through NGOs.)

15. It is also true that, with growing numbers of new, small NGOs arriving in complex emergency settings, inexperienced and young aid workers also are on the increase even as aid is professionalizing. Though inexperienced, this cadre of new aid workers nonetheless expects many of the same support systems and benefits (other than salary) enjoyed by the professional

156 *Mary B. Anderson*

workers. They expect to be protected, housed, fed, driven in NGO vehicles, and rescued, if the need arises. So the side effects of professionalization have affected the broad aid community to a large extent.

16. A few agencies have recently begun to change their policies with regard to local staff, ensuring them of safe evacuation when expatriate staff leave.

17. I cannot relocate this brief paper so cannot cite the author adequately. His sensitivity and thoughtfulness were impressive and challenging. I hope I someday find out who he is.

18. The corresponding change in attitudes of recipients mirrors the shifts cited here in aid worker attitudes. As one shifts, so does the other; the process is mutually reinforcing. I focus here only on the dilemma posed to aid providers because my intent is to understand better the moral challenges contained within the systems of aid delivery.

19. An exception is the uprising in Chiapas, Mexico, which was spearheaded by peasants to express their dissatisfaction with the continuing impoverishment and marginalization they experience in relation to central government and its policies.

20. Furthermore, many societies experience both poverty and injustice and do not go to war to correct them.

21. There are a few exceptions to this view, but in these cases (e.g., Israel and Palestine; East Timor and Indonesia; and Bhutan, to name a few) these wars preceded the end of the Cold War.

9

Hard Choices after Genocide
Human Rights and Political Failures in Rwanda

Ian Martin

UNHCR's mandate is the protection of bona fide refugees, not of mass murderers fleeing justice. . . . [UNHCR] allowed men and women responsible for genocide to evade justice and to continue to murder from a base established and run by the international community.—Rakiya Omaar, codirector of African Rights, "A Bitter Harvest," *Guardian* (London), 30 April 1997

Amnesty International has serious concerns about the role played by the international community, in particular UNHCR, in condoning the mass *refoulement* of refugees to Rwanda by neighboring countries. . . . Amnesty International deeply regrets that under pressure from the authorities in Rwanda, neighboring countries and donor governments, UNHCR has sacrificed basic principles of refugee protection.—Amnesty International, *Rwanda: Human Rights Overlooked in Mass Repatriation*, January 1997

The moral dilemmas that have followed the international community's failure to prevent or check genocide in Rwanda in 1994 have divided humanitarian organizations, human rights critics, and the staff of the United Nations' refugee agency themselves. Those who advance unambiguous positions with certainty seem to be able to do so only by limiting themselves, consciously or unconsciously, to a partial perspective. Those who grapple with all dimensions of an unbearable reality seem crippled in their ability to embrace with confidence any course of action. If we strive to confront, with as much objectivity as we can achieve, the different aspects of this reality, do we merely confirm the impossibility of reconciling conflicting humanitarian and human rights principles—and identify ourselves with the person who, when asked to provide directions, replied, "I wouldn't start from here"? Or can we look back to identify better paths that could have been chosen if principles had been better respected, finding the most principled route that can still be taken for a journey that cannot be abandoned?

Rwanda's Challenges

The Nature of the Genocide

The first and dominant reality, which more than all others determines the depth of the dilemmas, is the nature of the Rwandan genocide. The killing was highly organized at the national level, and the killers were controlled in their tasks by state officials: prefects, burgomasters, and local councillors. Militiamen arrived to take away contingents of victims with authorization signed by every administrative echelon. The army and the *gendarmerie* were heavily implicated, and a leading role was played by the extremist militia, the *Interahamwe*, but much of the killing was carried out by the ordinary Hutu peasants themselves. Some were directly coerced into killing by real threats to themselves, others subjected to orders or pressures they were unlikely to resist, but many were conditioned by years of anti-Tutsi indoctrination to be willing murderers. Yet it must never be forgotten that some stood out against these pressures and displayed real heroism in saving their Tutsi neighbors.[1]

The enormity of the Rwandan genocide consists first in the number of its victims, slaughtered by primitive methods in a short space of time. Over half a million were killed, and probably well over this number: one commentator calculates a daily killing rate at least five times that of the Nazi death camps over six weeks in April–May 1994.[2] But its enormity lies also in the numbers of its perpetrators: tens of thousands, possibly hundreds of thousands, murdered with their own hands. Among the guilty there were degrees of guilt—recognized in the law adopted in 1996 by Rwanda's Transitional National Assembly, which identifies "the planners, organizers, instigators, supervisors and leaders of the crime of genocide" and "persons who acted in positions of authority" as being in a category apart from ordinary perpetrators of homicide. The scale of the crimes simultaneously dictates the overwhelming need for justice and the impossibility of justice: the number of direct participants in crimes against humanity is beyond the capacity of any justice system to arraign and judge.

The Nature of the Exodus

The exodus of Hutu refugees into Tanzania, Zaire, and Burundi was also unparalleled in its combination of scale and speed, and in its nature. The first influx into Tanzania in April 1994 saw 170,000 cross the border in the first few days, and the number of refugees in Tanzania eventually swelled to over 500,000. The largest exodus, of some 850,000 into northern Kivu province of Zaire, took place over only five days in mid-July. A third major outflow, into southern Kivu and Burundi, brought the total outside Rwanda to around two million, and it would have been greater if hundreds of thousands had not remained internally displaced in the Humanitarian Protection Zone established by French troops under U.N. authority.

This exodus can be characterized as a politically ordered evacuation. The tendency of Hutu peasants to conform collectively to the orders of their leaders has been frequently remarked upon by those seeking to explain the manner in which they participated in the genocide: it operated again in the manner in which they left Rwanda. The administrative authorities sought to induce their populations to flee, warning them of massacres if they awaited the arrival of the Rwandan Patriotic Front (RPF), and there are reports of those refusing to leave being killed by the militia. The political motivation was clear in declarations by Hutu leaders; the army chief of staff commented that "the RPF will rule over a desert," and the leader of an extremist party boasted in exile, "Even if the RPF has won a military victory, it will not have the power. It has only the bullets; we have the population."

This is not, however, to deny that many, probably most, left of their own volition and in real fear of the RPF advance. Nor was that fear without any justification. In the years since the RPF had begun the civil war in 1990, massacres of civilians by its soldiers appear to have been few, but not unknown. Now the ranks of the RPF had been swollen by new recruits not conditioned by years of discipline; they were advancing through the horrific evidence of recent genocide, in which the families of some of the soldiers had perished. Reprisal killings occurred, in some cases amounting to massacres. The fleeing Hutu appear mostly to have anticipated revenge rather than awaited reports of the actual conduct of the RPF.

The Nature of the Camps

The former leaders kept almost total control of the population in the camps. The U.N. secretary-general reported in November 1994 that about 230 Rwandese political leaders were in Zaire, exerting a hold on the refugees through intimidation and the support of military personnel and militia members in the camps. The militia resorted openly to intimidation and force to stop refugees who were inclined to return to Rwanda. They and former Rwandese government forces personnel possessed firearms, and there were already reports of continuing military activity along the Zaire-Rwanda border.[3]

Nongovernmental organizations (NGOs) working in the Zaire camps were even franker. Former Rwandese authorities controlled almost all aspects of camp life, they reported, and used the distribution of relief items to reinforce their position. Refugees were being threatened, attacked, and killed for being "RPF spies" or for wanting to return to Rwanda: the militia carried out summary executions, public stoning, and other physical violence.[4] Most of the political leaders and former army and *Interahamwe* had fled to Zaire rather than to Tanzania, but the Tanzanian camps were also controlled by the former administrative authorities. When the UNHCR gave notice of the removal to the interior from the main Tanzanian camp of a former burgomaster, heavily implicated in the genocide, this was resisted by a machete-wielding crowd of 5,000 refugees that threatened and held hostage aid workers.

In November 1994 fifteen NGOs threatened to withdraw from the Goma (Zaire) camps, stating publicly:

- Under present conditions the UNHCR is prevented from fulfilling its mandate of protecting and assisting refugees.
- The work of humanitarian organizations is largely compromised due to the current power structure within the camps. When aid workers attempt to intervene on behalf of the victims of discriminatory practices, their lives are threatened.
- The relief operation is unsustainable. Refugees are denied the right to return to their homes, equal access to humanitarian aid, protection, and the guarantee of basic human rights. They remain hostages.

The U.N. secretary-general put to the Security Council options for addressing the issue of security in the Zaire camps. A peacekeeping force of 10,000–12,000 men would be necessary if the mandate were to separate out the former political leaders, military and militia, as well as to maintain security in the camps. Merely to establish security progressively without separation would require 3,000–5,000 troops (an estimate later revised upward).[5] Only one troop contributor (Bangladesh) was identified even for this lesser option. The Security Council thus returned the issue of camp security to the UNHCR, which contracted with the Zaire government to pay for the latter to provide a contingent of elite troops, with international trainers. On this basis, and with effective policing by the Tanzanians in their camps, a reasonable degree of security in the camps was achieved, but without the control of the former Rwandan authorities being broken. Moreover, the Zairian Security Contingent had neither the will nor the capacity to stop the flow of arms, military training, and cross-border incursions into Rwanda.[6]

Médecins sans Frontières (MSF)–France and the International Rescue Committee withdrew from the camps in late 1994, but most of the NGOs continued their work. The moral dilemma they faced is well illustrated by the different positions taken by different national sections of MSF. MSF–France stated, in announcing its November 1994 decision to pull out, that "the continued diversion of humanitarian aid by the same leaders who orchestrated the genocide, the lack of effective international action regarding impunity, and the fact that the refugee population was being held hostage, presented a situation contradictory with the principles of humanitarian assistance." MSF–Belgium and MSF–Holland decided to continue working in the camps "while at the same time continuously and publicly advocating for an end to impunity and improvements in the security situation for the refugees." But in August 1995 MSF–Belgium and MSF–Holland announced their own decisions to leave the camps. Medical humanitarian relief, they stated, was consolidating the situation in the camps, still controlled by those responsible for the genocide in Rwanda. Impunity still reigned: hardly any people had been arrested, and none brought to justice. The militarization in the region was continuing: "the setting is now still a launching pad for future military action." Now that the medical emergency was over, the negative effects of the relief activities were outnumbering the positive effects. The international community had failed to respond to MSF's advocacy efforts to put the situation on the international agenda.[7]

The Nature of the Insurgency

The implications of the character of the camps on the borders of Rwanda were of obvious and immediate concern to its new government. In a radio interview in December 1994, the vice president and minister of defense, Paul Kagame, said that unless the international community was capable of regaining political and even military control of the camps, it would keep helping "an army in exile preparing for war."

At first, that war was slow coming. Until late 1995, the challenges to Rwanda's security consisted chiefly of minor acts of sabotage and the placing of antipersonnel mines, mostly near to the Zaire border. From early 1996, however, insurgents were operating in larger groups, and a pattern of murderous attacks on local officials and isolated Tutsi civilians became evident. In June, Tutsi civilians were massacred in three different prefectures, and it became clear that the insurgency stemming from the Zaire camps had penetrated well inside the borders of Rwanda.

The numbers of Tutsi killed in these attacks may have been small in the context of the preceding genocide, but it is precisely in the context of the preceding genocide that the reaction of the Rwandan government, and of the genocide survivors operating as a critical constituency of that government, must be comprehended. For both perpetrators and victims, these attacks were a continuation of the genocide and evidence of an intention to pursue the goal of recovering control of a Rwanda from which the Tutsi had been eliminated. The initial response of the government was to launch in mid-1996 a series of counterinsurgency operations in which hundreds of unarmed Hutu civilians, presumed to be insurgents or the collaborators of insurgents, were killed. But it is likely that the firm decision to break up the camps by military action across the border in Zaire dates from this moment.

The Nature of Postgenocide Rwanda

In the absence of a forcible separation of the old leaders from the refugees in the camps, it was left to the UNHCR to do what it could to encourage voluntary repatriation through cross-border visits and an information campaign designed to counter the propaganda of extremists asserting that returnees would be killed. The UNHCR also worked to improve conditions in the receiving communes, as did the Human Rights Field Operation in Rwanda (HRFOR) of the U.N. High Commissioner for Human Rights regarding the human rights conditions for return.

The human rights situation inside Rwanda made reassurance in the face of extremist propaganda difficult. RPF killings of Hutu civilians during their advance from April to July 1994 at least belonged to the period of active conflict and the immediate aftermath of genocide, but fresh reports after the new government was installed played further into the hands of the extremist Hutu leadership opposing return. A UNHCR team that carried out interviews with people inside Rwanda as well as with recently arriving refugees in the camps in August and early September 1994 alleged a continuing pattern and practice of atrocities aimed at the Hutu population in certain parts of the country. These findings were repudiated by the U.N. peacekeeping operation UNAMIR, which had at last deployed around the country, as well as by the government. But media reports of these findings, and then of the intervention of the U.N. secretary-general to ensure the suppression of any "report" by the UNHCR, were well publicized, especially in the camps. The reports of human rights NGOs publicly documented Rwandan Patriotic Army (RPA) killings, but not on the scale estimated by the UNHCR team. Its guilt for its failure to stop the genocide and its goal of refugee repatriation combined to render the international community reluctant to play into the extremist propaganda in the camps by giving credence to such reports and to acknowledge the real human rights disincentives to return. Yet it was precisely sustained human rights pressure and assistance that were necessary to create a moral basis for encouraging return.

There was a modest return of Hutu refugees in the early months of 1995, but human rights violations in Rwanda dealt repatriation efforts another blow when thousands of internally displaced people were killed in the forcible closure of the last camp in southwestern Rwanda. The government had lost patience over joint efforts with the U.N. and the NGOs to bring about the closure of the camps. These efforts had some success, but as voluntary returns slowed, a divergence grew between those in the international agencies who stressed the Rwandan responsibility to create conditions to encourage voluntary return, most notably acceptable arrest procedures, and the government, which felt its sovereignty and security threatened by camps containing a hard core of militia implicated in the genocide and receiving humanitarian assistance. This situation was thus a microcosm of the larger situation developing with the refugee camps across Rwanda's borders. In April 1995 the RPA launched a military action to close the Kibeho camp that became a bloodbath. The government admitted to only 338 dead, but U.N. and other agency estimates put the toll upward of 2,000. The deaths occurred in the presence of UNAMIR troops, mandated to contribute to the security and protection of displaced persons. It was officially stated that UNAMIR could use force only to defend U.N. lives; the May 1994 mandate was in fact ambiguous in permitting UNAMIR to "take action in self-defense against persons or groups who threaten protected sites and populations." But it was inconceivable that a U.N. presence discredited by its failure to resist genocide would fight the RPA: so the U.N. was again humiliated by its impotence, while severe damage was done to the human rights credentials of the new government.[8]

From 1995 until the massive return of late 1996, the risk that a refugee returning to Rwanda would fall victim to a targeted killing was in fact small. The contrary perception in the camps was hugely exaggerated, but it was fed both by isolated killings by undisciplined RPA soldiers and by indiscriminate killings of Hutu civilians in counterinsurgency operations or in reprisal for soldiers' deaths. And if there could be no absolute assurance on this score, far less could refugees be honestly advised to discount the risk of arbitrary arrest and detention in horrific, life-threatening conditions, with no prospect of prompt or fair trial.

It was at first inevitable, in the absence of any functioning judicial system, that those accused of acts of genocide would be arrested outside any legal procedures by soldiers and local administrative authorities. Despite the training and deployment of judicial officials, most arrests were still being made outside legal procedures when the mass return of refugees took place in late 1996: some denunciations of individuals' involvement in genocide were clearly well founded, others abusive, and the judicial machinery was not strong enough to distinguish between the two and order releases. Prolonged detention in Rwanda is a life-or-death issue: thousands of detainees have died in grossly overcrowded prisons or local *cachots* (lockups), where conditions defy description. In early 1997 the number of untried detainees passed 100,000 and despite improvements in medical care and some expansion of prison capacity, horrific deaths from suffocation continued to occur in lockups. When genocide trials began at the end of 1996, many of the defendants were not represented by lawyers, and other serious doubts arose about their fairness.

Legitimate concerns of refugees considering return related not only to life and liberty but also to property: their ability to recover land and homes in a densely populated country to which over 700,000 Tutsi refugees had returned in the first year after the war ended. But beyond this loomed the general reluctance of Hutu refugees to return to what they perceived as a Tutsi-dominated Rwanda. When this reluctance represented a fear of justice for personal complicity in genocide, it merited little sympathy. But others were entitled to question, in the light of the recent experience of Burundi as well as Rwanda's more distant but living history, the nature of political power in the present and future Rwanda. The formal multiparty and multiethnic character of the Government of National Unity could not conceal an overwhelming concentration of power in Tutsi hands, which strengthened at the center after government changes in August 1995. It was strongly reflected in local administrative and judicial authorities, as well as in the continued military dominance that the insurgency only intensified.

The Nature of the Crisis in Eastern Zaire

The beginning of the end of the refugee camps came with two successive eruptions in eastern Zaire. Rwandese Hutu refugees who spread outside the camps in northern Kivu entered into simmering intergroup tensions over land between Banyarwanda and groups indigenous to the region. Zairian Tutsi who fled into Rwanda in the early months of 1996 reported that the new arrivals had poisoned long-peaceful relations with their Zairian Hutu neighbors: The *Interahamwe* from Rwanda set out to kill Tutsi, not merely to expel them from their land.

Over many years, the Zairian authorities had sought to exclude long-settled groups—Zairian Tutsi known as Banyamulenge in southern Kivu, as well as Hutu and Tutsi Banyarwanda in northern Kivu—from citizenship and political power. In September 1996 open conflict broke out between the Zairian army and Banyamulenge militia. The balance of power quickly shifted to the Banyamulenge and those fighting with them, the Alliance of Democratic Forces for the Liberation of Congo-Zaire, led by Laurent Kabila. Rwanda acknowledged that Zairian Tutsi had fought and trained with the RPA but initially denied that its own forces were fighting inside Zaire. It was only in July 1997 that Rwandan vice president Paul Kagame confirmed that Rwandan "mid-level commanders" had led the Alliance forces throughout the successful rebellion that went on to topple Mobutu, that Rwandan troops had participated in the capture of major cities, including Kinshasa itself, and that Rwanda had provided training and arms for the Congolese rebels before the campaign had begun.[9]

It became clear that Rwanda had seen in the Banyamulenge crisis the opportunity to put into effect an operation it had been preparing since mid-1996 to end the security threat on its border, by breaking up the camps and leaving at least the east of Zaire under sympathetic control. Rwanda had repeatedly pointed out that the camps had become the base for armed insurgency in continuation of the genocide. It had warned publicly as well as privately that it would have to act if the international community failed to do so. Rwanda's acknowledged objectives were to dismantle the camps and destroy the rebel structure. Thus, refugee camps were attacked, and the fighting set off a massive return of refugees into Rwanda and Burundi. The Hutu army and militia retreated, forcing some of the refugees to remain with them; others scattered further into Zaire to escape the conflict.

Amid concern that another major humanitarian disaster had begun, the U.N. Security Council authorized a Canadian-led multinational force to be launched to bring humanitarian aid to those at risk in eastern Zaire. From the outset it proved almost impossible to define its mission in a way that could realistically assure troop-contributing governments that they would not be drawn into local conflicts. As refugees flooded back to Rwanda, the governments of Rwanda and the United States swiftly maintained that the refugee issue was virtually at an end, and the mission was aborted. In fact, hundreds of thousands of refugees had scattered into Zaire, many to be the victims of slow extermination by famine and disease or to be deliberately eliminated by the Alliance troops on suspicion of being the hardcore of *génocidaires*; some survived to be repatriated to Rwanda over the following months. NGOs found themselves confronting new dilemmas, as humanitarian aid was used to lure refugees out of the forests, to their deaths at the hands of Rwandan or other Alliance forces. UNHCR and the refugees law principles on which its work is based were, according to the UNHCR's own testimony, abused and brushed aside to a degree never seen before: inside and outside the UNHCR, some felt that the agency itself had not stood firm enough on these principles. Humanitarian and human rights organizations maintained that there were mass killings of unarmed men, women, and children, sometimes but not always in the company of armed elements. One U.N.-mandated investigation into these abuses was rejected by the new government of the Democratic Republic of Congo; a second was confronted with a succession of obstacles and had barely begun its work by the end of 1997.

The Nature of Repatriation and Reintegration

The mass return from Zaire was one of three major induced repatriations to Rwanda. The first, of some 75,000 refugees, occurred from Burundi in July–August 1996. Starting in mid-November 1996, an estimated 750,000 Rwandans joined the flight from fighting in Zaire back into Rwanda. Some expressed themselves as relieved to return, saying that they would have chosen to return long before if they had been free of the threats and pressures of their leadership; others were obviously fearful of what awaited them. Then, in December, Tanzania decided to compel the return of Rwandan refugees, and the UNHCR cosigned a government statement setting an imminent deadline, with no reference to any process for considering the cases of those who feared return. Some 500,000 were repatriated, with the UNHCR explaining its cooperation in what was undeniably a forced repatriation on the grounds that without political support from the international community it was in no position to oppose this and decided not to abandon the refugees on their way home.[10]

The initial reception of the returnees was monitored by both the UNHCR and the U.N. Human Rights Field Operation in Rwanda. Government directives that arrests for alleged involvement in the genocide should not take place until returnees had reached their home areas and case files had been completed were largely respected, but by mid-January over 2,000 of the returnees from Burundi and at least 6,800 of the returnees from Tanzania and Zaire had been detained. Some returnees were involved in an increasing incidence of killings and other attacks on Tutsi, and at least 100 returnees had been killed by members of the local population or soldiers in incidents reported to U.N. human rights officers before their monitoring was severely restricted in early February, after the murder of five U.N. staff and other killings of expatriates. The security situation inside Rwanda quickly worsened, with increasingly confident attacks by larger groups of insurgents and hundreds of deaths of Hutu civilians in RPA counterinsurgency operations or reprisals.

Failures and Deepening Dilemmas

It is undeniable that for over two years the international community fed and otherwise supported camps that were the base from which those who had perpetrated genocide pursued a murderous insurgency. It is equally undeniable that the international community welcomed or condoned a repatriation of refugees that was mostly involuntary or induced by the failure of protection, to conditions in Rwanda where some have been or will be killed or the victims of other human rights violations. Could it have been otherwise?

The Failure to Halt Genocide

Betrayals of human rights principles by the Rwandan actors and by foreign governments began long before the genocide, but the deepest betrayal lies in the genocide itself and the refusal to intervene to prevent or halt it. Although no one—including the RPF—predicted the scale of the killings that were to come, strong warnings had appeared. Following NGO reports on massacres in Rwanda, the Hutu regime of President Habyarimana acceded to an April 1993 visit by the U.N. special rapporteur on extrajudicial, summary, or arbitrary executions. In his report he described massacres of civilian populations that, he said, could constitute genocide; the involvement in these ethnic killings of political militias; the existence of a "second power" alongside that of the official authorities; and the "pernicious role" of Radio Rwanda in instigating several massacres. He recommended that a mechanism for the protection of civilian populations against massacres should be set up, including international teams of human rights observers and a civilian police force.[11]

When only weeks later the peacekeeping operation UNAMIR was mandated by the Security Council, no attention seems to have been given to this analysis or recommendations. The Arusha Peace Agreement, signed by the Habyarimana government and the RPF on 4 Au-

gust 1993 to create a power-sharing transitional government, provided for a "Neutral International Force," whose mandate would go
so far as to "guarantee the overall security of the country" and "assist
in the tracking of arms caches and neutralization of armed gangs
throughout the country."[12] The actual mandate given to UNAMIR
was the more limited one of "monitoring" the security situation, although it did extend as far as "to contribute to the security of the city
of Kigali."[13] Even the modest force strength of 2,548 recommended
by the secretary-general led to Security Council pressure for a reduction and economies: no human rights component or officers were included, and the U.N. was as always constrained from providing an
official intelligence unit, although Belgium financed directly a small
unit attached to its UNAMIR contingent. Nevertheless, strong warnings of growing and impending violence were sent to U.N. headquarters, especially when in January a senior government official gave details of plans for killings of politicians, Belgian peacekeepers, and
Tutsi if the implementation of the Arusha Peace Agreement pro-
ceeded. Following this, and again on three occasions in February, the
UNAMIR force commander, General Romeo Dallaire, requested permission to carry out cordon-and-search operations to seize arms:
these were turned down by New York.[14]

There is every reason to believe that, once the genocide had been
launched, a rapid reinforcement of the U.N. operation, with a Chapter VII mandate to protect civilians, could have checked its course,
without suffering heavy casualties at the hands of the Rwandan
armed forces or militia.[15] What was lacking was in part a failure to
interpret the situation correctly—most of the media portrayed the
killings as mutual ethnic violence, and diplomatic attention focused
on seeking a further cease-fire between the government forces and
the RPF, rather than on the protection of civilians in government-
controlled areas. Even more, however, it was a failure of political
will. The Belgian withdrawal of their peacekeepers after ten had been
murdered, French sympathy for the Habyarimana regime and antipa-
thy to the RPF, and U.S. determination to impose its interpretation
of the lessons of Somalia on the Security Council as a whole played
leading roles in this failure; but very few governments, most of them

African, can be credited with a heartfelt desire to see the international community respond robustly.

The Resulting Dilemmas

Once the genocide had occurred, the full application of human rights principles to the resulting situation became literally impossible. They required that the perpetrators of genocide be brought to justice but that they be investigated and arrested by due process of law, held in decent conditions of detention, and given a prompt and fair trial. They required that refugees with a well-founded fear of persecution be given protection, able to make voluntary decisions to repatriate without being compelled or intimidated into either returning or remaining. They required that those guilty of crimes against humanity be arrested and brought to justice and that those waging armed conflict be excluded from refugee protection. They required that insurgents still engaged in genocidal murder be combatted by security forces fully respecting the principles of humanitarian and human rights law. They required that all citizens of Rwanda not convicted by process of law could enjoy freedom of expression and freedom from discrimination and could expect to enjoy full political rights.

It is not hard to focus on any one of these absolute requirements and demonstrate the failure to respect or fulfill it. It is harder to suggest what actions could have led to the least unacceptable compromises of objectives that were simultaneously unachievable or can best reconcile conflicting principles today.

The Failure to Protect and Exclude from Protection

The French *Operation Turquoise*, operating under U.N. authority, should have been mandated to detain those who were prima facie organizers of genocide and to disarm those crossing international borders out of Rwanda. In fact, however, the French, and Zaire in particular among neighboring states, facilitated the cohesive migration of the political, military, and administrative leadership that had launched and carried out the genocide and did little to disarm its fighters; Zaire became complicit in their rearming.

Once the most immediate humanitarian needs—checking the cholera epidemic and providing basic food and shelter—had been met and the refugee camps were recognized to be under the control of the *génocidaires*, the international community should have assumed an obligation that would and could not be fulfilled by Zaire alone: excluding those implicated in crimes against humanity and those engaged in armed conflict from protection as refugees. The prime responsibility for the failure to fulfill this obligation rests with the Security Council, which alone could apply the necessary military force, and not with the UNHCR. The UNHCR did urge international action, but after the Security Council had turned its back on its own responsibilities, the agency failed to speak out as strongly or continuously as it should have done to confront the international community with the reality it preferred to ignore. The moral burden cannot be left with the humanitarian NGOs, the best of which agonized over the choice of abandoning the needs of children and other innocent refugees or knowing that their assistance in part fueled a continuing conflict. Either the U.N. member states should have faced up to the secretary-general's recognition that military action was necessary to remove the leadership from the existing camps, or international assistance to the camps should have been progressively cut off, then reprovided for those who chose not to return to Rwanda in camps to which arms and leading genocide suspects could have been denied admission.

The Failure of Impartial Justice

An impartial justice should have been a higher priority for international assistance to Rwanda. This would have required not only greater resources but a greater willingness to ask unwelcome questions about the ethnic composition of the new justice system: even to recognize that, in the special circumstances of postgenocide Rwanda, justice required non-Rwandan participation, as well as appropriate representation of both Hutu and Tutsi among the judges and the judged. Most donor governments have been more willing to condemn detention conditions of extreme inhumanity than to assist in ameliorating them; yet they would only be right to support an overall program that offered the early release of the many detainees against whom there is no evidence, and due process of law in all future arrests, rather than the continuing growth of the detainee population.

The most guilty must be punished, but in a manner that gives their peers no excuse to deny the justice of their punishment. Any equation of Tutsi killings of Hutu with the genocide against the Tutsi should be rejected, but the contrite acknowledgment that such killings have occurred—before, during, and since the genocide—and the pursuit of justice for their victims, too, would be the foundation of true reconciliation.

The international community failed to play adequately the part in the pursuit of impartial justice that it claimed for itself. The early history of the International Criminal Tribunal for Rwanda was a shameful failure of both commitment and competence.

The Failure of International Assistance

The new Rwanda needed both more assistance and more criticism than it received, and only a willingness to deliver the former would have made the latter morally and politically acceptable. It needed the Marshall Plan its new leaders sought, but, even if donor states had been ready to deliver this, such a commitment of resources could be the basis of future stability only if those leaders had embarked on a genuinely inclusive political strategy. It has become less possible to believe in such a strategy as Tutsi control of national and local power has tightened. The early idealism of those who believed that they could transcend ethnic distinctions in building a new Rwanda would have had a greater chance of prevailing within the government if the international community had acted to remove the security threat that strengthens the hand of hardliners and had delivered assistance more promptly, generously, and efficiently.

Morality and Hard Choices

The Rwandan genocide left a situation in which the absolute application of human rights principles to its different aspects was impossible, and what has happened since has moved us farther away from being able to reconcile their conflicting requirements. The failure to do the right thing when it is difficult can be expected to deepen the later dilemmas and make still less possible the avoidance of compromises of principle in practice.

Yet morality requires that no part of the truth is evaded and no principle unacknowledged. The Hutu leadership that was truly implicated in the genocide has no claim to a future political role, but Rwanda's government at all levels must become representative of and accountable to all its people. A brutal insurgency must be combatted, but it must not become the excuse for deliberate or unnecessary killings of civilians. Refugees must be fed and protected, but those who do not qualify for protection must be excluded from it. Those guilty of crimes against humanity must be arrested and prosecuted, but their conditions of detention must meet minimum standards of humanity, and their trials must conform to basic standards of fairness. Each of these principles is extraordinarily difficult to respect in practice in the circumstances of Rwanda. Yet the extent to which each is or is not being respected must be confronted with honesty by both Rwandan and international actors, and this examination must lead to efforts to come closer to all of them together. Actors in the real world must not allow themselves to be paralyzed when they cannot adequately serve every moral imperative, nor must they indulge in the absolutism of partial vision or exclusive choices. It is morality, after all, that requires them to identify and support the least bad of the remaining choices.

Notes

1. On the nature of the genocide in Rwanda, see Gérard Prunier, *The Rwanda Crisis: History of a Genocide* (New York: Columbia University Press, 1995), 237–65.

2. Prunier, *The Rwanda Crisis*, 261–65.

3. "Report of the Secretary-General on Security in the Rwandese Refugee Camps," U.N. document S/1994/1308, 18 November 1994; reproduced as Document 99 in *The United Nations and Rwanda, 1993–1996* (New York: United Nations, 1996).

4. Médecins sans Frontières/Doctors without Borders, *Breaking the Cycle*, 10 November 1994.

5. "Report of the Secretary-General on Security in the Rwandese Refugee Camps," U.N. document S/1994/1308, 18 November 1994; and "Second Report of the Secretary-General on Security in the Rwandese Refugee Camps," U.N. document S/1995/65, 25 January 1995; reproduced as Documents 99 and 111 in *The United Nations and Rwanda*.

6. Médicins sans Frontières/Doctors without Borders, *Deadlock in the Rwandan Refugee Crisis*, July 1995.

7. "Additional Info on MSF Holland Will Leave the Refugee Camps in Zaire and Tanzania," MSF-Holland, Amsterdam, 28 August 1995.

8. For a detailed account of the positions and events surrounding the closure of the camps inside Rwanda, see Stephanie T. E. Kleine-Ahlbrandt, *The Protection Gap in the International Protection of Internally Displaced Persons: The Case of Rwanda* (Geneva: Institut Universitaire de Hautes Études Internationales, 1996). See also Médecins sans Frontières, *Report on Events in Kibeho Camp*, April 1995.

9. John Pomfret, "Rwandans Led Revolt in Congo," *Washington Post*, 9 July 1997.

10. "The U.N.'s African Refugee Dilemma," interview with the UNHCR director of international protection, Dennis McNamara, *International Herald Tribune*, 10 March 1997.

11. "Report by the Special Rapporteur on Extrajudicial, Summary or Arbitrary Executions on His Mission to Rwanda, 8–17 April 1993," U.N. document E/CN.4/1994/7/Add.1, 11 August 1993; reproduced as Document 20 in *The United Nations and Rwanda*.

12. "Peace Agreement between the Government of the Republic of Rwanda and the Rwandese Patriotic Front," 3 August 1993, Annex VI; reproduced as Document 19 in *The United Nations and Rwanda*.

13. Security Council Resolution S/RES/872 (1993), 5 October 1993; reproduced as Document 20 in *The United Nations and Rwanda*.

14. Joint Evaluation of Emergency Assistance to Rwanda. *The International Response to Conflict and Genocide: Lessons from the Rwanda Experience*, Study 2, "Early Warning and Conflict Management" (Copenhagen: Steering Committee of the Joint Evaluation of Emergency Assistance to Rwanda, 1996), 35–40, and 66–71. See also Charles Trueheart, "U.N. Alerted to Plans for Rwanda Bloodbath," *Washington Post*, 25 September 1997.

15. This view has been most authoritatively supported by the Carnegie Commission on Preventing Deadly Conflict, after it convened an international panel of senior military leaders: *Preventing Deadly Conflict: Final Report* (New York: Carnegie Corporation, December 1997), 6.

10

Refugee Camps, Population Transfers, and NGOs

Rony Brauman

T he second generation of the humanitarian movement emerged during the 1970s, amid the conflicts of the postcolonial era. Undoubtedly triggered by the proliferation of violent situations and the population movements that were their direct result, the humanitarian boom was amplified and accelerated by the existence of television, which rose to ascendancy among the media during the same period. Fleeing for their lives or to escape oppression, thousands of civilians found themselves penned up in camps, dependent on purveyors of international aid who gradually managed to organize themselves in this new environment. Between 1976 and 1982, the number of refugees registered by the United Nations High Commissioner for Refugees (UNHCR) rose from three million to eleven million, almost all of them from the third world and, with the partial exception of the Vietnamese "boat people," all taking refuge in other third world countries. The picture seemed clear: on one side violence and arbitrary behavior; on the other the distress of civilians who were the innocent victims of predators. As they ventured into unfamiliar terrain and began to operate in the camps, the volunteer relief workers sent in by the nongovernmental organizations (NGOs) initially saw their universe as a simple one, divided by a line separating good from evil, the world of solidarity from the world of violence.

Before long, however, this pious vision began to blur. The first difficulties arose at the Cambodian border, where a long string of refugee camps was set up following the Vietnamese troops' victorious entry into Phnom Penh in January 1979. The retreating Khmer Rouge forces had taken tens of thousands of civilians with them to provide slave labor and serve as human shields. After months of wandering through the forests and mountains in the west of the country, their numbers decimated by famine and disease, they managed to cross the border and find refuge in Thailand. Other Cambodians quickly followed them into exile, fleeing both communism and foreign occupation.

Very soon the various border camps controlled by the Thai army became not only the center for all kinds of trafficking between Thailand and Cambodia but also political and military bases where the anti-Vietnamese counteroffensive was organized. Nationalists, communists, and Sihanouk supporters rapidly used them as veritable sanctuaries where combatants were recruited and trained. The civilian economy also prospered as people came from all over Cambodia to purchase consumer goods otherwise unobtainable in a country devastated by the Khmer Rouge and plundered by the Vietnamese.

It should be remembered that at the time—until 1989—the Khmer Rouge was the legal government of Cambodia, a government that was subsequently expanded to include other anti-Vietnamese resistance movements. This led to a situation unique in history: the legal government was in a refugee camp, while the "real" country had no international representation. Apart from the Soviet Union and its satellites and allies, no one had recognized the new Phnom Penh regime, which had come to power in Vietnamese army troop carriers and whose links with the outside world depended essentially on the channels of international aid.

Each of the political factions opposed to the Vietnamese had its own camps, which were kept under more or less strict control, with the support of the Thai authorities. There was a fair amount of freedom in the Khmer People's National Liberation Front (FLNPK) camps (Site 2, the largest of these camps), while those run by Sihanouk supporters a few dozen kilometers to the north were under more rigorous control. The Khmer Rouge camps, situated on the southern

Khmer-Thai border, were closely supervised by Pol Pot's political apparatus.

The Use of Aid for Political Leverage on the Cambodian Border

After the initial phase, during which the need to respond to the emergency overrode all other considerations, problems and contradictions began to appear. The humanitarian organizations, many of them newly formed and completely lacking in political experience, were now faced with a situation in which aid was at the center of complex political maneuvering. Remaining in the camps would mean training medical auxiliaries while knowing full well that many of them would go off to fight in the ranks of the anti-Vietnamese forces; it would also mean tolerating thefts and occasional wholesale misappropriation of medical supplies carried out under the protection of the Khmer camp administration. Humanitarian agencies had to decide whether they could agree to work in camps controlled by the Khmer Rouge, knowing that behind the window dressing its ways had not altered at all since its defeat.

Some NGOs, such as Handicap International, viewing the Khmer Rouge camps (e.g., Site K) as ordinary refugee camps, decided to set up operations there. Others, including Médecins sans Frontières (MSF), of which I was president during this period, refused all contact with the Khmer Rouge but soon realized that transactions of all sorts were constantly going on between the various camps, including, naturally, the transfer of "humanitarian goods" such as food and medicine. These were in the majority. A third group of NGOs, under the leadership of Oxfam U.K., felt that a precondition for assisting the Cambodian people was the restoration of normal relations between Cambodia and the international community, a move that they saw as indispensable for the rehabilitation of this devastated country. Accordingly, they argued in favor of recognizing the Phnom Penh government as the only entity representing Cambodia and refused to maintain any presence in the border camps. They naturally backed up their action in the field by lobbying the media and international institutions, explaining that nothing significant would be accomplished as long as the festering abscess of overassisted border camps remained and as long as the real center of power in Cambodia was boycotted by the rest of the world.

These questions gave rise to stormy debate within the different NGOs as well as among them. Although the issue lost its edge as time passed, it was not actually resolved until 1992, when the border camps were dismantled and the UNHCR organized the repatriation of the refugees to Cambodia under the Paris-Jakarta accords. MSF was one of the organizations that fiercely defended the necessity of remaining in the border camps (notably Khao-I-Dang and Site 2) despite everything, although it still refused to work in the Khmer Rouge camps. It believed that the Khmer Rouge ideology did not leave any room for humanitarian activity and precluded the possibility of extending any aid worthy of the name to those who needed it. In MSF's view, any operation carried out under the authority of the Khmer Rouge could be nothing more than a sham and a facade designed to improve their public image while bolstering the Angkar's ability to control its own population. Although the working conditions in the other camps were far from satisfactory, MSF felt they were more or less acceptable. Moreover, an initial mission to Phnom Penh in the summer of 1979 had convinced MSF that the aid sent to Cambodia was not reaching the population but passing directly into the hands of the Vietnamese authorities. The large-scale misappropriation of aid later reported by the press led us to take an outspoken stand against the regime: in February 1980, in cooperation with such agencies as the French *Action Internationale contre la Faim* (AICF) and the American International Rescue Committee, MSF organized a "March for the Survival of Cambodia" along the Khmer-Thai border. This closed the country's doors to MSF for many years.

The aim of the march was to draw international attention to this country that was being portrayed in the press as a "convalescent," slowly recovering under the attentive ministrations of Hanoi. In reality, Cambodia was being colonized and plundered by Vietnam, as the reports of refugees attested. The organizers of the demonstration knew that there was no prospect of their being allowed to enter the country in the foreseeable future, but they felt that some symbolic action was essential at that moment in time. Indeed, the march attracted wide coverage by the international media and helped open the eyes of the public to the true nature of the Phnom Penh regime.

Thus, MSF, like the defenders of the Phnom Penh regime, relied on mainly political arguments to justify its position. In its view, invoking humanitarian principles was pointless as it could not have restored the essence, the symbolic significance, of humanitarian aid in such a politically charged context. In other words, MSF was passing judgment on the different parties to the conflict, selecting the one with which it was willing to work and rejecting those (the Phnom Penh government until 1988 and the Khmer Rouge ever since) with which it felt it could not cooperate.

However unsatisfactory such a position may be for a humanitarian organization, MSF was—and remains—convinced that under such circumstances, in which political considerations overrode all else, it was better to espouse a political position actively than to support it by default. In short, MSF preferred to define its own stance vis-à-vis the different powers in the region; since it had to sup with the devil, it chose to sit with the devil who would let it use the longest spoon. The choice, then, was not between a political position and a neutral position but between two political positions: one active and the other by default.

Turning Point in Ethiopia: Aid Can Kill

Neutral or partisan, humanitarian or political, at least some action was possible in relation to Cambodia; there was some scope for giving practical effect to one's principles by maintaining a presence and doing useful work for the refugees. The Ethiopian famine and population transfers, on the other hand, brought the humanitarian movement up against a problem of quite a different magnitude, in that humanitarian aid was used as a weapon against those for whom it was intended, with the indispensable—though admittedly passive— cooperation of the NGOs on the spot. The significance of this episode in the history of humanitarian action justifies extended discussion of it here.

A general review of the historical context is in order. In 1983–1984, a drought struck the entire Sahel, from Mauritania to Sudan. Sporadic food shortages and even actual famine appeared in the affected countries, which launched international appeals for aid. Ethiopia, although as hard hit as other countries, did nothing, despite the alarming reports that were beginning to filter in via the armed opposition movements in Tigray and Eritrea. In early 1984, the head of the Ethiopian Relief and Rehabilitation Commission (RRC)[1] did ask for emergency food aid at a U.N. Food and Agricultural Organization (FAO) meeting. Virtually nothing came of this, however, owing to the Ethiopian government's refusal to allow an assessment mission to visit the affected region. The Addis Ababa government did not want to admit that there was a famine, because such an admission would cast a pall over celebrations marking the tenth anniversary of the overthrow of the Negus, scheduled for October 1984. At a session of the World Food Council held in Addis Ababa in June 1984, Colonel Mengistu's lengthy opening address contained only a brief reference to the situation in his own country: "Ethiopia is currently suffering from the serious drought that has struck most African countries, and the situation is getting worse. The revolutionary government has taken concrete, immediate measures to rehabilitate the victims of a drought resulting from abnormal world climatic conditions."

A sinister irony can be seen here by anyone who remembers that it had been Haile Selassie's own criminal negligence that had led to the terrible famine of 1973, in which 200,000 people died. Only after the vastly expensive tenth-anniversary celebrations were over was the BBC television documentary "Seeds of Despair" broadcast, sending shock waves around the globe and triggering a phenomenal mobilization of humanitarian forces. NGOs from all over the world proposed their services, many Western governments offered logistic resources and money, the European Community released hundreds of millions of ecus, and the most celebrated rock stars organized the "concert of the century," which took place simultaneously in Wembley, U.K., and Philadelphia, U.S., and was broadcast live by every television network in the world. Colonel Mengistu certainly could not have foreseen the scale of this surge of solidarity, and, given his past, he was probably surprised to find himself absolved of all responsibility, as though the famine decimating his people had no connection with his policies.

What is more, far from showing the slightest regret about the terrible suffering endured by its people, the Ethiopian junta attacked the international community, accusing it of turning a deaf ear to the desperate appeals issued by Addis Ababa—although until then not a single journalist or independent assessment mission had been authorized to visit the affected areas. These accusations were leveled precisely when the humanitarian mobilization was gathering momentum, in the winter of 1984–1985.

This set the tone for what was to come. The disaster became a propaganda tool and a bargaining chip in Ethiopia's relations with the international community: a bargaining chip because the victims, at the mercy of their government, were to become a valuable resource in terms of funds in hard currency; and a propaganda tool because the famine was presented as resulting from the combination of a natural disaster—lack of rain—and the cynicism of the powerful and affluent of this world, who were indifferent to the suffering of the Ethiopian people. The most surprising aspect was that no one bothered to challenge this version of the facts, although the reality was clearly very different. The drought played a considerable part in the appearance of food shortages, but the cataclysmic extent of the famine was due to very human reasons: on the one hand, the government's program of land collectivization, the nationalization of agricultural production and marketing, and totally irrational taxation systems; on the other hand, the war and repression in the north of the country—the famine zone—with the attendant destruction of crops, confiscation of livestock, and forcible recruitment of manpower into the army. An additional factor was the bureaucratic compartmentalization of the country, which prevented regions enjoying surpluses (and there were some) from supplying those with shortages. All these circumstances explain why a moderate drop in precipitation—no more than 20 percent compared with the average of previous years—should have had such tragic consequences in this deliberately and artificially weakened society.

It was a long time before this political reality finally became apparent, not because of the secrecy enveloping it but because no one really wished to see it. The spectacle of suffering relegated the causes of that suffering to the background, and the humanitarian credo ruled out any speculation about them. The pressing need for emergency relief eclipsed all other considerations. This is understandable from the NGOs' point of view but raises serious questions about the meaning and the limits of their action. For at that point, according to official communications in Amharic (translated by the BBC, so universally accessible), those in power in Ethiopia were seeking to construct "the first authentically communist African society" and to create a "New Man." In the implementation of this grandiose project, no weakness on the part of the country's administrators would be countenanced, as Colonel Mengistu kept repeating in his interminable speeches.

And indeed, the government's social surgery was carried out without flinching. Population transfers began in January 1985. The RRC's Ethiopian teams, with whom the foreign NGOs had been working on good terms, were set aside, and the whole aid system was placed under the authority of the Workers' Party, which had been established three months earlier on the tenth anniversary of the revolution. In practical terms, this meant that aid distributions were made dependent on "voluntary" departure for the "new economic zones" in the south of the country. Propaganda teams made the rounds of the relief camps to extol the merits of these new lands waiting to be conquered, but their persuasive abilities were evidently limited since it was blackmail and violence that ultimately propelled the new "pioneers" south.

At first, none of the NGOs understood what was happening. Relief workers would see the militia arrive at dawn, encircle part of the camp, and round up as many people as it could pack into its trucks (some of which had been "borrowed" from NGOs). They witnessed harrowing scenes of mothers trying to hang on to their children, families torn apart by club-wielding militiamen, men being driven off at gunpoint to unknown destinations. At Korem, the main camp where MSF was working, members of the organization observed the new party official putting pressure on the disaster victims: confiscating blankets and part of the food supplies, he authorized distributions only to those who "volunteered" to go south. Given these survivors' physical weakness and the biting cold of the high, wind-scoured plateaux, this ploy was indeed a deadly means of blackmailing the entire population. Because of the mountainous terrain and the prevailing winds, the areas affected by the drought were sharply demarcated, often bordering on other regions where harvests were normal, albeit subject to tax collectors' relentless attentions and the other depredations mentioned previously. Various NGOs and the United Nations World Food Programme (WFP) attested to the existence of abandoned "ghost towns" where crops had been left rotting in the fields. All the inhabitants had been rounded up and sent to resettlement zones.

All this was gleaned in bits and pieces by NGO volunteers, who could not make sense of the general picture. Were these practices an abuse of power by overzealous, sadistic officials, or were they part of some incomprehensible strategy of terror? Moreover, while a number of NGOs, together with the U.N., were describing the relief operation in Ethiopia as a "success story," commending the government's bold measures and the determination and efficiency of the authorities, tens of thousands of Ethiopians were fleeing to neighboring Sudan and Somalia, venturing into a hostile environment to escape the humanitarian paradise that had been promised them. Very few people wondered why this exodus was taking place.

When the press began to draw attention to these forced displacements, the main aid donors (the European Economic Community and the United States) expressed reservations about, and even opposition to, the relief operation, asserting that their aid should not be used to displace communities within the resettlement zones. These statements were commendable but had no real effect on the ongoing population transfers and the deployment of aid, since in the field the NGOs, the U.N., and the main embassies concerned—those of the United States, Canada, France, Italy, and India, among others—were much more accommodating toward the authorities. As in Cambodia, some championed the government for basically ideological reasons, as communist "fellow travelers." These were the only ones operating from an intellectually coherent position, because they believed that those dark days merely reflected a violent and unjust world order and would ultimately give way to a rosy future. This theory, espoused by a minority at the time, collapsed with the Berlin Wall and is only mentioned here as a historical curiosity.

The issue of forced population transfers created a split between humanitarian organizations that approved of the program (including

Oxfam, War on Want, and World Vision) and those that either did not know what to think or criticized it privately while considering it none of their business (such as the Save the Children Fund, Concern, AICF, and MSF during the first year of the crisis). These internal debates had no outward effect, however, because all the organizations concerned explained that it was a process having nothing to do with themselves or their activities. In their view, therefore, they bore no responsibility whatsoever.

Shocked by the violence of the resettlement program, NGO volunteers were murmuring their condemnation of the government's brutal methods but considered that their humanitarian duty lay exclusively in their day-to-day work. For them, the humanitarian volunteers' overriding aim was to extend a helping hand to the victims of disaster while refraining from making any judgments—necessarily political—about the surrounding circumstances. Taking part in controversies over the host government's decisions would mean violating the pact of neutrality and excluding themselves from the humanitarian scene. The general conclusion seemed to be that children tortured by hunger should not pay the price of political disputes. While a minority of NGOs endorsed the resettlement program as a mark of political support for the Ethiopian government, the majority took the opposite view or were undecided but did not express their opinions for reasons of humanitarian neutrality.

What these two positions shared, despite their apparent differences, was their adhesion—active in one case, passive in the other—to the government's policy, justified by the conviction of the organizations concerned that they already knew where the common good lay. During the first half of 1985, MSF belonged to the second category, together with most of the other NGOs. It and its counterparts found the government's methods unacceptable, but it was not insensible to the rationale of preventive action. After all, policies of territorial development have their virtues and their opponents, and this particular policy might be as valid as any other.

Curiously enough, what NGO volunteers failed to see was that the people concerned—the Ethiopian rural communities—did not want to leave their lands and villages. Or rather, they could see it at each roundup (otherwise, why were police roundups necessary?), but this observation did not give rise to any judgment. The violence used aroused the spectators' indignation without influencing their view of the population transfers in general. They did not really grasp the situation until they had read the reports on two surveys taken among Ethiopian refugees in Sudan and Somalia regarding the reasons for their flight.

Incidentally, a strange and significant phenomenon should be noted: while hundreds of millions of dollars were pouring into Ethiopia, not a single official aid agency would agree to provide the few thousand dollars necessary to carry out such surveys—probably because all concerned were aware, more or less consciously, that the refugees' accounts would disturb everyone's peace of mind. And, indeed, the surveys showed clearly that the Ethiopian people's suffering was the result of a reign of terror in which international aid played an essential role. The presence of humanitarian workers served the government's purposes in at least two respects. First, it inspired confidence in the people, who believed that these foreign witnesses afforded them some degree of security in the distribution centers. This view encouraged more of the starving population to gravitate to those centers. Second, it led aid donors to assume that the relief operations were being carried out properly, since the NGOs in the field, which enjoyed freedom of movement and speech, said nothing to make them think otherwise.

Their silence was a great boon to the government, which did not hesitate to draw attention to it every time the resettlement program was challenged. Thus, contrary to what the NGOs wanted to believe and what they wanted others to believe, silence could not be equated with neutrality in such circumstances, since the government turned their silence into approval. The Ethiopian government, caught in the spotlight of the international media and dependent on international aid for its survival, was in fact in a shaky political position. It is quite conceivable (though, of course, unprovable) that vigorous protest against the deadly resettlement policy might have secured its suspension, if not its termination. After all, the Dergue had signed an agreement with the United Nations stipulating that population transfers would be on a voluntary basis and would preserve family unity. In theory this commitment allowed the U.N. to exert pressure on the

Ethiopian government and even to issue public protests, but the U.N.'s local hierarchy chose to ignore the problem, giving its seal of approval to the entire Ethiopian relief and development policy. The NGOs, which were treated like pawns on a chessboard, could have extricated themselves by jointly asserting their determination not to do anything contrary to the expectations of the population they were trying to help. Taken together, as things stood in 1985, they carried a great deal of moral weight of which the government had to be aware, and as a group they probably could not have been expelled. None of them, however, wanted to take the risk. For them, remaining in the field, at whatever cost, was an absolute priority that no public stance could be allowed to endanger.

As the sole protester, MSF was expelled from Ethiopia on 2 December 1985 but continued to campaign against the population transfers, which were suspended in autumn 1986. According to the estimates of Cultural Survival, backed up by MSF's own observations, these transfers cost 150,000 people their lives, with the total human cost of the famine amounting to some 700,000–800,000 people. Although the NGOs were clearly not responsible for the resettlement policy, it is equally clear that their silence made them passive accomplices. Yet the old dilemma—principles versus action, abdication versus compromise—could have been resolved with a real chance of success in this particular case.

The Ethiopian famine was a milestone in the recent history of the humanitarian movement and its complex relations with those in power: it was an occasion when humanitarian action failed to live up to humanitarian principles. The manipulation of public compassion and humanitarian aid did not begin in the 1980s, however. Major precedents include the famine in the Ukraine in 1921, used by Lenin to hasten recognition of his regime; the Nazi propaganda machine's manipulation of the Red Cross during World War II; and the exploitation of the genocide theme during the war in Biafra. Humanitarian aid has been used as a tool of totalitarian propaganda throughout the twentieth century, from the aftermath of World War I to the genocide in Rwanda.

What distinguished Ethiopia and ushered in a new era for humanitarian action was the tangible proof that humanitarian assistance, like

any other human activity, could be turned against its supposed beneficiaries and cause more harm than good. If the humanitarian agencies, private or intergovernmental, had refused to play the role assigned to them by the government, and if they had denounced the fact
that the government was misleading the outside world by speaking in
their name, the scale of the resettlement program would have been
considerably reduced. In that year the humanitarian movement lost
its innocence. The population transfer program itself—which was in
fact modeled on Stalin's 1930s nationalities policy—was nothing
new; what was new was its context, its sources of support, and its
implications. In other words, what was new was the emergence of a
"victim strategy" that no longer belonged to the tradition of sacrifice,
the tragic offering on which every political community is founded,
but that had more to do with pity and tending to the needs of suffering humanity. It was this same process of reducing individuals to their
biological common denominator that led to the surprising convergence of three positions that should have been irreconcilable: the liberal technocrats of the World Bank, the humanitarian organizations,
and a totalitarian power.

The NGOs' invocation of neutrality was, as we have seen, nothing
but a rhetorical device, since they had already been enlisted in the
service of government policy. The very logic of the war that the government was waging against its own people ruled out the establishment of any haven sheltered from the conflict. As in most modern
conflicts, humanitarian neutrality lost all real significance.

The Aid Business

Beyond the considerations stemming from the specific political context in Ethiopia, it should not be forgotten that humanitarian action
is also a market. We cannot hope to understand the NGOs' reactions
and policies without taking into account their business interests, their
need to promote their image, their communication requirements, and
the market shares that they feel they have to win and maintain. The
mainstays of their relationship with the public and the donors—that
is, with the market—are the generosity of their intentions, the trans-

parency of their accounts, and, more recently, their technical expertise in the field.

The events in Ethiopia, however, showed that all these qualities offered no guarantee that their operations would not be hijacked and turned into vehicles for lies and oppression. This is why protesting was problematic: besides involving a painful process of self-examination, it created difficulties with the NGOs' main donors, their institutional sponsors. Being the bearer of bad tidings always entails the risk of being identified with those bad tidings, which is why, in this age of instant communication, "charity shows" must have a happy ending: the child is torn, *in extremis*, from the grip of hunger and adversity, thanks to international solidarity. But the real world does not always offer the happy ending characteristic of the virtual world of communication and marketing. Confusing those two worlds, taking for granted that the sincerity of their intentions and the technical efficiency of their operation were guarantees of its virtue, the NGOs resolved the ethical dilemma by ignoring it.

The crucial question that humanitarian agencies must ask in such circumstances is whether it is possible to create a space within which the spirit of humanitarian action can be preserved. Such a space is essential to the establishment of proper relations with those we are there to help. When the distribution points and the practical arrangements for providing aid are decided by and under the exclusive control of the government, when individual relations between relief workers and the assisted populations are orchestrated by the political authority, that space disappears. Humanitarian aid then becomes a tool at the exclusive disposal of the authorities, a sort of selective maintenance service for biological organisms who become increasingly dependent on those authorities. In such circumstances relief workers are more like zookeepers than representatives of human solidarity. There is no universal formula for determining whether the necessary space for humanitarian action exists, but organizations that are aware of its importance and of the danger of taking action when it does not exist can be alert to the manipulation and reversals to which humanitarian operations are always susceptible.

In Bosnia and Herzegovina, for example, the refugee problem was not an unfortunate consequence of the conflict but the actual objective of war. In organizing shelter for refugees and making their exile less painful, the humanitarian agencies were both playing into the hands of the "cleansers" and carrying out their humanitarian mission. And that mission was only necessary at all because the Serb extremists' strategy of conquest and racial hegemony had been accepted de facto by the European powers. Western governments used the spectacle of the humanitarian organizations in action as an opiate, or rather as a technique designed to create the illusion that this "ambulance diplomacy" adopted by the Europeans was in fact determined opposition. This is what both the UNHCR and the NGOs meant when they used the term "humanitarian alibi" to denounce Europe's abdication in the face of the first conflict to erupt on its soil since World War II.

Villages destroyed, medical facilities in ruins, a population left shaken and vulnerable, widespread hardship—all the usual scenes of war were there in Bosnia and Herzegovina. Yet the people in those villages were not victims but conquerors and colonizers who had chased out the original Muslim residents. Under these circumstances, providing aid for "resettlement" amounted to providing direct support for ethnic cleansing, because it facilitated the influx of occupiers from Serb regions unaffected by the war.

With rare exceptions—notably assistance to refugees and support for civilians who had gathered in the enclaves—humanitarian aid in the Bosnian conflict was swept up in the vortex of the war, diverted from its objectives, stripped of most of its content and purpose, and manipulated by all sides. MSF, for example, set up permanent teams in the beleaguered Muslim enclaves of Srebrenica and Gorazde to help the distraught population. The practical utility and symbolic force of their presence seemed clear; yet here again appearances were deceiving, because access to those enclaves depended, of course, on the Bosnian Serb authorities, who intended to extract as many advantages as they could out of this temporary concession to the U.N.

After the fall of Srebrenica and the ensuing massacres, however, the situation changed. It could be believed at the time that by offering symbolic protection a foreign presence could give some substance to the idea of a "security zone," quite aside from the material assistance provided. Today, however, the question arises as to whether those humanitarian workers helped maintain the illusion of international protection and thus encouraged the refugees to remain in the enclave rather than seek a safer refuge somewhere in the government zone. The presence of a United Nations Protection Force (UNPROFOR) battalion was undoubtedly the primary source of this illusion. But by moving in by its side, MSF was endorsing UNPROFOR's message and therefore also bore some responsibility for misleading the population, even if it was not party to the deception.

Unfortunately, the intention, however humble, to do good is usually accompanied by a feeling of omnipotence: not a pathological conviction that moral forces will overcome all obstacles by their sheer virtue but rather an excessive and rather smug faith in the morality of humanitarian action. In other words, the insouciance that permits humanitarian agencies, in their guise of selfless saviors, to remind governments and other authorities of their responsibilities without pondering their own.

The very object of humanitarian action—both constituting its main strength and setting its structural limits—is to try to combat suffering directly, irrespective of its political roots or historical context. Yet humanitarian workers are under a compelling moral obligation to mistrust this premise, to be aware of the risk that any such program may rebound against those for whom it was intended. This obligation is very widely disregarded, since the humanitarian movement seems largely oblivious of the positive ethical implications of refusing to act. "Oh, why didn't we ever say no?" wonders Solzhenitsyn throughout *The Gulag Archipelago*, reminding us that acquiescence may be abdication and refusal may be courage. He emphasizes what Hannah Arendt observed during the Eichmann trial: that mechanical obedience is nothing but unavowed adherence, a sacrifice of judgment, and hence a necessary condition for the unthinkable.

Consequently, deciding to act means knowing, at least approximately, why action is preferable to abstention. Any plan of action must incorporate the idea that abstention is not necessarily an abdication but may, on the contrary, be a decision. Experience has provided enough evidence of this: in humanitarian action as in other spheres, intentions can easily be turned against their objectives. But the contexts in which humanitarian aid is mobilized make this realization particularly difficult, since emergency situations encourage the substitution of reflex for reflection. Reinforcing the institutional mentality mentioned earlier, the time constraints inherent in emergencies blur the distinction between activism and action, between the end and the means. The humanitarian organizations—failing to take steps to restore that distinction, to rebel against sentimental conformism, and to resist the lures of marketing—tend simply to go through the motions, reducing their operations to logistic deployment accompanied by pious slogans. Their mission deserves—indeed, demands—better than that.

Note

1. The RRC, set up following the 1974 famine, employed 17,000 officials, many of whom did outstanding work in the field—at least when they were authorized to do so.

11

Bringing War Criminals to Justice during an Ongoing War

Richard J. Goldstone

The complexities of interethnic/religious civil wars, the most prevalent form of modern-day war, with their devastating and vicious consequences for whole civilian populations, has forced the international community to reassess its traditional responses to and mechanisms for the resolution of conflict. Indeed, the last decade or so has seen significant developments in the sphere of international peacekeeping, with the international community adopting new and innovative solutions to recent crises. Central to these recent paradigmatic shifts in international conflict resolution techniques has been the acknowledgment that the creation of a political, economic, and social environment conducive to peace and stability is essential to any successful peace initiative.[1] Following from this acknowledgment, and building on the vast strides made in the field of international human rights law, has come the recognition that the establishment of democracy and the securement of human rights are essential to the pursuit of peace. Yet, despite all the recent emphasis on progressive theories of conflict resolution, the precise role that the enforcement of human rights can and should play in conflict resolution still remains shrouded in controversy. This was brought to the fore in 1993 with the launching of one of the more controversial recent peace initiatives of the United Nations—the establishment by the

Security Council of the International Criminal Tribunal for the former Yugoslavia (ICTY).[2]

Perhaps unwittingly, by establishing an international criminal tribunal for the prosecution of war criminals as a peace mechanism, the Security Council sparked an important moral, legal, and philosophical debate on the relationship between peace and justice. This debate is timely and hopefully will lead to a more informed and thorough understanding of the interrelationship of these two concepts to guide future international initiatives. The aim of this chapter is to articulate and develop that debate. While the chapter deals with the broad moral and philosophical issues inherent in the subject matter, its purpose is not so much to expound on jurisprudential aspects but rather to provide clarity from a policy perspective. In it I draw on my personal experience in the field.

The ICTY Established as a Peace Mechanism

The establishment of the ICTY was unusual in many respects. It was the first time that a truly international criminal court was set up by the international community to prosecute gross violations of human rights[3]—despite the fact that since World War II, both before and contemporaneous with the outbreak of war in the former Yugoslavia, the international community has witnessed numerous horrific incidences of war crimes and gross human rights violations. Most significant however, and at the heart of the controversy surrounding its establishment, is the fact that the ICTY was set up *as a mechanism for the restoration of peace while the conflict continued to rage in the former Yugoslavia.* This set the ICTY apart conceptually from the only other multinational precedents for the prosecution of war criminals—the Nuremburg and Tokyo tribunals—which were set up *after* the end of World War II *as a consequence of peace* (a peace obtained, it should be emphasized, through the unconditional surrender of the Axis powers).

The ICTY, on the other hand, was established by the Security Council in terms of its Chapter VII powers to help restore international peace and security to the war zones of the former Yugoslavia.[4]

Many seriously questioned the appropriateness of the Security Council establishing a tribunal for the prosecution of war criminals in the context of the ongoing conflict in the former Yugoslavia. Such a step, they argued, was counterproductive to initiatives aimed at promoting a negotiated settlement. Particularly at the time of the negotiations being held in Dayton, Ohio, in November 1995, many politicians and commentators argued that in fact peace and justice were in opposition and that the work of the ICTY was doing more to retard peace than to promote it. Many questioned how the international community could expect a peace settlement to be negotiated when the political and military leaders involved in the negotiation process were the very people indicted or under investigation by the tribunal. How, so the logic went, could one expect that such leaders would negotiate a peace agreement when one of the consequences of that agreement would be their prosecution and possible life imprisonment for war crimes?[5]

None, however, of those critics who had criticized the establishment of the ICTY have challenged the essential morality or ethical desirability of prosecuting war criminals—indeed, none of them has disputed the validity of the underlying premise that where there have been gross human rights violations, morality demands that justice be done. Rather, their challenge lies in the political expediency and morality of pursuing such justice during the life span of an ongoing conflict at the apparent expense of a negotiated peace and the lives of further innocent victims. According to these critics, despite the compelling moral imperative involved in the prosecution of war criminals or the pursuit of justice, there is a limited time and place for such a moral imperative—the delicate stage of negotiating an end to hostilities is not such a time. The issue raised by these critics is really the incompatibility of pursuing a negotiated settlement in tandem with the prosecution of war criminals. In the minds of these critics these two policy objectives are incompatible and cannot be pursued together. In their minds the choice is a clear one: there is no option but to pursue a negotiated settlement whatever the indirect moral or ethical implications of such a choice may be—it is better to negotiate an end to war with war criminals, even though it may mean for the time being sacrificing their accountability, than to doggedly pursue justice at the expense of peace. It will be my argument that a closer examination of the moral and political issues, as well as a closer examination of the specific facts of the former Yugoslavia, do not support this proposition.

Peace versus Justice

Perhaps the most eloquent and trenchant recent criticism of the ICTY is the one by an anonymous author published in a recent edition of the *Human Rights Quarterly.*[6] The author's essential premise is summed up in the following statement:

> The quest for justice for yesterday's victims of atrocities should not be pursued in such a manner that it makes today's living the dead of tomorrow. That, for the human rights community, is one of the lessons of the former Yugoslavia. Thousands of people are dead who should have been alive—because moralists were in quest of the perfect peace. Unfortunately, a perfect peace can rarely be attained in the aftermath of a bloody conflict. The pursuit of criminals is one thing. Making peace is another.[7]

The author's argument is based on a conceptual paradigm that juxtaposes justice and peace. It conceives of justice and peace as mutually independent of one another. In this paradigm justice, on the one hand, seems largely concerned with the business of the past (as opposed to the present and the future). It sees justice as being primarily designed to achieve retribution for the abuses of the past and satisfaction for victims of the past. Peace, on the other hand, is conceived of as largely concerned with the present (as opposed to either the past or the future). Peace is the preservation of life through the cessation of present hostilities. Put differently, according to this argument the prosecution of war criminals is largely an exercise concerned with hangovers of the past, an exercise that pales in significance when compared with (what should be) the overriding concern of the international community during an ongoing conflict—the achievement of a cease-fire and cessation of immediate hostilities.

Much needs to be said about this argument, and because it goes to the heart of the debate, I will spend much of the rest of this chapter responding to it. Let me start by saying that, though at first blush the argument is a compelling one (who, after all, would challenge the proposition that to preserve life is the overriding and overwhelming principle that must guide us in all our attempts to resolve conflict?), it is an argument that does not bear close scrutiny. It is an argument that because it is founded on simplistic notions of peace and justice fails to identify the essential relationship between peace and justice. If we are to conceive of peace as this anonymous author does, then we have learned nothing from the last few decades of struggle in the field of human rights and conflict resolution. If we conceive of peace as understood by this author, then although we may stave off the ravages of war for a while, we are unlikely, in the greater scheme of things, to save more lives. For this reason, we should not too easily be persuaded by it.

The Relationship between Peace and Justice

The quest for perfect justice or perfect peace is a futile one. There is no magic recipe for achieving the one or the other. So the anonymous author quoted earlier is right when he or she says there is no perfect peace. Decisions as to the best or most appropriate policy for the resolution of any conflict are always complex and difficult and will always have to take into account many varied factors—historical, political, socioeconomic, and frequently military. But, having said that, there is one truth about peace and justice that history has revealed and that it will continue to drive home until we finally take heed. At some times and under some circumstances the relationship between peace and justice is so profound, peace and justice are so inextricably bound up with one another, that "peace" negotiated in the absence of the pursuit of justice will be worth little more than the paper an ensuing peace agreement is written on. Such a hollow, imposter peace often does nothing more than usher war back to haunt its beneficiaries in a guise more brutal and with a ferocity that few could anticipate. The examples are so notorious and so many that it is hardly necessary for me to cite any, but for the sake of completeness, we only need to look to Rwanda, where the fragile Arusha Peace Agreement of 1993, which negotiated an end to the hostilities of 1990–1993 in Rwanda, was soon shattered by the horrors of the 1994 genocide.[8] Surely such a peace is not the peace the international community should pursue?

It is one thing to reject the senseless pursuit of a nonexistent *perfect* peace; it is quite another to reject or dismiss the pursuit of a *meaningful, lasting,* and *effective* peace. Lasting and effective "peace" cannot and should not be equated with "making peace," in the sense of a few war-weary leaders getting together around a table to negotiate a peace agreement in order to gain political advantage. It is all too easy to "make" such a peace but unfortunately often very difficult to implement and carry it out. It will not work where the political, military, social, and economic conditions for reconciliation and nation building are not present. As I will illustrate later with a discussion of the conditions in the former Yugoslavia at about the time of Dayton, justice very often is one of the keys necessary to facilitate effective peace.

It is perhaps appropriate at this point to reemphasize that when I talk of justice, I do not talk of it in any prescriptive sense. Justice in one context may mean the criminal prosecution of political and military leaders by an international tribunal, either in conjunction with or as a substitute for national criminal prosecutions, in another it may mean the adoption of a national or international truth commission.[9] Key to all of these mechanisms is the exposure of the truth and acknowledgment of the suffering of the victims, coupled with official imposition of responsibility upon identified perpetrators and relevant sanctions, even if only moral, psychological, or political.

What, then, is it about justice that is so vital, so necessary to peace? Although justice had much to do with retribution, and therefore with the past, this does not mean that this is where the purpose and role of justice end. Justice, retribution, and their achievement or lack of it can have a significant impact on the future. In the Balkans violence and conflict have been erupting periodically over a span of over 600 years. Never, until now, during those centuries was anyone meaningfully brought to account for the atrocities that have been committed. Instead, anger and hatred continued to feed on the legacy of past atrocities, fueling further cycles of violence. Without the tempering effect of retribution, people will continue to hate, and hatred will continue to cause people to take the law into their own hands. This is only human.

The official acknowledgment and satisfaction that is achieved through justice and retribution becomes all the more important in contexts such as the former Yugoslavia and Rwanda where the conflict contains a religious or ethnic component. Without the individualization of guilt that ensues from an official judicial or quasi-judicial process, the danger arises that whole ethnic, religious, or even political groupings will be labeled with guilt and become the targets of anger and hatred, resulting in a dangerous collective guilt syndrome. Indeed, this is what has happened historically in both the former Yugoslavia and Rwanda. Whole ethnic groups were saddled with responsibility because of the acts of some individuals belonging to the group—with disastrous consequences.[10] Such collective or group guilt dehumanizes whole peoples, providing fertile ground for abuse by evil political opportunists. It is a genocide or massive crime against humanity in the making.

Justice and retribution therefore have as much to do with the present and the future stability and sanity of a society as they do with satisfying legitimate claims based on the past. This is especially so in a traumatized society where the anger and the hurt run so deep that they cannot easily be forgiven or forgotten. In the words of the chairperson of the South African Truth and Reconciliation Commission, Archbishop Desmond Tutu:

> [E]xperience worldwide shows that if you do not deal with a dark past
> . . . , effectively look the beast in the eye, that beast is not going down
> quietly; it is going, sure as anything, to come back and haunt you horrendously. We are saying we need to deal with this past as quickly as
> possible . . . then close the door on it and concentrate on the present
> and the future.[11]

What the previously quoted anonymous author also neglects to consider is the deterrent effect of justice, and by so doing he or she fails to appreciate the broader purpose and role of its pursuit. In my experience, there is only one effective way to thwart criminal conduct and violence, which is through good policing and the implementation of justice. In any society a direct relationship exists between the effectiveness of the criminal justice system and the crime rate. If would-be criminals believe that there is a healthy prospect of their being apprehended and punished for their criminal activities, they will think twice before embarking on such criminal conduct. This principle of deterrence is fundamental to domestic systems of law and order, and it is no different in the international context. If political and military leaders believe that they will likely be brought to account by the international community for committing war crimes, that belief in many cases will have a deterrent effect. Between the Nuremburg and Tokyo war crimes trials and the establishment of the ICTY, a singular failure was committed on the part of the international community to enforce humanitarian law. Politicians and military leaders with grandiose political and military aspirations could be confident that they were free to fight their wars in blatant disregard of the law of war that the international community had so painstakingly built. If they were safe in their own countries, they had nothing to fear from any external agency. But no longer so if the international community takes a forceful stand on the enforcement of humanitarian law. In the former Yugoslavia some signs have emerged that the advent of the ICTY caused some military leaders to tread more carefully.[12] Unfortunately, the lack of political will on the part of leading Western nations to support and enforce the orders of the tribunal probably deprived the tribunal of any of its potential deterrent effect. It is not the mechanism of the tribunal that is at fault in this regard or lacking but the deficiency in international political will. I shall return to this issue later in the chapter.

Another important purpose served by the implementation of justice in a society victim to massive and widespread human rights abuses is that it can help expose the institutions and practices most responsible for them. In some cases, a study of gross human rights abuses reveals a systematic and institutional pattern of gross human rights violations. In this way it tends to refute popular misconceptions about the nature and causes of such massive violations—that they are arbitrary and sporadic occurrences of bloodlust or the like. In exposing the institutions and practices responsible, such a study makes an important contribution to the future dismantling of such institutions. This has already been the experience of the ICTY in relation to the conduct of the Bosnian-Serb administration. A good illustration is the exposure of the systematic nature of the slaughter of Muslims by the Bosnian Serb Army that took place at Srebrenica after it fell under Bosnian Serb control in July 1995. When the mass graves at Srebrenica were discovered, Bosnian Serb army spokespeople stated that the graves contained the bodies of men killed during battle. However, the exhumations conducted by the office of the prosecutor exposed the lies in these claims. Most of the persons buried in these mass graves had been shot in the back of the head with a single bullet, with their arms bound behind their backs. This is not the way in which people die in the ordinary course of battle.

Similar systematic patterns in other administrations within the former Yugoslavia are also emerging. It is certainly also the experience of the Truth and Reconciliation Commission in South Africa where the evidence being led is credibly exposing the systematic and institutionalized nature of covert security force operations in South Africa during the apartheid era. No longer can those responsible deny the existence of such operations and the systematic nature of their activities. The same is also true of the experience of the United Nations International Criminal Tribunal for Rwanda in Arusha. The evidence being collected and led by the prosecutor's office is revealing the planned and systematic nature of the genocide that occurred in Rwanda in 1994, helping dispel the ignorant and at times racist assumptions about the causes and nature of the events of 1994. Without such exposure, the systems and institutions responsible for gross human rights violations remain protected behind a veil of secrecy free to continue their practices in the future. It is naive for anyone to assume that in a transitional society such institutions and practices will die a natural death. Without exposing and dismantling such institutions and those who are responsible for them, little hope remains of eradicating such abuses from a society.

Finally, the pursuit of justice also plays the important role of providing a more accurate and faithful record of historical events than would otherwise be the case. The importance of this point should not be underemphasized. Without an accurate record of history, the unconscionable attempts by revisionists and political opportunists to use and abuse history for future evil ends will be facilitated. The manipulation and distortion of history through a virulent propaganda campaign was arguably one of the most significant institutional mechanisms used by the warmongers in the former Yugoslavia and Rwanda to instigate the genocidal acts that were committed during the respective wars in those territories. The state-controlled media in both the former Yugoslavia and Rwanda before and during the wars abounded with blatant lies, half-truths, and distortions of history and current events in order to sow the seed of fear, hatred, and anger necessary to galvanize whole communities for war and prepare them for the commission of "ethnic cleansing." Similarly, one of the main instruments used by the Nazi government to pave the way for the crimes committed against its Jewish population and other persecuted groups was a massive, finely tuned propaganda machine. In its judgment against the major Nazi war criminals, the International Military Tribunal at Nuremburg emphasized the role that this propaganda campaign had played in the commission of the crimes for which the defendants were found guilty.

To sum up, the message is that the implementation of justice is vital to ridding a society of the root causes, the very evils responsible for human rights atrocities. Mechanisms or policy options designed to root out such causes of conflict should therefore not be dismissed as idealistic schemes with no meaningful relation to peace. A peace accepted by a society with the willingness and ability to heal, with the willingness and capacity to move itself beyond the abuses of the past, is the only really viable peace. Such is the peace that the international community should be seeking to promote. A peace masterminded by and in order to accommodate the concerns of vicious war criminals defiant of all fundamental international law prescriptions or norms is no such effective or enduring peace.

Incompatibility of Negotiations and Prosecutions: Case Study of the Former Yugoslavia

I have argued that there is, in many instances, a critical relationship between peace and justice. But still, what of contexts like that of the former Yugoslavia—the context of an ongoing war? Can there be any significant positive relationship between peace and justice when one is attempting to negotiate a peace with indicted war criminals? Although justice may be important to lasting peace, any lasting peace is after all dependent on *the negotiation* of a peace. And while you maintain the threat of prosecution, there will be no such negotiations for peace, so the critics argue.

Events in the former Yugoslavia have, in fact, proved quite the opposite. The Dayton peace process *affirmed* in a number of different ways the positive contribution of the work of the ICTY to the peace process. Indeed, specific evidence suggests that without the work of the ICTY—without the indictment of Radovan Karadzic and Radko Mladic by the ICTY and their consequent isolation by the world community—there would have been no Dayton Peace Agreement. The Dayton peace talks were held in November 1995, just two months after the massacre at Srebenica. Even for a people numbed by the consecutive horrors of a few years of the Bosnian war, the events at Srebenica were of such a calculated and brutal nature that they could not be overlooked. Srebenica firmed the resolve of the Bosnian Muslim government not to sit at a negotiation table with the leaders of the Bosnian Serbs. To do so would have been both morally and politically indefensible.[13] Only through the work of the tribunal was it legally and politically possible for the international community to insist on excluding Karadzic from the Dayton peace talks. Contrary to the assumptions of many critics of the ICTY, the work of the tribunal had already by that stage made a significant impact. Although Karadzic and Mladic have yet to be arrested and prosecuted, their indictment for genocide and crimes against humanity by a legitimate international institution did with time lead to their moral and political censure and international isolation. Even their one-time ally, if not coconspirator—Milosevic—had to turn his back on them because of the international pressure brought to bear on him. Furthermore, even assuming that Karadzic had been present at the Dayton peace talks, I am convinced that a peace agreement, or at least a peace agreement of the nature of the Dayton Peace Agreement, which is in many respects a remarkable peace agreement,[14] would not have ensued. The

Dayton peace process would have collapsed through the obstructionist presence of Karadzic.

The Dayton peace process, therefore, only goes to prove that it
cannot be accepted as a foregone conclusion that the indictment of
political and military leaders will necessarily seriously stall a peace
process. On the contrary, it has every opportunity of serving as a
catalyst for the successful resolution of a peace process. Furthermore,
it also goes to prove that *who* one negotiates with[15] may be material
to the type of peace that will eventuate. Not only may it be morally
indefensible to negotiate with leaders responsible for unspeakable
atrocities, but it may also be politically and pragmatically indefensible. For a negotiation process to give rise to a *worthwhile* peace agreement, a basic level of good faith, mutual trust, and commitment is
necessary. When the parties you are negotiating with have time and
time again notoriously and willfully violated the most fundamental
norms of humanity, it is in my mind difficult, if not impossible, ever
to obtain that level of trust. I hear the refrain, "But if these are the
leaders of an important constituency, how can we avoid negotiating
with *them?*" As you cannot choose your family, so you cannot choose
the leaders you have to negotiate with. But history teaches us that
leaders come and leaders go. There is nothing immutable about the
political process. Indeed, we all know that the political process is a
fickle one. Political support is based on (assumed) legitimacy and capacity. Few people would, if they knew the truth of the ambitions and
associated misconduct of leaders responsible for genocide and crimes
against humanity, long continue to support such a leader. If this is
crediting humanity with too much, then I rely on the alternative that
few would long continue to support a leader who, because of his or
her international political condemnation and isolation, is unable to
represent her or his constituency meaningfully in the international
community or who, even worse, has brought on his or her constituency military, diplomatic, economic, and cultural sanctions and embargos.

Still, the objection persists that the process outlined here takes time.
It takes time to get the international community sufficiently activated
to take the necessary steps to ensure such legal and political isolation
of indicted war criminals. And in a war time costs lives. This point is
indeed true. But once again I wish to stress that the fault does not lie

with the policy or the mechanism—it lies with the lack of political will of the international community. To the extent that the international community does not have sufficient will to enforce a policy, no policy, as simple and self-evident as it may appear—not even the apparently tried and tested policy of pursuing negotiations—will work. Referring back to the example of the Yugoslav conflict, if one considers the whole life span of the conflict, it did not take long for a final peace settlement to be reached after the international community *finally* resolved to take a more forceful stand against the aggressive policy of the Bosnian Serbs and ordered NATO air strikes. Had such a firm, aggressive stance been taken in conjunction with supporting, to the fullest, the work of the tribunal earlier on in the conflict, it is highly likely that a durable peace could have been achieved much earlier. Referring back to the arguments of the anonymous author quoted at the beginning of this chapter, he or she argues that the reason that it took so long for a peace agreement to be negotiated in the Bosnian conflict was because the international community blindly, arrogantly, and perhaps hypocritically insisted on human rights guarantees, later to be compounded with the misguided decision to indict Bosnian Serb leaders for war crimes. This is surely to give *too* much credit to the potential effect of the indictments by the tribunal! For, as pointed out by many others elsewhere, the failure to conclude a successful peace agreement before Dayton was due to a number of converging factors—including the overwhelming military strength of the Bosnian Serbs that enabled them to hold out as long as they did. To assume that it was largely the weak threat (given the then lack of political support for the tribunal's work) of effectively being held accountable by the international tribunal, which stood in the way of a peace agreement, is to assume far too much. Such assumption is to undermine the complexity of factors that interplay to determine the life span of any conflict.

To conclude, I believe that the policy of effectively pursuing justice *can* make a major contribution to the achievement of a lasting and durable peace. It would be naive to suggest that the pursuit of justice *on its own* can and will achieve as much. Pursuit of justice *has* to be accompanied by the firm resolve of the international community to put an end to the conflict effected through the use of economic, diplomatic, *and military* sanctions. Furthermore, when I talk of pursuit of justice by the international community, I mean a proper and firm commitment to such an objective. I do not mean the establishment of an ineffective, underfunded, understaffed, and toothless institution with no means for the enforcement of its work. By international justice, I do not mean the useless charade of a paper tiger. Let me conclude by quoting the following words from Juan Mendez:

> Redressing the wrongs committed through human rights violations is not only a legal obligation and a moral imperative . . . [i]t also makes good political sense.[16]

Notes

1. In particular, see Boutros Boutros-Ghali's, "Agenda for Peace-Preventative Diplomacy, Peacemaking and Peacekeeping," adopted in June 1992 (reproduced in International Legal Materials 31 [1992]: 953), in which he emphasizes that the enhancement of respect for human rights and fundamental freedoms, and the promotion of sustainable economic and social development, are essential to the promotion of enduring peace.

2. This was followed eighteen months later by the creation of the Rwanda tribunal (ICTR). Although a discussion of the Rwanda tribunal is relevant to this discussion and will inform the chapter, because of the extraordinary circumstances surrounding the establishment of the ICTY, the focus of the discussion will be on the ICTY.

3. The Nuremburg and Tokyo tribunals cannot be classified as truly international tribunals representing the collective interests of the international community. Rather, they were an example of a few victor states joining together to exercise collectively their individual criminal jurisdiction. This point is well illustrated by the fact that these tribunals did not have broad jurisdiction to prosecute all violations of humanitarian law committed during World War II but only had limited jurisdiction to prosecute violations committed by individuals representing the defeated Axis powers.

4. The ICTY was established by Resolution 827 of the Security Council. In this resolution, having determined that

> the widespread and flagrant violation[s] of international humanitarian law occurring within the territory of the former Yugoslavia, and especially the Republic of Bosnia and Herzegovina, including reports of mass killings, massive, organized and systematic detention and rape of

women, and the continuance of the practice of 'ethnic cleansing,' . . . constitut[ed] a threat to international peace and security,

the Security Council resolved that

> in the particular circumstances of the former Yugoslavia the establishment as an *ad hoc* measure . . . of an international tribunal and the prosecution of persons responsible for serious violations of international humanitarian law would . . . contribute to the restoration and maintenance of peace.

5. See, for example, Anthony D'Amato, "Peace vs. Accountability in Bosnia," *American Journal of International Law* 88 (1994): 500.

6. Anonymous, *Human Rights Quarterly* 18 (1996): 249.

7. Anonymous, *Human Rights Quarterly,* 258.

8. Prior to the 1994 genocide, Rwanda, like the former Yugoslavia, had been victim to numerous vicious outbreaks of violence that had gone unaccounted for.

9. Certain crimes, such as those committed in the former Yugoslavia and Rwanda, threaten the very moral and legal foundations of the international community and also cause tremendous dislocation to surrounding states. They therefore demand prosecution by an international tribunal. Furthermore, often the judicial systems in states recovering from massive human rights abuses will be incapable of meting out impartial and effective justice. Rwanda provides an excellent example. Post-1994 Rwanda has little in the way of a functional criminal justice system and is struggling to deal with the tens of thousands of suspects in custody in Rwandan prisons. As a result, those who are being tried are not being given the benefit of a fair trial, as judged by international standards.

10. As an example, many radical right-wing Bosnian Serbs continue to hold all Croats responsible for the massacre of an unknown number of Serbs during World War II by Nazi Ustashi extremists.

11. Archbishop Desmond Tutu, "Healing a Nation," *Index on Censorship* 1972, no. 5 (September/October 1996): 39–43. Reprinted with permission.

12. Just as an example, a military leader of the Croatian (HV) troops was reported, during the 1995 Croatian military offensive to recapture the Serb-held Drajina in Southern Croatia, to have warned his soldiers to act within the limits of humanitarian law.

13. This point was confirmed recently by the Bosnian ambassador to the United Nations and former Bosnian-Herzegovinian foreign minister, Ambassador Sacirby, at a meeting of the International Peace Academy, which I addressed in New York on 2 October 1996. The ambassador stated there that, without a doubt, had Karadzic been free to attend Dayton, the Bosnian gov-

ernment would not, in the aftermath of Srebrenica, have participated in the Dayton proceedings.

14. The Dayton Peace Agreement is a comprehensive agreement composed of a principal General Framework Agreement and twelve annexes, including a Constitution for the Republic of Bosnia-Herzegovina, an Agreement on Human Rights, and an Agreement on Refugees and Displaced Persons. It also incorporates, by reference, a number of other international agreements, including many international human rights instruments. It provides for, among other institutions, a constitutional court and a commission of human rights, and it places strong emphasis on the protection and enforcement of human rights and the rebuilding of civil society.

15. This is not to pass any judgment on the credibility of Milosevic, who many argue was, in fact, the one-time mastermind of the whole Yugoslav conflict. It is also categorically not intended to pass any judgment on the question of his legal responsibility for any events that have taken place in the Yugoslav conflict. The point is simply that, because Milosevic, by the time of the Dayton peace process, had politically distanced himself from the Bosnian conflict, he had less of a direct interest in the results of the peace process and therefore was a potentially less obstructionist presence than Karadzic.

16. Juan E. Mendez, "In Defense of Transitional Justice," in *Transitional Justice and the Rule of Law in New Democracies*, A. James McAdams, ed. (West Lafayette, Ind.: University of Notre Dame Press, 1997), 1.

12

Moral Reconstruction in the Wake of Human Rights Violations and War Crimes

José Zalaquett

How does a population build or reconstruct a just society following civil war or a dictatorship that engaged in massive human rights violations?

Since the return to civilian rule in Argentina in 1983, this dilemma has become a key issue of public ethics and governance in a growing number of countries that are going through what has come to be termed a transitional period. By this it is meant a political change toward democracy or at least toward a more benign form of government.

Following the Argentinean case, other transitions to democracy have attracted considerable international attention, including those of Uruguay, Chile, El Salvador, Guatemala, the Czech Republic, the former German Democratic Republic, Poland, Uganda, and South Africa. In most of these cases, the problem of how to deal with the abuses of the past and how to forge national unity and democratic institutions has largely been handled internally (allowing for the particularities of the unification of Germany and the division of Czechoslovakia), notwithstanding the international attention vested on these processes. Partial exceptions are El Salvador and Guatemala, where the United Nations played an important role in facilitating the peace accord between the contending parties and in implementing some key agreements, such as the establishment of truth commissions for the investigation of past crimes.

These transitions have prompted the emergence of a whole new field of practical expertise and scholarly inquiry. It is referred to with expressions such as "truth, justice, and reconciliation," "transitional justice,"[1] "the fight against impunity," or variations thereof. It has engaged national and international governmental and nongovernmental organizations (NGOs) and the participation of experts, activists, and scholars in a variety of fields, including, prominently, the law, ethics, moral theology, history, psychology, forensic medicine, and social and community services. It has captured the attention of mass media and public opinion. Arguably, it has become one of the preeminent contemporary issues of political ethics.

In parallel, since the end of the Cold War, the international community—the United Nations and world powers as well as the media, NGOs, and other international opinion makers—has wrestled with the humanitarian problem of how to stop and prevent the recurrence of wars characterized by ethnic cleansing, major war crimes, and genocide in places such as territories of the former Yugoslavia, Rwanda, Burundi, and the Chechen Republic. Unlike the cases grouped under the label of transitions to democracy, in these situations at least one of the contending parties sees itself as a separate nation or aims to achieve independence from the other(s). Another difference is that in these cases the intensity of the conflicts and the loss of life have been so severe as to create in the international community a shared sense of extreme humanitarian emergency.

The notion of humanitarian intervention has thus developed in the last few years. It means generally the intervention, including armed operations, by the United Nations or other international bodies, with the participation or support of major powers, to stop the warfare, assist the victims, and hopefully help in a process of peacemaking and institution building that may prevent human rights violations and war crimes from recurring. Humanitarian intervention may also be understood in a broader sense, to include United Nations involvement in situations of lower-intensity conflict, such as El Salvador and Guatemala, although these cases are usually studied under the rubric of "transitions to democracy."

A wealth of expertise and studies has also developed around the issue of humanitarian intervention. This field has recently been associated with studies and initiatives aimed at establishing ad hoc and permanent international criminal courts to prosecute and try war crimes and crimes against humanity.

Both streams of studies and experiences—that of transitions to democracy and that of humanitarian intervention—have developed relatively separate from each other. Yet both encompass common ethical dilemmas and should be considered in terms of their relationship to one another. I examine some of these dilemmas in this chapter.

Difficulties in Applying the Post–World War II Normative Framework

The general problem of how to build a decent society in the wake of war and crime is certainly not new. It was at the center of the Allies' efforts to build a democratic order in Germany and Japan, and indeed an international order, after World War II. Yet the stream of complex transitions to democracy of the last fifteen years has brought to the fore novel, wrenching moral and political questions.

The initiatives taken by the Allies and by the nascent United Nations in the aftermath of World War II left a legacy of moral mandates, international norms, and institutions. They include the moral imperative to bring to justice the perpetrators of the gravest crimes; the legal notions of crimes against peace, war crimes, and crimes against humanity; the Universal Declaration of Human Rights, the Geneva Conventions, and other major human rights and humanitarian instruments; and the establishment of human rights commissions and committees within the United Nations and regional intergovernmental bodies.

This legacy was later enlarged, as a result of the international human rights movement that started in the 1960s and subsequently spread to most regions of the world. International norms and specialized intergovernmental bodies and courts were developed even further. Human rights became a household notion.

The moral mandates and international norms established in the postwar period have been generally invoked as the framework to judge the policies applied by incoming governments or by the international community to deal with a past of grave human rights violations. In the main, this framework calls for punishment for crimes against humanity and war crimes, reparations to the victims or their families, the preservation of memory, and the erection of institutional safeguards against the recurrence of such atrocities.

However, the political transitions to democracy of recent years in countries of Latin America, Central Europe, and Africa and the efforts to establish a durable peace in places such as Bosnia have stressed how difficult it can be to apply that postwar framework—in particular, the duty to punish the perpetrators of grave crimes. One of the main reasons has been the lack of sufficient power. Unlike the outcome of World War II, none of these political changes was brought about by a complete military defeat of the forces that transgressed basic norms of humane behavior. As a consequence, in the countries concerned the perpetrators have remained a force to be reckoned with. They have managed, to different degrees, either to establish legal or institutional barriers against justice, before they relinquished power, or to wield enough pressure to secure total or partial impunity for their crimes, after a change of government, a truce, or a peace accord.

Yet, it must be noted that however much a decisive defeat of the perpetrators of grave crimes is to be desired, a victor's unfettered power creates, as history shows, a situation that is in itself a danger against justice.

Moreover, the conflict between morally desirable ends and political feasibility is not the only difficulty. There is often a tension between similarly desirable goals, such as justice versus reconciliation or social peace. These objectives are not necessarily in contradiction. Rather, as it is frequently argued, justice may be seen as a precondition for reconciliation or a stable peace. But in practice it is hard to harmonize fully such goals. Furthermore, unsurmountable practical complications may arise—even if there is no lack of political power—to investigate most of the crimes committed during a period of great chaos and upheaval and to give fair trial to innumerable defendants.

Such difficulties vary in complexity and intensity depending on a number of factors. These can relate to the nature of the problem that leads to the armed conflict, political strife, or dictatorial rule; the gravity and enormity of the human rights violations or war crimes committed during such periods; and the character of the eventual truce, peace agreement, or political transition.

As to the nature of the problem, first, it is widely assumed that divisions caused by political or ideological differences are, as a rule, less arduous to overcome than conflicts that stem from racial, ethnic, or religious divisions. A cursory comparative analysis of recent experiences would seem to buttress such an assumption. Former bitter enemies in Uruguay or Chile or in countries of Central Europe may now be seen sitting in the same Parliament and otherwise ostensibly accepting the right of the other to coexist and compete within the workings of a democratic system. It is harder to imagine the contending religious and ethnic groups in Bosnia or the Hutus and Tutsis in Rwanda achieving similar understanding.

However, though ideological persuasion seems on the whole to be less immutable than traits of identity such as nationality, ethnicity, or religion, most generalizations of this kind tend to be superficial. The very divide between ideological conflicts and religious or ethnic enmities is often a simplification. Ideology, political allegiances, social and class interests, membership of a group defined by religion, ethnicity or other traits of identity—these are all factors that may combine or clash in different and sometimes shifting ways to create profound "them versus us" splits between groups or communities.

The gravity and endurance of the confrontational stance of adversary groups or communities appears to be related to a number of other factors, such as whether there is a long history of serious grievances among them; the extent to which the respective political system allows the different groups to try to advance their rights and interests within the existing legal and institutional arrangements; and, related to the latter, whether the various groups or communities may see each other as forming part, in the end, of the same nation-state, whatever their respective desire for autonomous status or national privileges.

Second, the extent and gravity of the crimes committed is, needless to say, a key factor to be considered when deciding how to address the past. Demands for justice are generally commensurate with the gravity of the offense. Crimes such as "disappearances," which prolong the uncertainty about the fate of the victims and the whereabouts of their remains, have given rise to a particularly strong and enduring clamor for truth and justice. Truth is also demanded the loudest concerning other secret crimes such as unacknowledged political assassinations and torture. Thus, official "truth commissions" in countries such as Argentina, Chile, El Salvador, and South Africa have focused mainly on such crimes.

Demands for punishment may be less intense where both or all sides to an internal armed conflict have engaged in similar transgressions and they reach a negotiated peace, as they may have a shared interest in impunity.

Third, the particular mode of the eventual peace agreement or political transition determines to a great extent the nature and degree of the restrictions new governments or the international community will face in their efforts to deal with past abuses. The following is a tentative typology of situations, drawn from contemporary examples[2]:

1. Significant political constraints are absent owing to the fact that the perpetrators of past abuses suffered a complete military defeat by insurgent forces or by an outside power (the defeat of the Nazi and Japanese regimes in World War II; the overthrow of Somoza in 1979 by the Sandinistas and their complete control in Nicaragua, before the contras raised in arms against them).

2. The armed forces representing the previous government have lost legitimacy and cohesiveness because of a military humiliation outside their territory, but they retain control of armed power within their land (Greece, following the Turkish invasion of Cyprus, in 1974; Argentina, after its defeat in the Falklands War in 1982).

3. Military rulers allow for a civilian government to come to power, following a negotiation or under terms imposed by them (Uruguay in 1984; Chile in 1989–1990).

4. After a gradual process of political opening, the worst violations become part of the relatively distant past, and a measure of popular forgiveness ensues (Brazil in the late 1970s and 1980s; Spain in the last years of Franco's rule).

5. Following the fall of a dictatorship, a new civilian government must face continued armed struggle against its former allies and must rely, to fight them, on the strength of the military that supported the previous dictatorship (the Philippines under the Aquino government, after the downfall of the Marcos regime).

6. Ethnic, national, or religious divisions stand in the way of pacification, and the new government may find it difficult to engage in widespread prosecutions without exacerbating divisions that may threaten peace or national unity (Uganda under the Museveni government; Rwanda).

7. Past abuses were committed by agents of an omnipotent state involving, at different levels, countless perpetrators; moreover, the military and civil servants of the past regimes may have to be counted on for the continued operation of basic state functions (Russia and the communist regimes of Europe).

8. Peace accords are reached after protracted internal armed conflict without a clear victor (El Salvador and Guatemala).

9. The case of South Africa, on account of the regime of apartheid imposed on it for decades, is in a category of its own and does not fit well in the situation described in point 6.

Content of the Policies Applied or Advocated in Different Countries

Amidst these difficulties, many of the countries concerned or the international community have attempted to address past violations of human rights and humanitarian norms in various ways. They have studied the experience of other countries, sometimes very systematically. As a consequence, certain solutions, such as truth commissions, tend to repeat themselves.

Since the overthrow of the Somoza government in Nicaragua in 1979, which was followed by massive trials of people accused of complicity with the defunct regime, hardly any clear-cut case has occurred of complete military defeat of the forces accused of having committed humanitarian abuses. Thus, the recent transitions have been marked by different degrees of constraint—political or otherwise—imposed on the new governments.

One consequence is that there have been few trials and convictions for past crimes. Only in Argentina were the top leaders of the previous regime brought to justice, during the Alfonsin administration, but they were later pardoned by President Menem, after serving only a few years in prison.

Several countries instituted official truth commissions to investigate the worst crimes (particularly concealed ones) and published their findings. In other countries, accounts of the political repression of the past were disseminated by church organizations and other nongovernmental groups.

In countries of Central and Eastern Europe, nongovernmental groups have taken a number of initiatives to preserve the collective memory about the deeds of the former communist regimes. Few trials have taken place. However, in some of those countries official procedures were instituted to identify and disqualify for public office or civil service people who collaborated with the respective secret police.

The need for society as a whole to acknowledge the truth and for the groups and individuals responsible for past crimes to admit to their wrongdoing has been stressed in most countries. Admission of past wrongdoing has been rare. An exception is South Africa, where amnesty is being offered by the Commission on Truth and Reconciliation in exchange for detailed confession of politically motivated crimes.

Reparations for the victims or their families have been made in many countries. They include symbolic measures, payment of compensation, and health and educational assistance.

Special mention is due to the involvement of the United Nations and the international community in some cases. In El Salvador and Guatemala, the United Nations facilitated the peace accords that included, among other agreements, the establishment of truth commissions.

War crimes and crimes against humanity in Bosnia prompted the establishment of the International Criminal Tribunal for the Former Yugoslavia in 1993. Again, in the absence of a state or international force sufficiently capable and willing to attempt to arrest people accused of committing such crimes, few have been brought before the international court. In 1994, the United Nations established the International Criminal Tribunal for Rwanda.

It is fair to say that two main threads may be distinguished among those who have commented on these developments, although both sides tend to acknowledge the other's main points, and their differences are mostly matters of emphasis. Some writers stress the obligations and responsibilities placed on governments and individuals by international law, particularly the law of human rights and international humanitarian law. Others, though agreeing about the moral and legal imperativeness of such obligations, tend to focus on the problem of how to achieve the best possible results in situations in which full compliance with them does not seem feasible. They stress that such an approach is also guided by moral principles and the ethics of responsibility.

Both threads revolve around a legacy of ethical and legal norms that stemmed from the traumatic experiences of World War II and the professed resolve of the international community not to countenance such atrocities. The experience of recent years has been enriching that legacy with contributions from other viewpoints or traditions. As a result, elements of what may eventually emerge as a new normative framework to address these questions begin to suggest themselves.

Insufficiency of the Approach that Emphasizes the Legal Obligations of States

As mentioned earlier, much of the debates and measures adopted or proposed in situations of political transition are couched in legal terms or ethical concepts closely related to the law. The most pertinent legal principles and institutions are those of criminal law. They are established for the protection of certain values.

The very existence of criminal law and the importance of its effective application are, of course, rooted in the need to bar behavior that a particular society deems most prejudicial to the values it seeks to protect. Criminal law must be applied to uphold the rule of law and mete out justice. Punishment is justified as a preventive measure—insofar as it may be deemed to deter future crimes—or as retribution that fits the offense. Society as a whole has an interest in the punishment of crimes; victims and their families have a right to legal remedies.

Notwithstanding these points, the law also seeks to attain other values, which may be in partial conflict with the need to punish harmful behavior. For instance, the law seeks to achieve certainty about the content of its norms and the right of every person to be protected against arbitrary prosecution and punishment. These values give form to the principle of legality, according to which no behavior may be treated as a criminal offense and no penalty may be applied unless they have been previously established by law. The accused person also has a right to be presumed innocent unless proven guilty in a fair trial. Standards for a fair trial have traditionally included the requirement that the tribunal be impartial and established by law prior to the offense that is to be judged.

Another value many domestic legal systems seek to achieve is the ultimate settlement of outstanding legal situations. The rationale of the institution of statutory limitations is that it is convenient for society and anyone liable to be prosecuted not to have unsettled legal situations for an indefinite period of time.

Yet other relevant values are forgiveness and the need for social peace and reconciliation, which serves as justification for measures of leniency, such as amnesties, pardons, and immunity from prosecution.

The conflict among these values has been obviated by international law with respect to the gravest crimes. After World War II, judicial rulings and United Nations conventions and declarations have established the parmountcy of the need to punish crimes against humanity and war crimes, over the other traditional legal principles and institutions that may be at play. Thus, these crimes are always punishable under international law, and no statutory limitations apply to them. A narrow understanding of the principle of legality does not apply to these crimes, either, as they are punishable under international law even if "such acts do not constitute a violation of the domestic law of the country in which they were committed."[3] Also, international ad hoc military tribunals were established after the facts in the aftermath of World War II to prosecute major war criminals in Europe and the Far East and again in recent years, as mentioned earlier, to deal with major crimes committed in former Yugoslavia and Rwanda. However, the principle of presumption of innocence and other standards for a fair trial are still valid under international law, regardless of the gravity of the alleged offense.

In different countries, those responsible for war crimes and grave violations of human rights have attempted to avoid accountability for their acts by a variety of means. As long as they can rely on their force as governments or as groups controlling certain territory, they may attempt to conceal or deny their worst crimes and otherwise secure their impunity by their sheer hold on power. Prior to leaving power, they often pass amnesties and other legal measures of leniency or else press for them after a change of government has taken place. They and their supporters would naturally argue for the legal validity and political convenience of such measures and affirm the preeminence of domestic law over international law.

International organizations, concerned scholars, and national activists who fight for justice in the countries concerned would stress the paramountcy of international law and interpret it progressively on any unclear points.

The solid historical, moral, and juridical foundations of this legacy of international law cannot be denied. Yet, it is not conducive to confront the issues of justice, truth, and reconciliation in ambiguous political situations solely from that standpoint.

The first problem is that a legal approach presupposes that new governments can exercise the power of a sovereign—that is, the power states must have to enforce the law and judicial decisions. Such force must be greater than that of any member of society and certainly greater than the force criminal defendants may wield. At the international level there is no such sovereign power. So, the rulings of an international court will not be followed unless concerned states are willing to surrender suspected criminals within their territory or lend their power to attempt to arrest them in another territory.

New state authorities in countries where the perpetrators of past crimes are still a force to be reckoned with can therefore be said to have restricted sovereign powers to confront the past. In practice, these restrictions seldom take the form of open armed resistance against judicial decisions. Rather, there usually are legal measures of impunity that domestic parliaments are incapable or unwilling to repeal, for fear of political consequences, or domestic courts are reluctant to declare invalid, for similar or other considerations.

Advocates of justice for past crimes would insist that governments keep attempting to bring the perpetrators to justice, or they would point out that even if the new authorities cannot reasonably do so, that does not absolve the state from its responsibility under international law to compensate the victims and that, at any rate, individuals responsible for crimes against international law may be prosecuted by other states or international bodies. Correct as these views are from a legal standpoint, the problem of insufficient power to enforce the law does remain.

The second question concerning the insufficiency of a purely legal approach is that the criminal justice model, including individual prosecutions and fair trials, has developed historically as an integral part of functioning legal systems. In normal periods, transgressions of the law are to be expected, to some extent. They do not bring down the existing legal system and political order but rather mobilize its defenses, particularly the institutions of criminal justice.

Criminal justice is, then, a means to enforce and preserve an existing legal and, indeed, moral order. It is not an instrument designed to rebuild a just society after a major breakdown of the existing order (or to build a just order in places where none had existed before). This point certainly does not imply that criminal justice is useless in such situations. On the contrary, to punish major crimes is an important and in some cases indispensable component of the policies to be applied during a period of political transition. But the central question is determining what measures are most conducive, in each case, to the purpose of building or reconstructing a just society. That is a crucial issue of political ethics.

The Political Ethics of Foundational Times

The question raised at the outset of this chapter belongs to what may be termed a foundational time in politics (which is really a time for refoundation in most cases). This foundational time may be said to be a period when societies intently address social-contract kind of questions—that is, matters concerning the very basis of the political system they are about to build, rebuild, or transform and how, on such grounds, political compromises can be justified. From a stand-point of political ethics, the ultimate purpose of a foundational time is to construct or rebuild a moral order—that is, a just political system.

As I have written for a forthcoming publication:

> The way a nation deals with questions of values during a foundational time has a seminal importance because it may mark the particular nation's culture and its institutions for years to come. The new government and indeed the whole nation must face the past because it impinges on the present and on the future. Of course, governments must also be concerned about the present—transitions can be fragile and the possibility of major backlashes is often a distinct one. Finally, they must aim at securing a future of peace and national unity where there was conflict and political polarization. Many of the specific measures and policies adopted during a transition, such as reports from truth commissions or trials, have a bearing simultaneously on the legacy of the past, on the present and on the future.[4]

Although normal times, meaning the adequate functioning of an established political system, are expected to be the rule, times of deep crisis, which may eventually be overcome through a new foundational process, do occur in the life of most nations. International law has attempted to regulate times of crisis or emergency. Human rights law does allow states to derogate from certain of their obligations in "time of public emergency which threatens the life of the nation . . . to the extent strictly required by the exigencies of the situation."[5] In practice, states invoke this kind of provision, more often than not, as a pretext to impose political restrictions, but that does not deny the reality of genuine crisis to which specific sets of ethical and legal rules apply. International humanitarian law is in its entirety a normative system designed to regulate a time of crisis—international or internal armed conflict. This explains the unique character of this branch of law and its norms.

However, neither international law nor domestic legal systems contain specific rules for a foundational time, because law itself is one of the components of the order to be founded or rebuilt. True, some standards of political ethics may be said to have achieved international moral and legal ascendancy, such as the ethical parmountcy of a democratic system of government, based on popular sovereignty and participation, the rule of law, and respect for human rights. Yet democracy—or, more generally, a just political system—is a goal to strive for during transitional situations, but no generally accepted ethical or legal blueprint exists for how to achieve such goal.

Arguably, the experience of recent transitions may gradually contribute to the formulation of a generally acceptable framework or a set of guidelines for such periods of political foundation or refoundation.

Major components of this possibly emerging framework will still come from international law. Meanwhile, ideas from other disciplines or traditions have been advanced. They include religious doctrines about forgiveness and views about the psychology of healing and reconciliation. All such contributions are giving shape to this increasingly distinctive field called "truth, justice, and reconciliation."

Of the three concepts included in that expression, truth is perhaps the one that has been elaborated the most through recent experiences. I have argued[6] that during a political transition the policies designed to address the past must be based on as full and public as possible a disclosure of the truth about repressive practices and specific instances of the gravest forms of victimization. The truth must be established in an official, impartial manner, so it may be generally accepted and incorporated as part of the nation's historical memory. When human rights violations have been committed on a massive scale, the truth must reveal both the overall working of the repressive machinery and the fate of individual victims of the worst crimes. Different methods may be required to account for these distinct but related aspects of the truth.

It is important for the truth to be not only known but also acknowledged by all institutions and individuals concerned and by society at large. Acknowledging the truth implies both admitting the veracity of the facts accounted for and recognizing that they amounted to wrongdoing. This contributes to affirming the value of the norms that were violated, which is particularly important during a foundational period.

Justice has several connotations: (1) the vindication of the victims' memory and good name, (2) the need to compensate the victims' families, and (3) the punishment of the perpetrators.

Reconciliation suggests a degree of magnanimity. Yet forgiveness cannot be equated with blanket impunity. The doctrines of forgiveness from major religions emphasize a number of steps: the wrongdoer must admit what he or she did, acknowledge that it was evil, repent and resolve not to do it again, and compensate those who were wronged. If these steps are taken, the perpetrators themselves would be accepting the norms transgressed, thus contributing to reaffirming basic values during a foundation period.

In reality, legal amnesties or pardons are a form of societal forgiveness. Whether and how the victims of abuses or their families may forgive are intimate matters that cannot be the direct object of policy making. Given policies, though, may influence the inclination of individuals to forgive.

Moreover, the cases of genuine, spontaneous contrition are actually rare. When admissions of guilt do occur, they are usually motivated by a desire to obtain a lesser penalty or an amnesty, as is currently the case in South Africa, where thousands have applied for amnesty for politically motivated crimes in exchange for confession.

While a genuine contrition may be morally superior to one dictated by self-interest, the authorities or the legal system have no way to gauge the subjective disposition of the persons who acknowledge their wrongdoing. For the purpose of publicly reaffirming key values during a foundational time, the external steps of acknowledgments must suffice.

How far may clemency and forgiveness legitimately go? It may be asserted that amnesties and other measures of leniency are legitimate if the truth is known and acknowledged. However, the moral mandates etched in the conscience of humankind and imperative norms of international law after World War II demand that war crimes and crimes against humanity always be prosecuted. These norms should not be tampered with.

Yet, must it always be understood that all measures short of trials and criminal punishment for these crimes are illegitimate and tantamount to impunity?

The case of South Africa comes to mind. Inhuman acts resulting from the policy of apartheid have been characterized as crimes against humanity by the Convention on the Non-Applicability of Statutory Limitations to War Crimes and Crimes against Humanity. However, the parties to the negotiation that led to the dismantling of apartheid agreed on amnesties for politically motivated crimes. Later, the Mandela government decided that widespread prosecutions for such crimes might adversely affect the efforts to build a multiethnic democratic society on the basis of national reconciliation; mere forgetfulness and impunity, however, would equally jeopardize such a goal. The government thus established the Commission on Truth and Reconciliation, which has held innumerable public hearings and considered, as already mentioned, thousands of applications for amnesties in exchange for open admission and detailed information about wrongdoing.

Does this civic ritual of public exposure and shame count as punishment? The example of South Africa suggests it might well do. It may be true that the rule about punishment of war crimes and crimes against humanity is cast in nearly absolute terms. But reality shows that in some situations to follow that rule to the last may be detrimental to the very process of founding a just order. For this reason the International Military Tribunal conducting the Tokyo trials decided to spare Emperor Hirohito. In other cases, full application of that rule may not only be dangerous to peace but next to impossible, as it would be in Rwanda.

Again, these caveats do not justify any rush calls to attenuate the severity of the international norms about punishment for such crimes. Rather, they should spur the interest to learn from the experiences of countries that struggle with the difficult issue of attempting to build a just society on the ashes of war and crime.

International and domestic initiatives to achieve moral reconstruction may be mutually reinforcing, if the respective participants show sensitivity for each other's views. But in the end, it will be the internal efforts that will determine the quality and sustainability of the outcome.

Notes

1. *Transitional Justice,* ed. Neil J. Kritz, is a three-volume compilation of writing and documents on this topic (Washington, D.C.: United States Institute for Peace Press, 1995).

2. For variations of this typology, see José Zalaquett, "Confronting Human Rights Violations Committed by Former Governments: Principles Applicable and Political Constraints," in *State Crimes: Punishment or Pardon* (Washington, D.C.: Aspen Institute, 1989); and an essay I also wrote, to appear in a forthcoming book to be published by the Woodrow Wilson International Center for Scholars, Washington, D.C.

3. Article 1, Convention on the Non-Applicability of Statutory Limitations to War Crimes and Crimes against Humanity.

4. See note 2.

5. International Covenant on Civil and Political Rights, Article 4.

6. See "Confronting Human Rights Violations" in *State Crimes;* also, "Balancing Ethical Imperatives and Political Constraints: The Dilemma of New Democracies Confronting Past Human Rights Violations." The Mathew O. Tobriner Memorial Lecture, *Hastings Law Journal* 43, no. 6 (August 1992).

13

The Morality of Sanctions

Larry Minear

The issues treated in this volume are complex, situated as they are at the intersections of colliding moral imperatives. Economic sanctions are no exception. They enjoy a privileged place in the United Nations Charter and in the tool kit of diplomats. Carefully crafted, adroitly applied, and well managed, they represent an effective expression of international law and assertion of international human rights and humanitarian values. Avoiding the resort to military force may spare civilian populations wide-ranging and inhumane consequences.

However principled in concept and design, sanctions have nevertheless often failed to achieve their eminently legitimate objectives. Even when successful, they have often occasioned one degree or another of hardship among civilians in the targeted country. The same United Nations that imposes economic coercion then dutifully moves to relieve the associated suffering. The world body that seems morally schizophrenic in causing wounds that it then binds up would appear morally irresponsible were it to leave such suffering unattended.

The extent to which economic sanctions place political and humanitarian imperatives on a collision course was dramatized at a workshop in December 1995 that was part of a U.N.-commissioned study on the humanitarian impacts of economic sanctions. Officials with Security Council–related responsibilities urged researchers to avoid recommending any constraints on the imposition of sanctions by the council in the pursuit of its political objectives. U.N. aid officials, by contrast, wanted a powerful floodlight of condemnation focused on the inhumanity of such measures. Each group claimed the moral high ground.[1]

This chapter examines the morality of sanctions. It views sanctions not as a clash between coercion and compassion but rather as a challenge of managing the tension between principles. After a review of the changed international political climate in the wake of the Cold War, the chapter examines recent experience with multilateral sanctions, with particular attention to the difficulties they create for humanitarian interests. It concludes by observing ways in which a more nuanced understanding of the convergence between political and humanitarian interests would benefit both.

The Changing Political Environment

The passing of the Cold War has brought a fundamental shift in the traditional understanding of the relationship between political and humanitarian imperatives. For decades, international responses to human distress had been calibrated according to the location of the suffering and the politics of the host authorities. "Anyone who examines the historical record of communism must conclude," a florid editorial in the *Washington Times* in the mid-1980s opined, "that any aid directed at overthrowing communism is humanitarian aid."[2]

International policy generally reflected such editorial polemics. Nicaraguans, Cubans, Vietnamese, Angolans, and other civilians under communist control in the "third world" were denied life-saving assistance by the United States–led "first world" and received special help from the Soviet Union and its "second world" allies. By the time East-West confrontation peaked in the 1980s, the third world and its urgent human needs seemed little more than a battleground for first and second world ideologies. Multilateral humanitarian and economic assistance, heavily politicized, suffered accordingly. Ideology infiltrated the international refugee regime, with refugees from communism welcomed in the West, which shunned those fleeing right-wing dictatorships, and vice versa. Very little assistance was genuinely neutral, impartial, and independent.

With the ebbing of Cold War tensions, humanitarian concerns during the past decade have attained a new and higher profile. The deprivation of the essentials of life and the abuse of human rights have come to be viewed as threats to international peace and security, justifying the exercise of economic and military force under Chapter VII of the U.N. Charter. Humanitarian extremity and human rights abuses have figured prominently in U.N. interventions in such internal conflicts as Bosnia, Somalia, and Rwanda. Such action no longer requires the political consent of crisis-affected countries.

The changes in the global environment themselves reflect political and humanitarian forces. Major humanitarian crises, politicized and/or masked during the Cold War, have become more visible and accessible during the 1990s. "As the atom is to nuclear physics, the nation-state was supposed to be the basic unit of international politics," observed Peter J. Fromuth. "Yet since the end of the Cold War, the pent-up hatred and frustration of nationalist, ethnic, religious and other forces have exploded, splitting the nation-state atom and sending shock waves across the international system."[3] Eroded sovereignty and greater permeability of national borders have opened new space for humanitarian action. At the same time, complex moral issues, including identifying criteria for interventions and consistency among them, have edged toward the center of an expanding international stage.

The newly perceived importance of human need reflects changes in the humanitarian as well as the political ethos. The first post–Cold War decade has witnessed growing assertiveness by humanitarian interests themselves. Aid organizations have welcomed the new attention to humanitarian concerns within the corridors of power. The explosion of humanitarian need has produced exponential growth in the size and scale of the international humanitarian enterprise. Widespread disaffection with governmental action and a new sense of the importance of the institutions of civil society have contributed to a higher international profile for relief action and actors.

Yet the reality that heightened human need has caught the attention of policy makers has been, according to aid groups themselves, a mixed blessing. Humanitarian interests, applauding the fact that human deprivation and human rights abuses have come into their own, have also warned against the accompanying dangers of politicization. Threats to humanity, they have pointed out, create their own imperative for action quite apart from perceived connections to top-drawer political issues of international peace and security. Moreover, as the locus of post–Cold War conflicts has shifted from interstate to intrastate, requiring a more diverse international tool kit, aid organizations have cautioned against substituting short-term, high-profile relief assistance for measures that tackle the underlying causes of conflict and recurrent instability.

Ironically, some of the same nongovernmental organizations (NGOs) that were consenting handmaidens of Cold War geopolitics now challenge governments for lack of decisive political and military action. Demands for more coercive and firm pressure on reprobate regimes now often originate in humanitarian quarters. The sea change is particularly striking in the United States, where private relief groups no longer rely on ritual incantations of their nonpolitical nature to rationalize their unwillingness to challenge inhumane government policies. Yet their growing outspokenness about the impacts of donor and host government policies on civilian populations has been slow to be reflected in more savvy humanitarian programs in the field. Cold War chickens coming home to roost are no more welcome in the humanitarian than in the political henhouse.[4]

The adoption in 1997 of a convention to ban the production and use of land mines represents the latest and most dramatic example of the post–Cold War reevaluation of humanitarian imperatives in relation to political-military necessity. It demonstrates a new level of effective advocacy by humanitarian and other groups, now graced with a Nobel Peace Prize that in turn lends greater political force to a humanitarian *cause célèbre*. Yet reversing the traditional preemption of humanitarian imperatives by political interests would not have been possible without converging political pressures. These included leadership by key "middle powers" such as Canada, Norway, and South Africa; a well-orchestrated coalition that enlisted active and retired military personnel; the well-documented contribution of unexploded ordnance to the destabilization of peace agreements around the post–Cold War world; and the heightened role played by the media.

These twin trends—the higher humanitarian component in political decision making and the greater assertiveness of humanitarian interests in the political arena—have converged in the world's highest political body. In recent years, the U.N. Security Council has not only invoked humanitarian values as a rationale, or rationalization, for its actions. It has also demonstrated a new openness to hearing from humanitarian interests themselves.

Access to the council for the U.N.'s own humanitarian organizations had traditionally been closely guarded by the U.N. secretary-general.[5] Member states had been the sole point of access to the council on matters of concern to NGOs and government aid agencies. Beginning in 1997, Secretary-General Kofi Annan encouraged the U.N. Department of Humanitarian Affairs (DHA) to play a more visible and direct role vis-à-vis the council. Moreover, the council itself has sought wider input. In February 1997, members received an informal briefing by three NGOs on the crisis in the African Great Lakes and, in June 1997, on the preliminary findings of the sanctions study referenced earlier.

Newfound interest in things humanitarian, however, has yet to be reflected consistently in Security Council action. Indeed, the post–Cold War repositioning of humanitarian action in relation to political priorities has not resulted in a new "balance." Even an appropriate figure of speech to describe the evolving relationship has yet to be devised. It is in this new and still-fluid context that debate about the morality of sanctions takes place. That debate draws strength from the current repositioning of humanitarian and political concepts and interests; it also contributes to the changing political environment.

Humanitarian Action on Unfriendly Political Ground

Recent sanctions episodes provide a rich set of experiences. They range from highly specific (selective embargoes of arms trade, transport, communications, financial transactions, cultural and sports exchanges) to more comprehensive measures that ban virtually all international intercourse. Some sanctions are imposed by a single government (e.g., the United States against Cuba), others by a coalition of governments (the Economic Community of West Africa against Liberia), and still others by the United Nations Security Council (against Libya) or the U.N. General Assembly (against South Africa).

Some sanctions originate among governments within a given region (e.g., the Organization of American States [OAS] against the military regime in Haiti) and are then embraced by the United Nations. Others (against Southern Rhodesia) originate with the U.N. itself. Most are against countries, although political factions such as the Khmer Rouge in Cambodia or UNITA in Angola have themselves been targeted. Sanctions have been crafted to advance such highly moral political objectives as reversing international aggression, reinstating elected regimes, punishing terrorism, and condemning human rights violations.[6] Some respond to, or win, constituencies within target countries; others never garner such support or lose it over time.

Although history provides far more examples of unilateral or coalitional than multilateral sanctions—more than half of all sanctions to date have been of United States origin—multilateral sanctions have become much more frequent in the post–Cold War era.[7] Of the sixty-some cases of sanctions during 1945–1990, only those against Southern Rhodesia and South Africa were multilateral in nature. In the 1990s, however, the Security Council has imposed or maintained sanctions against South Africa, Iraq, the former Yugoslavia, Somalia, Libya, Liberia, Haiti, Angola, Rwanda, Sudan, and Sierra Leone.

Irrespective of their nature, origin, and scope, sanctions involve issues of moral legitimacy and political effectiveness. Moral issues are most thoroughly joined by when global legitimacy is conferred through the U.N. action, even though the U.N. imprimatur does not necessarily make for greater efficacy. Multilateral action highlights tensions between widely shared political objectives and universally affirmed moral principles, particularly when coercion is associated with serious humanitarian consequences.

Unilateral sanctions should not, however, be held to a less rigorous standard. The health consequences associated with the U.S. embargo against Cuba have been no less serious than those associated with the

OAS/U.N. embargo against Haiti. The toll in Haiti, however, flowed from an action graced with the formal endorsement of the international community, not from the political agenda of a single country. U.S. economic pressure to isolate Cuba and others deemed hostile to its national security interests deserves close scrutiny in its own right, although that is beyond the focus of the present chapter.

Sanctions and Suffering

Multilateral sanctions have three major kinds of negative humanitarian impacts: they increase human suffering, they complicate the ability of humanitarian organizations to provide succor, and they politicize humanitarian activities. Varying by degree from episode to episode, these impacts are nevertheless sufficiently recurrent and serious to call into question the moral legitimacy of sanctions as an appropriate instrument of international policy.

First, sanctions increase the distress of civilian populations. That result is indelibly clear in the case of Iraq, where, since their imposition in August 1990, U.N. sanctions have had wide-ranging and far-reaching impacts. Analysts do not disagree on the extent to which the health and welfare of the Iraqi population have eroded during this period: all key social and economic indicators have shown alarming deterioration. They differ, however, on the extent to which sanctions themselves—as distinct from economic mismanagement, war damage in the 1990s by Iran or in 1991 by the Allied Coalition—are implicated. Most agree that though sanctions are not the sole cause of the continuing misery, they bear a heavy responsibility for the deteriorating condition of civilian populations.[8]

The Iraq experience is far from unique. Sanctions have also created a widening circle of suffering in Serbia and Montenegro, Haiti, and other settings where such coercion has been applied and maintained. In fact, they are designed to force policy changes even at the risk of civilian hardship and, indeed, precisely through generating pressure on such regimes. That civilians suffer therefore comes as no surprise. The fact that in South Africa, Rhodesia, and Haiti, large segments of civil society welcomed sanctions as a means of changing conditions of apartheid or military rule gave them added moral legitimacy. However, the linkage between sanctions and increased suffering was not in dispute.

The premise that political gains will be achieved by extracting civilian pain does not prevent supporters of sanctions from claiming that such suffering is unintended. Yet as new sanctions are imposed and as experience with their effects multiplies, protestations of ignorance become less intellectually persuasive or morally dispositive. "The amount of information available today on the devastating economic, social and humanitarian impact of sanctions," concluded a U.N. study, "no longer permits [policy makers] to entertain the notion of 'unintended effects.' "[9]

Proponents of sanctions argue that however inevitable the pain, the political gains involved justify such suffering. That calculus, however, raises both empirical and moral questions. A review of the political effectiveness of sanctions in South Africa, Iraq, Serbia/Montenegro, and Haiti suggests that such measures can be said to have achieved their objectives only in South Africa. Incalculable pain in Iraq has not forced changes in national policy; instead, sanctions have allowed the regime to tighten its grip. Sanctions against the former Yugoslavia leveraged support for the Dayton Peace Agreement, which reduced the level of civilian suffering, although a durable and just peace remains elusive. In Haiti, the restoration of democracy was produced not by three years of sanctions but by the threat of military intervention.

The associated moral questions are troubling as well. While politicians and policy analysts talk of the pain-gain "equation," the use of human suffering as a political element in a calibrated calculus raises serious moral issues. These are particularly acute to the extent that the persons who suffer are generally poorer segments of societies and often persons largely without influence over their governments' policies.

In the application of sanctions, proportionality is essential: civilian pain must be offset by political gain in order to be countenanced. However, the reality that political gains are often elusive and ephemeral while social and political impacts are prompt and ongoing renders such equations anything but precise.

When sanctions achieve political objectives that themselves have a clear moral component, the ethical issues associated with their use are reduced. Yet even when sanctions produce the desired political change, the attendant suffering is not thereby automatically justified. Indeed, the creation of civilian suffering as a political change agent is highly questionable. In January 1998 fifty-four U.S. Catholic bishops appealed to President Clinton for the immediate cessation of sanctions against Iraq, observing that "they violate the human rights of Iraqi people, because they deprive innocent people [of] food and medicine, basic elements for normal life."[10]

Sanctions figured prominently in the challenge by the Iraqi government in late 1997 to the presence of American nationals on United Nations weapons inspections teams. Some diplomats and analysts found vindication of more than six years of sanctions in Iraqi insistence on their lifting. Sanctions provided the leverage, they said, to prevent the development of lethal weapons. In seeking to prevent the creation of weapons of mass destruction, the international community clearly enjoyed the moral high ground.

Yet the showdown produced Baghdad's grudging and only temporary compliance with continued U.N. weapons inspection but not with Security Council resolutions passed at the end of the Gulf War. In fact, the crisis shifted the spotlight from the importance of sanctions to their inability to produce the desired political change. In the process, the human toll of sanctions was highlighted in ways that implicated not only the policies of the Iraqi authorities but also the limitations of the U.N. program that allowed the proceeds from limited sales of Iraqi oil to purchase humanitarian necessities.

Reflecting the experience in Iraq and elsewhere, sanctions are coming to be viewed as morally viable only to the extent that their likely impacts are reviewed in advance, their actual impacts monitored closely, and the extent of civilian suffering proportionate to political gains. Governments themselves now speak increasingly of the humanitarian limits of sanctions, acknowledging the need for clearer and more restrictive parameters to govern their use. Such limits are in keeping with international law, which prohibits starvation of a civilian population. The evolving consensus also reflects a growing awareness that in responding to what is often perceived as short-term political problems, sanctions create long-lasting obstacles to reconstruction and development.

Concern to minimize civilian pain is also fueling attempts to devise what have come to be known as "smart sanctions." These are measures that target reprobate regimes and their supporters, thereby avoiding more indiscriminate impacts. While an approach is of course unobjectionable in principle, the jury is still out on whether approaches more discriminating in their choice of targets will also be more effective in their results. The secret to the success against South Africa lay not in the precision of sanctions but in their comprehensiveness.

Sanction proponents also note that sanctions are one element in a series of incremental measures legitimized by the U.N. Charter. Although the charter does not require that military force be invoked only after sanctions have been tried, the human costs of sanctions, it is widely believed, are less serious than those that might result from military action. Thus, the prevailing thinking is that application of military force to advance such objectives as reversing international aggression, reinstating elected regimes, punishing terrorism, and condemning human rights violations should be used only when sanctions have failed.

The view of sanctions as an alternative to military force, however, requires review, as does the assumption that military action is necessarily less civilian-friendly or morally justifiable than economic coercion. Rather than representing an alternative to war, sanctions against Iraq laid the political groundwork for the use of force. Imposed in August 1990, they had begun to make themselves felt by January, when the Security Council nevertheless approved military action. Moreover, although airstrikes may have avoided major "collateral damage" to civilians, seven years of sanctions have ravaged the essential infrastructure that military action had largely spared.

Sanctions and Succor

In addition to widening human suffering, sanctions make it more difficult for humanitarian organizations to respond. They restrict exports to, and imports from, targeted countries. Comprehensive sanctions block all transfers and transactions, affecting the essentials of day-to-day civilian life. Focused sanctions—for example, those that embargo arms transfers, cultural exchanges, or tourist travel—leave generally unaffected such economic transactions as the importing of food and medicines essential to the health of civilian populations.

In authorizing sanctions that affect trade flows, the Security Council normally makes special provision for certain items to continue to reach targeted countries. Such "humanitarian exemptions" represent, in effect, "the hinge between using sanctions to achieve political objectives, on the one hand, and safeguarding the rights of civilian populations in targeted countries, on the other."[11] Aid organizations and commercial suppliers that import basics such as food and medicines thus may continue to do so. Without pass-through provisions that spare humanitarian indispensables, the morality of sanctions would be seriously undermined.

Yet in practice humanitarian exemptions have exacerbated rather than eased the moral issues. What should be considered "humanitarian"? Food staples for the general population, along with supplementary food for infants and pregnant and lactating women, clearly qualify, but what of luxury foods, alcoholic beverages, or tobacco? Are the ingredients of food production such as seeds, tools, fertilizer, and pesticides themselves humanitarian? Medicines are essential, but should fuel and spare parts for the refrigerators to store vaccines be included? What of disposable hospital supplies, kidney dialysis machines, blood program supplies, spare parts for operating room equipment, and family planning and AIDS prevention devices? Widening the circle further, what of retirement annuities from former employers, newsprint, and electricity for civilian installations? So-called "dual-use" items needed by aid agencies such as computers, two-way radios, and the fuel for vehicles engaged in distributing and monitoring relief supplies create special problems.

Framing and managing humanitarian exemptions represents a quagmire, complicating the already problematic moral landscape of sanctions themselves. Neither the political nor the humanitarian institutions within the U.N. system have common definitions of what should qualify as humanitarian. Political interests favor a strict-constructionist approach, whereas humanitarian agencies are more expansive. Individual U.N. agencies are strong advocates for including items within their own specializations (e.g., women and children, food and agriculture, health and medicine, refugees, family planning, and education). Because the Security Council has no definitional template or standard language, each new episode is undertaken without juridical or moral sextants.

Definitional disarray is compounded by administrative difficulties. The Security Council sets up a separate sanctions committee for each episode, each composed of a representative of each of the council's fifteen member governments and with its own secretariat of U.N. staff. Meeting behind closed doors, each committee establishes its own ground rules and procedures, reflecting its particular perception of the humanitarian and political situation. Procedures based on consensus or "no objection" give individual governments enormous power.

Processing exemption requests has become a nightmare for all concerned. U.N. aid agencies as well as NGOs have had to commit considerable time and resources to preparing and monitoring exemptions applications. For U.N. secretariat staff, the workload is formidable. During a period of almost four years, the Yugoslavia committee, meeting in formal sessions almost 100 times, received and processed some 140,000 applications, most involving essential items for import by aid or commercial organizations.[12] The delays experienced on the operational end in each successive crisis are well documented, although over time some of the kinks are worked out of the review process.

The lack of clear and consistent guidelines, whether from one crisis to the next or even for a given crisis, has created confusion among humanitarian groups and commercial suppliers. In a letter to their headquarters from Belgrade, officials of the World Health Organization (WHO), the U.N. High Commissioner for Refugees (UNHCR), and the International Federation of Red Cross and Red Crescent Societies noted, "While the sanctions in principle do not cover medical supplies, in practice they have contributed to breaking the health care system. . . . [A]ll health care institutions in all parts of the country lack vital drugs, equipment and spare parts." Alerting their headquarters, they said, was part of their "ethical obligation" to call attention to "the detrimental effect of the sanctions on the health of the people and on the health care system of the country where we work."[13]

Sanctions often challenge the professional and personal ethics of those practicing humanitarian vocations. Faced with day-to-day challenges in environments of proliferating human need, aid personnel frequently see sanctions and associated administrative problems as their nemesis. The important policy objectives that sanctions are seeking to advance often become obscured by the operational difficulties that they create.

Such problems are compounded by the heightened difficulties faced by aid agencies in the sanctioned countries themselves. These include increases in the climate of insecurity affecting aid activities and personnel, in lawlessness and black-marketeering, and perhaps also in repression of minority or dissident groups. In Haiti during the sanctions period, an inoculation campaign and other health activities were suspended for fear of attacks on those using and providing such services. Government suspicion of humanitarian activities may also increase their vulnerability. Although such difficulties exist in many countries experiencing internal armed conflict, they are heightened when sanctions are applied.

External and internal difficulties combine to create major problems for humanitarian actors. Increased suffering associated with sanctions coincides with decreased ability to provide succor. An official of the International Federation of Red Cross and Red Crescent Societies, recalling his experience from Iraq in particular, observed that "the magnitude of the impact of sanctions is so large that [the offsetting humanitarian contributions] of any and all relief programs are dwarfed by comparison."[14] A WHO official, based on his experience in Belgrade, stated, "Sanctions make the life of humanitarian organizations almost impossible."[15] In Haiti, "sanctions were more damaging to humanitarian organizations than to the regime against which they were invoked."[16]

Difficulties notwithstanding, the essentials of survival must be ensured. Such essentials not only encompass the staples of food, medical care, and shelter for vulnerable groups but also extend to the infrastructure needed to sustain the health and welfare of the civilian population. In a concession to the political constraints of the circumstances, however, ingredients to support longer-term development in a target economy would probably not merit inclusion. Inputs intermediate between emergency relief and longer-term development (e.g., seeds, fertilizer, educational materials) would qualify by virtue of their centrality to survival. The determination of what is to be allowed wherever sanctions are imposed would thus be less expansive than humanitarians advocate but also more inclusive than sanctions would support. Dual-use items would require special review. Standard operating procedures to facilitate rather than impede their provision are also indispensable.

There is, in short, no substitute for improvements in the definitional and administrative aspects of sanctions management. However, since even the most effectively functioning exemptions regime will be overmatched if it is expected fully to offset sanctions-associated need, the fundamental issue remains that of sanctions as an instrument of policy rather than how sanctions arrangements are managed.

Sanctions and Politicization

The challenge of meeting increased human need despite circumscribed institutional capacity is complicated by the politicization of assistance activity—the third respect in which sanctions situate humanitarian action on tricky ground. Politicization takes place within the United Nations itself, in the perceptions of the authorities and populations of targeted countries, and among contributors to relief activities.

First, sanctions set the U.N. system against itself. As noted in a recent comment by a U.N. committee, "sanctions should always take full account of the provisions of the International Covenant on Economic, Social, and Cultural Rights." In actual practice, however, "While the impact of sanctions varies from one case to another, . . . they almost always have a dramatic impact on the rights recognized in the Covenant."[17] The impacts of sanctions also exist in tension with other international legal safeguards, including the Geneva Conventions and Protocols, the Universal Declaration of Human Rights, and the Convention on the Rights of the Child.

Political interests, both among member states on the Security Council and its sanctions committees and in the U.N. secretariat's political department, place humanitarian action within a carrot-and-stick framework. Assistance levels and humanitarian exemptions are expanded or contracted as reward or punishment for political intransigence or concessions. Strict constructionist definitions of humanitarian assistance and exemptions keep humanitarian activities on a short leash, with aid efforts viewed as threats to effective sanctions and aid workers not as team players but as apologists for sanctioned regimes.

For their part, aid officials ground their action on humanitarian law and human rights, which, they point out, are not derogated when sanctions are imposed. They see humanitarian action as devoid of political agendas and thus undermined when permission is withheld—or even when it is granted—as an element in a larger political calculus. They view the secrecy of the sanctions committee review process as contrasting starkly with the transparency of humanitarian action. That process requires all but U.N. organizations and the International Committee of the Red Cross (ICRC) to solicit approval via member state intermediaries, yet another political intrusion. The friction between political and humanitarian actors is palpable.

Second, perceptions among political authorities and beneficiary populations are affected by sanctions. The linkage with sanctions of the U.N.'s own humanitarian organizations and their partners has transferred their unpopularity to aid efforts. Aid activities in Serbia and Montenegro lost credibility as a result of the perception that, as one NGO expressed it, "[h]umanitarian organizations here are on the bad side" of the conflict.[18] While association with the U.N. embargo against the Federal Republic of Yugoslavia was a liability in Serbia and Montenegro, association of humanitarian activities with ineffectual U.N. military action in nearby Bosnia undercut aid efforts there. The perception problem was so excruciating that aid officials based in Croatia with responsibilities for Bosnia-Herzegovina had business cards printed that omitted their Zagreb address.

Yet the problem was one not only of perceptions but also of reality. Although the sanctions committees function behind closed doors and without public accountability, their rulings and dynamics do become widely known not only among insiders in New York but also in the wider circle of humanitarian organizations and constituencies in recipient countries. The restrictive approach taken by the United States and the United Kingdom to humanitarian exemptions for Iraq is no secret. The former held up a UNICEF shipment of health kits on grounds that scissors could double as weapons.[19] The U.S. and the U.K. have micromanaged the administration of the humanitarian component of the oil-for-food program set up under Security Council Resolution 986. Small wonder that those in targeted countries view humanitarian activities as extensions of political agendas.

Third, sanctions over time also affect perceptions of human need and obligation. It is difficult for governments to ostracize a regime and express solidarity with its people through assistance activities. In practice, the punitive animus of sanctions often clashes with the instincts that animate relief assistance and human rights protection. Indeed, the level of resources committed to countries under sanctions have proved difficult to sustain year after year, although available data do not establish whether appeals for programs in countries targeted by sanctions have experienced greater difficulty over time than other headline humanitarian emergencies.

Politicization of donor involvement also blunts the perceived obligation among those who impose sanctions to come quickly and effectively to the aid of those affected. Those who impose sanctions usually issue ritual disavowals that their target is a given regime and that they have no quarrel with innocent civilians. However, because member states provide contributions for multilateral and bilateral humanitarian programs on a voluntary rather than assessed basis, each government is free to weigh its responsibilities and make its own financial commitments to populations living under pariah regimes.

Those who underscore moral obligations are often faulted for downplaying the behavior that unleashes the use of economic or military pressure. "If a target regime doesn't avail itself of the option provided by the Security Council," remarked a senior official in the U.N.'s Department of Political Affairs in a discussion, "humanitarian organizations must criticize the regime rather than the Security Council." There is no doubt that sanctions, whatever suffering they may cause, are not the illness but the medicine for the illness, however much a regime may seek to scapegoat the doctor and the attendant medical staff. Yet the international community is more directly implicated in the suffering associated with its own policies than if only the actions of the host authorities were involved. Even if a regime shifts responsibility for the misery of its population to the outside world, the moral obligations of the international community do not cease.

Often those targeted with sanctions are without particular concern for, or accountability to, their own populations. Paradoxically, sanctions are likely to be more effective in settings where a regime is responsible and accountable, yet such are seldom the regimes against which sanctions are imposed. Whether through the conceits of the regime or the dynamics they unleash, sanctions often shift the focus from the crime to the punishment and from the punishment to the punishers. "Does a regime's refusal to help its own citizens give the international community ethical license to exact punishment on an entire civilian population, particularly the poor and the young?"[20] Those who use a given weapon must take responsibility for its consequences, however limited their influence over its repercussions.

In sum, the moral character of the policy objectives that sanctions are designed to serve exist in tension with the recurrent humanitarian problems that sanctions entail. The reality that in situation after situation sanctions create major difficulties for civilian populations and aid institutions points toward their more sparing and discriminating use. Those who impose sanctions are morally obligated to avoid disproportionate harm and to come to the aid of the affected civilian populations. Neither human needs nor assistance to persons in distress should be used as political weapons. The negative humanitarian consequences of sanctions must be carefully weighed, monitored, and addressed.

Converging Political and Humanitarian Interests

The foregoing analysis has examined the extent to which humanitarian interests find themselves on unfriendly ground when economic sanctions are imposed. Operating within the political context and constraints of the Security Council, its sanctions committees, and U.N. member states, humanitarian interests are expected to cushion impacts of sanctions on civilians that are well beyond their ability to redress. Their ministrations are even viewed by some within the

United Nations and member states as a threat to the efficacy of their chosen political strategies. Meanwhile, those on the receiving end see their work as conveying a hostile political animus.

Despite such formidable difficulties, sanctions are not entirely or inherently hostile to humanitarian interests. When sanctions succeed, they lead to more humane and just conditions, with far-reaching benefits for civilian populations. In the case of South Africa, sanctions played a pivotal role in dismantling apartheid and establishing democratic governance. Efforts by the South African government and private sector to counteract the effects of the embargo through import substitution also led to expanded opportunities for employment among blacks.[21]

Even when sanctions do not succeed, as in Haiti, humanitarian values can be affirmed and humanitarian interests strengthened. Despite serious problems caused by sanctions for Haitian civilians and those seeking to assist them, international funding for some aid programs there increased during the 1991–1994 period, thanks to the increased awareness of the difficulties of life under the de facto regime. Sanctions need not represent an unmitigated disaster for humanitarian interests. The ledger sheet for any set of sanctions will have entries in both the plus and minus columns.

The sanctions debate at the United Nations, among governments and humanitarian agencies, and in academic circles is itself beginning to evidence changes in attitude on both the political and the humanitarian sides. Reflecting the new prominence of humanitarian concerns and the increased assertiveness of humanitarian interests described earlier, governments these days seem on their best behavior, or at least they are restraining their own negative political reflexes.

The General Assembly has approved recommendations designed to make sanctions more consistent, transparent, accountable, and humane.[22] In a 1995 letter to the president of the Security Council, ambassadors of the permanent five member states demonstrated the shifting balance between humanitarian and political concerns. "While recognizing the need to maintain the effectiveness of sanctions imposed in accordance with the Charter," they wrote, "further collective actions in the Security Council within the context of any future sanctions regime should be directed to minimize unintended adverse side-effects of sanctions on the most vulnerable segments of targeted countries."[23]

Such views gained credibility with a decision of the council related to Sudan, from which it sought to hasten the extradition of persons suspected of an assassination attempt on Egypt's president. The council's decision to delay a ban against international flights by Sudanese aircraft allowed the U.N. Department of Humanitarian Affairs to assess the likely impacts of such a measure on civilians and aid efforts. If the council eventually decides to proceed with sanctions, the report "has laid the groundwork for crafting eventual sanctions measures to mitigate adverse humanitarian consequences."[24]

In this instance and in responding to Iraq's treatment of the U.N. weapons inspection team in late 1997, the Security Council showed itself deeply divided on sanctions. In seeking advance information regarding the humanitarian impacts of such measures on Sudan, some governments were concerned that such increased solicitousness might set a precedent that would prove unhelpful, constraining the council's future freedom to act with dispatch.

The sanctions committees themselves have made strides in clarifying and simplifying their procedures. After delays of months in processing applications in the early days of the Yugoslav crisis, some of the hitches were out of the system by late 1995. The needs of the ICRC, which enjoys a high level of council respect and a special relationship to it, were accommodated earlier in that year with the approval of a blanket exemption for material used in its programs. Yet some governments remain wary. They continue to resist placing humanitarian activities outside the "carrot-and-stick" framework and tackling the real threat to the efficacy of sanctions that comes not from humanitarian succor but from smuggling, arms trade, and other illicit commerce.

Signs of change are also apparent on the humanitarian side. Aid agencies are taking a more sober view of the difficulties encountered in settings where international economic and military coercion is imposed. Gun-shy as a result of recent experiences with military humanitarianism, NGOs may also become more sanctions-shy in selecting venues for mounting their programs. Yet some senior humanitarian officials, like their political counterparts, still underestimate the magnitude and complexity of the problems created by sanctions. The U.N.'s schizophrenia is still real, although the patient's symptoms for the time being may have receded from severe to moderate.

Sanctions represent uncertain moral terrain both for political actors who are seen as tampering with the health and welfare of civilian populations and for humanitarian actors who are trying to function effectively in highly politicized surroundings. Nevertheless, the needs of civilian populations in such settings remain urgent; political and humanitarian imperatives alike require that they be met. In the quest for an international sanctions regime that will be an adequate match for reprobate regimes, consistency, transparency, and accountability will be the essential hallmarks.

In the final analysis, humanitarian and political interests are not as antagonistic as often supposed. The humanitarian and the political are not positioned at opposite ends of a playground teeter-totter, with advantages by one party gained at the expense of the other. Relevant experience from the Cold War and early post–Cold War eras suggests, however, that for humanitarian and political objectives alike to be accomplished, the fulcrum may need careful and deliberate repositioning nearer the humanitarian end.

Notes

1. See Larry Minear, David Cortright, Julia Wagler, George A. Lopez, and Thomas G. Weiss, *Toward More Humane and Effective Sanctions Management: Enhancing the Capacity of the United Nations System* (New York: United Nations Department of Humanitarian Affairs, October 1997).

2. "Resistance Aid, Not Party Games," *Washington Times* editorial, 10 May 1985, 9.

3. Peter J. Fromuth, "The Making of a Secure Community: The United Nations after the Cold War," *Journal of International Affairs* 46, no. 2 (Winter 1993): 344.

4. For a review of the embryonic effort in the mid-1980s by private U.S. relief groups to examine the political aspects of humanitarian action, see Larry Minear, *Helping People in an Age of Conflict: Toward a New Professionalism in U.S. Voluntary Humanitarian Assistance* (New York, D.C.: InterAction, 1988).

5. Secretary-General Boutros Boutros-Ghali discouraged undersecretar-

ies-general from dealing directly with the council, including the undersecre-tary-general for humanitarian affairs, a post created in 1992. However, even before Kofi Annan became secretary-general in January 1997, the U.N. High Commissioner for Refugees and other individual U.N. organizations dealt with the council on matters of special interest. For a number of years, the International Committee of the Red Cross has given the Security Council president monthly briefings on humanitarian issues.

6. For a more extended discussion, see Thomas G. Weiss, David Cort-right, George A. Lopez, and Larry Minear, *Political Gain and Civilian Pain* (Lanham, MD: Rowman & Littlefield, 1997). The volume also includes an extensive bibliography of literature on economic sanctions.

7. See Gary Clyde Hufbauer, Jeffrey J. Schott, and Kimberly Ann Elliott, *Economic Sanctions Reconsidered: History and Current Policy* (Washington, D.C.: Institute for International Economics, 1990).

8. For an analysis that connects the deterioration of the physical quality of life in Iraq principally to sanctions rather than to war-related damage, see Eric Hoskins, "The Humanitarian Impact of Economic Sanctions and War in Iraq," in Weiss et al., *Political Gain.*

9. Claudia von Braunmühl and Manfred Kulessa, *The Impact of U.N. Sanctions on Humanitarian Assistance Activities* (Berlin: Gesellschaft für Communication Management Interkultur Training, 1995), p. iii. The study was commissioned by the U.N. Department of Humanitarian Affairs.

10. Letter to President William J. Clinton, 20 January 1998, 2.

11. Minear et al., *Toward More Humane and Effective Sanctions Man-agement,* 37.

12. Letter dated 15 November 1996 from the chairman of the Security Council Committee Established Pursuant to Resolution 724 (1991) Concern-ing Yugoslavia addressed to the president of the Security Council, S/1996/946, para. 7.

13. Quoted in Larry Minear, Jeffrey Clark, Roberta Cohen, Dennis Gal-lagher, Iain Guest, and Thomas G. Weiss, *Humanitarian Action in the For-mer Yugoslavia: The U.N.'s Role, 1991–1993* [Occasional Paper 18] (Provi-dence, RI: Watson Institute, 1994), 94–95.

14. Quoted in Minear et al., *Toward More Humane and Effective Sanc-tions Management,* 11.

15. Minear et al., *Humanitarian Action in the Former Yugoslavia,* 94.

16. Robert Maguire, Edwige Balutansky, Jacques Fomerand, Larry Mi-near, William G. O'Neill, Thomas G. Weiss, and Sarah Zaidi, *Haiti Held Hostage: International Responses to the Quest for Nationhood, 1986–1996* (Providence, RI: Watson Institute, 1996), 49.

17. Committee on Economic, Social and Cultural Rights, "The relation-ship between economic sanctions and respect for economic, social and cul-tural rights," *General Comment* 8 (1997), paras. 1 and 3.

18. Minear et al., *Humanitarian Action in the Former Yugoslavia,* 100.

19. Larry Minear, U. B. P. Chelliah, Jeff Crisp, John Mackinlay, and Thomas G. Weiss, *United Nations Coordination of the International Humanitarian Response to the Gulf Crisis, 1990–1992* (Providence, RI: Watson Institute, 1992), 21.

20. Eric Hoskins, "The Humanitarian Impact of Economic Sanctions and War in Iraq," in Weiss et al., *Political Gain,* 141.

21. For a detailed discussion see Neta C. Crawford, "The Humanitarian Consequences of South Africa: A Preliminary Assessment," in Weiss et al., *Political Gain.*

22. Subgroup on the Question of United Nations Imposed Sanctions of the Informal Open Ended Working Group of the General Assembly on an Agenda for Peace, "Provisional Text," 10 July 1996.

23. Letter of 13 April 1995 to the president of the Security Council, S/1995/300, Annex 1.

24. Minear et al., *Enhancing the Capacity,* 8.

14

Moving in Vicious Circles

The Moral Dilemmas of Arms Transfers and Weapons Manufacture

Roger Williamson

Armed Conflict at the End of a Genocidal Century

It is perhaps surprising to discuss some of the dilemmas of arms transfers and weapons manufacture in a book on humanitarian intervention, since arms are designed to kill, injure, and threaten. But it is precisely these characteristics that make arms valuable for defense and deterrence. International law establishes a right to self-defense (Article 51, U.N. Charter). If the weapons supplied assist in the protection of the innocent, the arms trade can be a humanitarian intervention. If they assist in aggression or internal oppression, clearly they are antihumanitarian.

Two examples will help clarify this point. First, one could argue that the arms embargo on all parts of former Yugoslavia assisted the Serbs in their aggression by preventing the Bosnians from obtaining the weapons necessary for their self-defense. Arms embargos are usually considered a humanitarian measure, but here the effects were, arguably, antihumanitarian, making aggression easier. Second, concerning Namibia's struggle for freedom from apartheid South Africa, I recall hearing of a discussion in which a Namibian turned angrily to a Swede and said, "You Swedes with your humanitarian assistance.

251

How are we meant to defend ourselves against the South African army? With toothbrushes?"

It must be underlined, however, that the obvious intuition is usually right—that the humanitarian intervention relating to arms supplies is more often to restrict than to increase the supply of weapons into a conflict area. This can be a self-denying ordinance ("Whatever others do, we will not supply these weapons"), a negotiated position (e.g., by the European Union, possibly in the future on the basis of a European Code of Conduct), or international sanctions backed up by the United Nations.

This chapter seeks to show some of the many layers of the Faustian bargain entered into through the development of an arms industry and arms exports. Obvious unintended consequences ensue, such as ending up fighting enemies armed with weapons supplied by your own country or your allies—Britain confronting Argentina or the Allies and Iraq, for example. Anthropologist Marvin Harris encapsulates the irony of such unintended consequences in social matters. After documenting the negative effects of industrial production that aimed at improving lifestyles, he writes, "Twentieth century political and economic events reveal the same pattern of unintended, unanticipated and undesirable consequences: a war to end all wars followed by a war to make the world safe for democracy, followed by a world full of military dictators" (Harris 1989: 496). This has been a genocidal century, a "century of war" (Kolko 1994), an "age of extremes" (Hobsbawm 1994), with at least 100 million people killed in warfare (Sivard 1996: 18–91).

A pioneering Red Cross/Red Crescent Report, *Casualties of Conflict*, estimated that 90 percent of the 5 million war victims in 1988–1998 were killed in internal conflicts, and 90 percent of them were civilians (Ahlström & Nordquist 1991:19). Whereas 90 percent of the victims of war at the beginning of the century were military, now they are civilian.

This is the century of total war, in terms of both the capacity of armed potential and the collapse of any idea of preserving civilians from the effects of war. The arms trade is morally serious for many reasons. A central one is because it is civilians—noncombatants—who get killed in war, in overwhelming numbers. In the industrialized societies, we usually think of war either on the grandiose scale of the next threatened world war, the specter haunting Europe until the late 1980s, or as the armed forces of one country fighting the armed forces of another. But most postmodern wars are not like this. They are not so massive and ponderous that they must be dignified in a series of Roman numerals like volumes of an encyclopedia: World War I, II, III (discontinued). They are nasty, brutish, but often long, like the Sudanese civil war of 1955–1972 and 1983 to the present day (Assefa 1987; Saferworld 1994; Human Rights Watch 1994, 1996). The Third World War has been avoided, but war in the third world has continued. The "True Cost of Conflict," especially conflict far away in countries about which we know little or nothing, is usually radically underestimated (Saferworld 1994). Now much of the former Soviet Union faces many of the problems of postimperial dissolution and conflict.

Each year, the Stockholm International Peace Research Institute (SIPRI) publishes its authoritative yearbook, with a chapter on "Major Armed Conflicts." Such conflicts have caused a cumulative total of more than 1,000 battle deaths. In past years, there usually have been about thirty; the recent trend has been slightly downward. Of twenty-seven major armed conflicts active in 1996, twenty-two had started before 1989, when the Cold War ended (SIPRI 1997: 22). Hardly any of them, in recent years, have been between nation-states; the Iran-Iraq War and the Gulf War (Iraq against the Allies) are exceptions (SIPRI 1996: 15–30).

To quote from W. B. Yeats: "Things fall apart, the centre cannot hold." The nation-state, according to liberal theory, is a reasonably impartial allocator of scarce resources. But what if the resources are not there to allocate? We now even see wars in which the capture of the state is undesirable, since running the state is to take over liabilities rather than assets. States fall apart along ethnic/national, religious/cultural, and economic fault lines. Where two of these three dimensions or even all three coincide, trouble is in store. Kaplan's influential analysis of the coming anarchy, based on what he saw in West Africa, is a salutary warning. Armed factions and collapsed states could be the destiny of significant sections of the third world. The politics of identity has replaced the politics of blocs and nation-states. When this happens, the seeds are sown for complex emergencies—with the tragically familiar picture of hundreds of thousands of refugees leaving their homes, reports of massacres, ethnic cleansing, and, in some situations, the additional threat of famine. Here is the ready demand for weapons, for aggression or defense; here are conflicts that can be exacerbated by weapons. These are the killing fields, the complex emergencies such as Rwanda, into which the weapons flow.

The Extent of the Arms Trade

According to SIPRI, the period 1987–1990 marked a "precipitous decline" in arms sales. This downward trend slowed from 1991 to 1995 (SIPRI 1996: 463). Russian military production collapsed so that the 1995 level was only about 15 percent of the 1991 total (SIPRI 1996: 429). In 1995, Russian arms sales recovered considerably, meaning that the U.S. proportion of world arms sales fell from 56 percent in 1994 to 43 percent in 1995 (SIPRI 1996: 463–64). By 1996, Russia's supplies had recovered from 15 percent of the global total to 20 percent (SIPRI 1997: 269). Arms transfers are dominated by six suppliers, the permanent five (P5) members of the U.N. Security Council (China, France, Russia, the U.K. the U.S.) and Germany. The ten largest recipient countries shared between 50 and 65 percent of the purchases from 1986 to 1995, and the thirty largest between 85 and 95 percent (SIPRI 1996: 480). In 1996, China, South Korea, Kuwait, Taiwan, and Saudi Arabia accounted for 43 percent of the global total, with the three northeast Asian countries listed accounting for 30 percent of the world total (SIPRI 1997: 267).

The most reputable collectors of data agree that the trend in arms transfers has been a significant decrease from the peak of the late 1980s. Care must be exercised in using the data, because the monetary values of the different data collection systems varies widely. What can be compared is conclusions about the trends (upward and downward). There is a substantial agreement on whether acquisitions are increasing or decreasing among, for example, SIPRI, the International Institute for Strategic Studies (IISS), and the Arms Control and

Disarmament Agency (ACDA). The accounting procedures and values differ.

The latest data from the International Institute for Strategic Studies (the Military Balance 1997–1998) had the U.S. with a 42.6 percent market share in arms sales and Britain with 22.1 percent in 1996 (Black and Fairhall 1997). SIPRI had the U.S. share as 44 percent, with Russia in second place with 20 percent of a $22,980 million market based on constant (1990) U.S. dollars (SIPRI 1997: 267).

One of the most acute observers of trends, Lora Lumpe, director of the Arms Sales Monitoring Project of the Federation of American Scientists, isolated some dangerous developments within the overall downward trend for the period up to the end of 1994:

- Surplus equipment left over from the Cold War was sold (e.g., the equipment of the German Democratic Republic's forces; the U.S. selling $7 billion worth of surplus equipment).
- Because of the size of the surplus, top-of-the-line equipment including high-specification planes were for sale.
- Buyers were increasingly demanding the capacity to build their own equipment, not merely to buy weapons off the shelf.
- Cut-price rates were being offered, particularly as Russia sought to regain its market share.
- The lower level of monetary value of sales disguised the lethality of the portable arsenals and light weapons being transferred.
- The buyers' market also led to pressure to relax controls (Lumpe 1996: 13–14).

There are clearly difficulties in trying to limit arms transfers as part of an ethical foreign policy, as Robin Cook, the British foreign secretary, is finding. It would be easier to be ethical in a less cut-throat world. To illustrate this point, one could remodel "Prisoner's Dilemma" as "Arms Seller's Dilemma" by using game theory to design models showing likely responses. If one country were to decide radically to cut its arms transfers, some moral pressure would be placed on other countries to behave similarly. But opportunities would also increase for others to move into the gap in the market. The possibilities for coordination of international responses thus hinges on intangibles such as "political will," timing of elections and pressure over jobs, the standing of those pressing for limitation, the likely response of other competitors, and so on. The work of Andrew Pierre (1982), revisited by William Keller (1995), on President Carter's attempts to bring closer together human rights policy and foreign policy and, even under Cold War conditions, to work for limitation of arms transfers together with the Soviet Union provides a salutary lesson.

Dilemmas of Arms Production and Transfer

In this section, without elaborating on them, I will simply list thirteen dilemmas on this subject. Some may not be instantly illuminating, but I believe they are worthy of further thought as they encapsulate a number of the moral conundrums that we must address.

1. The Cold War has ended, but the age of war is not past.
2. We think of wars as the armed forces of country A fighting the armed forces of country B—but almost all postmodern wars are within countries.
3. There is a right to self-determination, but not every ethnic group can have its own state because that is a recipe for permanent warfare, especially in Africa where many of the inherited boundaries make little sense.
4. The state's monopoly of legitimate violence is an important step for civilization, but the state itself is often the biggest threat to people's security, through internal repression and exploitation.
5. Weapons are needed for defense, but more weapons do not necessarily mean more security, even for groups opposing a repressive state, since acquiring more weapons may provoke another turn in the spiral of violence.
6. War is an outmoded institution, but whenever a war occurs, powerful forces think it is advantageous, justified, or necessary.
7. There is a right to self-defense, but insistence on that right pro-

motes the demand for weapons and makes it harder to move beyond war as a means of solving disputes.

8. The five permanent members of the United Nations Security Council have the highest responsibility for world security, but they account for about 85 percent of the conventional arms transfers.

9. Arms control agreements address major weapon systems, but it is the portable weapons (machine guns, sniper rifles, land mines, etc.) that do most of the killing.

10. One side says, "Arms kill people"; the other side says, "People kill people"; but war is really a matter of weapons, warriors, and words.

11. The debate about limiting the arms trade is often polarized between those favoring limitations on the supply side and those favoring limitations on the demand side—but both are necessary.

12. A framework exists for careful assessment of just wars, but in crisis situations, these criteria are applied to justify almost any war.

13. Arms conversion is necessary, but there is never a good time for it. When arms sales are good, why do it? When arms sales are low, we need the jobs.

It would be possible to amplify this list even further. One point does need some additional comment, however brief—namely, the problem of intermediaries. The moral complications of the "middlemen" (and they are usually men) are that exporters can shift the moral responsibility onto the next link in the chain; end-user certificates will be produced to show that the supplier acted in good faith; suppliers can claim that even if they closed down this area of trade, others would not be so scrupulous; and so on. The official British Government Scott Inquiry into the "arms to Iraq" issue produced just such instances with Jordan. This is a tricky area and given the lucrative nature of the business is likely to remain so. It illustrates the need for greater transparency, strict penalties for abuse of the end-user or equivalent systems, and the importance of investigative journalism, even if cases can only be brought to light after the event.

Three Approaches to Arms Sales

In this section, I move to an analysis of the nature of the arms trade. Arms are not like other goods. They are designed to kill, injure, and threaten. What can we say about the morality of the arms market?

Free Market

This first category or argument is put up primarily to show how few people believe it. I have met only one person who argues for something like this view. He is Sam Cummings, the largest small arms salesperson in the world, who is engagingly (or alarmingly) frank in both his view of human nature and his sales philosophy. Few people really advocate anything approaching a free market. Cummings says (as he did when I debated with him on TV) that if governments really believed their rhetoric, this would dispose of almost all of the arms trade. They do not, so they are hypocritical. Why should he have more scruples? He will sell what he can make a profit from, within the laws of the land. The depths of human folly have not yet been plumbed. Cummings is a friendly, amusing, and urbane person. His sales philosophy and his pessimistic view of human nature fit well together. But there are other consistent worldviews, too.

Total Ban

The clearest case for a total ban on arms transfers is obviously a pacifist one. It is wrong to kill, maim, or injure other people. Therefore, by extension it is also wrong to threaten to do so. It is also wrong to possess the technology that would enable one to do so. It is therefore wrong to supply that technology to other people.

Anthony Sampson (1991: 386) in his classic book *The Arms Bazaar,* argues that the arms trade is the parallel for our times of the slave trade. If this is true, then the abolitionist case would hold. The morally correct position would then be to stop the arms trade, in an analogous way to the campaign during the nineteenth century by the slaves themselves, Wilberforce and other campaigners, parliamentary and public lobbyists. The slave trade was quite simply wrong and therefore had to be stopped. Sampson argues that the parallels are clear. With the arms trade as with slavery, the major powers could stop an economically lucrative trade that did immense human damage. Cardinal Basil Hume has advanced a similar argument, likening the arms trade to drug pushing. As with the heroin trade, the users become addicted. Others make money from this destructive dependency, and in Hume's view, the main blame is with the pushers—the major industrial powers.

These are rhetorical arguments with great emotive force, but in the last analysis they fall short. There are justifiable uses for weapons in defense and deterrence, whereas it is now overwhelmingly accepted that slavery is not a morally justifiable system. There are also controlled medical uses for drugs.

Responsible Limitation

If the preceding argument is accepted, we are now at a point where the argument for responsible limitation is the one that needs to be discussed. The question then becomes the formulation of detailed criteria and how to put them into practice. The key point is that arms are not like other goods. They are, by and large, engineering and electronics, but it is an ethically more serious thing to provide a weapon system than a washing machine or a car. Weapons are specifically designed to deter and, if necessary, to kill or injure. The conditional intention to kill someone is a serious matter. People can be killed and are killed by cars, but cars are not designed for that purpose. (Of course, to use a car deliberately to kill someone is seen as a crime—both capacity and intention are relevant—but cars are designed to get people from A to B.) The Vatican has therefore concluded "arms are not like other goods." Those who get the weapons have the main responsibility for how they are used. But the supplier also bears some responsibility.

Some sorts of weapons—weapons of mass destruction, unnecessarily inhumane and brutal weapons, those prohibited from transfer by international law—should obviously not be transferred. It is right to discriminate in the supply of weapons. Almost every country does so, at least by not providing them to their enemies or those who they think could be their enemies. The question then becomes what further criteria are needed.

An Approach to Responsible Limitation

In the Church of England report *Responsibility in Arms Transfer Policy,* the performance characteristics of the weapon are considered relevant. So is dual-use technology that can significantly enhance the aggressive and/or repressive capacity of a state. The third area is the intentions and capacity of the recipient. The report summarizes as follows:

• There is a right of self-defense.
• Weapons have legitimate uses, both threatened and actual.
• Since not all countries produce weapons, some supply of weapons is acceptable and, indeed, necessary.
• It is right to discriminate in the supply of weapons, in accordance with a realistic assessment of how they are likely to be used.
• Political judgment, informed by ethical evaluation, not commercial criteria, should play the key role in the decision whether to supply (Church of England 1994: 9).

The report also calls for an approach "generally acknowledged as being ethically responsible, transparent, publicly accountable and consistent" (Church of England 1994: 46). It is clearly directed toward the British national context but can easily be adapted to fit the international level, since the same criteria would apply (e.g., for the U.N. Security Council and General Assembly), regional groupings (the European Union), alliances based on economic power (the G7/G8), military cooperation (NATO, Organization for Security and Cooperation in Europe) or role within the international system (P5). The detailed criteria elaborated by the Church of England report are:

• subordination of commercial criteria to political and ethical judgment;
• clear separation between arms transfers and aid policy;

- refusal of arms transfers to countries engaged in or likely to engage in aggression;
- refusal of arms transfers to regions of tension, except to countries acknowledged to be under threat and insufficiently armed to be able effectively to exercise the right of self-defense (Article 51 of the U.N. Charter);
- removal of direct and indirect government subsidies for arms transfers;
- rejection of arms transfers to countries guilty of grave and consistent patterns of human rights violations or involved in unnecessarily high levels of arms spending (i.e., good government criteria);
- rejection of arms transfers to countries in breach of international law and those that refuse to participate in international arms control negotiations and respect international agreements;
- support for an international ban on the production and transfer of antipersonnel mines, including prohibition of their export from the United Kingdom; and
- development of both national and international approaches for responsible limitation of arms transfers (Church of England 1994: 46–47).

Togehter these criteria build up the sort of guiding principles needed to develop a responsible policy. They do not provide a neat, simple answer. But the problem is not of that kind—it is genuinely difficult. We can now explore some of the difficulties with the Church of England's criteria.

Economic Interest for Supply against Ethical Interest for Responsible Limitation

One example can be given of the difficulty of getting a country such as Britain, which is heavily dependent on the arms trade, to adopt a consistent ethical policy on this issue, in spite of proclamations by Tony Blair's Labour government of its intention to do so. The situation in East Timor shows that arms sales continue to countries even when they are illegally occupying a neighboring country. In contrast to the Allied mobilization against Saddam Hussein when Iraq marched into Kuwait, Indonesia's occupation of East Timor, now lasting well over twenty years, has not stopped the Indonesians from acquiring considerable quantities of weapons. The British government has tried to insist that the key issue is whether British Aerospace Hawk planes have actually been used in combat in East Timor (Saferworld 1997a). The key issue is why the British government is still prepared to confer international respectability on the Indonesian government in spite of this long-standing and grave contravention of international law.

Weapons Should Not Be Supplied to Areas of Tension, but They Are the Ones That Want the Weapons

The terminology "areas of tension" emerged from German legislation. At first sight, prohibition of exports to areas of tension seems absurd, naive, and other-worldly. Areas of harmony, sweetness, and light do not want to spend huge sums on the acquisition of weapons. The history of the arms buildup in the Middle East over recent decades is a salutary lesson. One dimension is the interplay between the Israeli-Arab tension and Cold War rivalry. A second is the readiness of major suppliers to provide, in a completely cynical fashion, weapons to Iran and Iraq to fuel their appalling war (Sweeney 1993; Timberman 1992). It was then hardly surprising that Iraq, having finished the war, having seen a blind eye turned even to the use of chemical weapons against its Cartouche citizens at Halabja, was prepared to risk the invasion of Kuwait.

Arms Embargos Look Moral but Can Have Undesirable Effects

The carefully defined proviso relating to an internationally recognized need for support in exercising the right of self-defense is of great importance. To ban totally arms transfers to regions of tension could have perverse consequences. A historical example can illustrate this. If such legislation had been in place in the United States at the beginning of World War II, Lend-Lease would not have been possible, and Britain could well have been defeated as a result. A more recent example is the case of Bosnia. Unarguably, in spite of the fact that Bosnia was undoubtedly in an area of tension, arms should have been provided to Bosnia to enable it to exercise effectively the right of self-defense under Article 51 of the U.N. Charter. If a country cannot defend itself effectively, if the international community cannot or will not do it, then there is a moral argument for arms supplies in order for that country to defend itself. The danger, as I argued myself at the time, is that this would, in the image used by former British foreign secretary Douglas Hurd, simply create a level killing field. It is necessary to call attention to such hard cases, because the ethical evaluation of arms transfers depends on the careful assessment of other possibilities for reasonably just resolution of a conflict. The just war criterion of violence as a "last resort" must also apply to the means of warfare.

What Right Do the Main Arms Suppliers Have to Sit in Judgment on the Good Government of Others?

A moral dilemma is implicit in the "good government" criterion. What right do the main arms suppliers (particularly the P5 and Germany) have to sit in judgment over other countries and determine what their defense needs are? The report of the South Commission (1990: 53) chaired by Julius Nyerere, provides a succinct answer: "only a few developing countries can rightly claim that their military expenditure is proportionate either to any external threat or to the resources at their disposal."

What Can Be Done? Toward a Pragmatic Program of Practical Steps

Most of prior argument here has centered on ethical dilemmas and should make clear that I hold out no hope for easy solutions. But steps can be taken, albeit of a pragmatic and cumulative nature. In some situations arms supplies are legitimate. The arms trade is big business. For these two reasons a total ban is neither ethically desirable nor practical. Yet the arms trade does immense damage. The only way forward is to try to limit it in a morally responsible way, through campaigning and negotiation, through pressure and agreement.

Banning Certain Categories of Weapon

Events have moved on since the criterion relating to land mines was formulated, and it clearly shows evidence of its U.K. domestic origin. What is wrong with land mines? An increasing consensus suggests that they should be banned because of their indiscriminate effects, the devastating consequences of preventing use of land for decades, and the return of populations after hostilities cease. Their military utility in certain circumstances is clear (e.g., for those seeking to control a long border with too few troops), which is why nothing short of an international ban will do. Even such a ban is not enough, since the mines also have to be cleared. Banning and clearing mines would be a significant step but would still leave many other types of weapon with which the killing will continue.

The international NGO coalition, stretching from Vietnam veterans, former military commanders, aid and refugee organizations, church groups, and others, has had a remarkable effect in galvanizing public opinion. The international campaign has been rewarded with the Nobel Peace Prize. Even princesses have endorsed the campaign against land mines: Christina Magnuson of the Swedish Red Cross articulated her concern publicly in 1993 (Magnuson & Sjöquist 1993), and Princess Diana braved public criticism from Conservative government spokespeople who called her (inappropriately in this context) a "loose cannon." The Canadian government mobilized support for its Ottawa declaration that was agreed in December 1997, in spite of U.S. failure fully to support it. Other candidates for banning include blinding laser weapons.

The Need for International Remedies

In Britain, the stock phrase used by advocates of less stringent arms transfer criteria is "If we don't sell them, somebody else will." Usually the name of the somebody else was supplied—the French, for example, particularly when Margaret Thatcher was prime minister, as she was immensely irritated that Britain's continental partners were out-performing the country in defense sales. This argument holds a germ of truth. It must be turned around: both national controls and negotiated multilateral controls are necessary. In this regard the work being done by such organizations as Saferworld in London to promote a European Code of Conduct is of great importance. They are also promoting a similar approach at the worldwide level with a panel of Nobel Peace Prize laureates, including Oscar Arias and former Archbishop Desmond Tutu (Saferworld 1997b). The U.N. Register of Conventional Arms Transfers also provides a good basis on which to build, although that so far is a means of recording rather than restricting arms sales. Its main limitations are that it is currently a reporting mechanism after arms sales have been made and that it only deals with the transfer of major weapon systems, not with domestic stocks and acquisitions. It is to be hoped that something similar to the U.N. Conventional Arms Trade Register in the small arms field will emerge as a result of the U.N. expert panel and other initiatives on this subject (Regehr 1997).

Concentrate on Small Arms and Portable Weaponry

Even in the most difficult area of this field—that of the portable weapons, which do most of the killing—things can be done. Bishop Dinis Sengulane, the Anglican bishop in Mozambique who was awarded the first peace prize of the All Africa Conference of Churches, told me of the approach adopted under a "swords into plowshares" scheme of the Mozambican churches. In a televised ceremony, people who returned machine guns were offered a bicycle or a sewing machine in exchange. With a wry smile, he said that no one who handed in any weapons was doing it on their own behalf; it was always for a friend. "But," he said, "does that matter?" The important thing is to take some of the weapons out of circulation.

Weapons can be removed from circulation by various other means. At first it seems a completely impossible task, but work headed by Virginia Gamba and conducted through the United National Institute for Disarmament Research (UNIDIR, Geneva) has looked at a number of postconflict situations (including Rhodesia-Zimbabwe, Croatia

and Bosnia-Herzegovina, Mozambique, and Cambodia) and concluded that immediately, right at the beginning of a postconflict phase
of reconstruction, possibilities exist for a limited period of aid-for-
weapons swaps or other incentives. Of course, difficulties emerge
with such approaches. If the period is too short, it does not have the
right effect. If it is too long, it can merely serve to create a market for
weapons. Disarmament of one group while others retain their weapons can be a recipe for renewed conflict, and so on. Interest is increasing in the field of microdisarmament and the transition from civil war
to reconstruction. This development is an encouraging sign and a
long-overdue response to the cries for help from countries devastated
by civil war and the development agencies that act as a "voice for the
voiceless" in the rich countries of the North, which supply most of
the weapons.

An important goal is to draw lessons from the land mines campaign
and look at how to devise a major campaign to close down the illicit
market in arms, particularly small arms (Federation of American Scientists 1997). This approach should be in governments' interest, even
though it is difficult, since, by definition, the illicit arms trade is illegal
somewhere. This task is, however, not so easy, given the lucrative
nature of the trade, the long delivery routes, and the difficulty of effectively controlling borders. The need for international cooperation is
very obvious.

Conclusion

It is hard to outline a program of viable practical steps. The human
suffering caused by the arms trade is on such a vast scale that moral
revulsion pushes one toward calling for a total ban. Careful analysis
indicates that this would be morally problematic. A healthy skepticism about the possibilities of limitation, particularly in a field so
lucrative as arms transfers, pulls in both directions—emphasizing the
need for, and the difficulty of, responsible limitation. Furthermore,
the design of an effective package depends on the readiness of other
actors to respond in consort. Surely in the rich world, at least, the
source of most of the weapons with which the killing is done, it is

possible to make some decisions—to rule out arms transfers to the dictators and murderers; to pay more for our own defense, if need be, rather than subsidize our defense at the expense of endangering others elsewhere through arms transfers (hardly a moral option); to develop socially useful products and invest in social infrastructure rather than sell more weapons to keep jobs. The economies of the rich world will not collapse if arms transfers are limited. Rich nations will not be unable to defend themselves unless they export large quantities of arms to fuel conflict elsewhere. Exported arms have at least a potential "boomerang effect," endangering the security of the supplier in some cases and creating population flows of refugees (Smith 1992). Conversion is possible—the world saw a massive reorientation away from military production after World War II. Both economies and workforces were reoriented toward civilian production.

The bottom line remains: arms are not like other goods. They are designed to kill, injure, and threaten. If we provide these weapons, we bear some responsibility for how they are used. That is why responsible and coordinated limitation of arms transfers is essential.

References

Ahlström, Christer, and Kjell-Åke Nordquist. *Casualties of Conflict: Report for the World Campaign for the Protection of Victims of War.* Uppsala: Department of Peace and Conflict Research, Uppsala University, 1991.

Assefa, Hizkias. *Mediation of Civil Wars: Approaches and Strategies—The Sudan Conflict.* Boulder, Colo.: Westview, 1987.

Black, Ian, and David Fairhall. "The Profits of Doom." *Guardian,* 16 October 1997, 17.

Church of England. *Responsibility in Arms Transfer Policy.* London: General Synod of the Church of England, 1994.

Federation of American Scientists. *Public Interest Report,* July/August 1997.

Harris, Marvin. *Our Kind.* New York: Harper, 1989.

Hobsbawm, Eric. *Age of Extremes: The Short Twentieth Century 1914–1991.* London: Abacus, 1995.

Human Rights Watch. *Civilian Devastation: Abuses by All Parties in the War in Southern Sudan.* New York: Human Rights Watch, 1994.

———. *Behind the Red Line: Political Repression in Sudan.* New York: Human Rights Watch, 1996.

Keller, William W. *Arm in Arm: The Political Economy of the Global Arms Trade.* New York: HarperCollins, 1995.

Kolko, Gabriel. *Century of War: Politics, Conflict and Society since 1914.* New York: New Press, 1994.

Lumpe, Lore. "The Military Burden," in *World Military and Social Expenditures 1996*, Ruth Leger Sivard, ed. Washington, D.C.: World Priorities, 1996.

Magnuson, Christina, and Börje Sjöqvist. "Mines—Weapons That Kill and Maim for Generations." In *Selling Weapons: A Deadly Business*, Börje Sjöqvist and Roger Williamson, eds. Stockholm: Swedish Red Cross, 1993.

Pierre, Andrew. *The Global Politics of Arms Sales.* Princeton, N.J.: Princeton University Press, 1982.

Regehr, Ernie. "Militarizing Despair: The Politics of Small Arms," *New Routes* (Uppsala, Life and Peace Institute) 4 (1994): 3–6.

Saferworld (ed. Michael Cranna). *The True Cost of Conflict.* London: Earthscan, 1994.

———. (ed. Malcolm Chalmers). *British Arms Export Policy and Indonesia.* London: Saferworld, 1997a.

———. *Network: Newsletter on Arms Export Controls.* London: Saferworld, Summer 1997b.

Sampson, Anthony. *The Arms Bazaar in the Nineties from Krupp to Saddam.* London: Hodder & Stoughton, 1991.

Sivard, Ruth Leger, ed. *World Military and Social Expenditures 1996.* Washington, D.C.: World Priorities, 1996.

Sjöqvist, Börje, and Roger Williamson, eds. *Selling Weapons: A Deadly Business.* Stockholm: Swedish Red Cross, 1993.

Smith, Dan. "The Sixth Boomerang: Conflict and War," in *The Debt Boomerang*, ed. Susan George. London & Boulder, Colo.: Pluto Press with the Transnational Institute, 1992.

South Commission. *The Challenge to the South: The Report of the South Commission.* Oxford: Oxford University Press, 1990.

Stockholm International Peace Research Institute. *SIPRI Yearbook: Armaments, Disarmament and International Security.* Oxford: Oxford University Press, 1996.

———. *SIPRI Yearbook: Armaments, Disarmament and International Security.* Oxford: Oxford University Press, 1997.

Sweeney, John. *Trading with the Enemy: Britain's Arming of Iraq.* London: Pan Macmillan, 1993.

Timmerman, Kenneth R. *The Death Lobby: How the West Armed Iraq.* London: Bantam, 1992.

15

A Future, If One Is Still Alive

The challenge of the HIV Epidemic

Elizabeth Reid

Inside and outside situations of conflict, the HIV virus acts like, or is felt to act like, a terrorizing force. It does not strike randomly, but one does not know where or when it will next appear. It rarely attacks singly but infiltrates in clusters. Eighty percent of affected families have more than one member infected with HIV, usually both husband and wife, and often a number of children. In many affected families, three generations of women are infected. It penetrates homes, families, communities, and workplaces. It terrorizes whole populations.

It undermines intimacy, love, moral and bodily integrity, respect, and trust, unraveling the fabric of interpersonal relations and social cohesion in its wake. It "targets" leaders, teachers, and health workers, those whose work symbolizes shared values and aspirations but whose wealth, social position, and mobility have led many of them to become infected. It produces demoralization and fear as people fail to find ways to speak about it or to react and protect themselves. The resulting social and economic dysfunctionality relentlessly leads to mistrust, the refusal of intimacy and sexuality, interpersonal violence, political unrest, destitution, and conflict.

HIV in Situations of Conflict

In humanitarian emergencies, the virus spreads even more rapidly than in nonconflictual situations. Yet rarely in situations of conflict, or even postconflict or demobilization, is attention focused on the symbiotic relationship among violence, displacement and brutality, their psychosocial effects, and the spread of the HIV epidemic. Other pressing priorities take precedence; HIV can, maybe should, be done "later."

It is rare indeed that bandits, soldiers, or terrorized communities organize to respond to the epidemic. It is equally rare to find humanitarian organizations or peacekeeping forces supporting them in such an endeavor. Why is there this lack of action?

The rapidity with which the HIV virus can spread is difficult for people to conceive. In one country, Swaziland, infection rates went from 4 percent of the adult population to 21 percent in one year, 1994, in peacetime. In situations of conflict it spreads seemingly indiscriminately to humanitarian workers, children, health workers, police, teachers, peacekeepers, soldiers, mercenaries, bandits, rebels, warlords, and others. The death HIV causes is not immediate. It is protracted, occurring maybe a decade or so after infection, often long after the conflict has ended. The effect of the sudden spread of the virus in Swaziland, for example, will be a sudden increase in illness and death in the population, but not for another five to ten years.

In this, it is dramatically unlike epidemics in which the time from infection to death is only a matter of days and so causality and effect are pressingly visible. Is it this feature of the HIV epidemic, this long period between infection and death, that impedes effective programming during humanitarian emergencies?

Imagine a summary execution in which the person executed stands up, walks away, and continues to live for maybe another seven to ten years before dropping dead, at some unpredictable time, from the wound inflicted during the execution. Acts of summary execution are morally condemned, but what would be the content of the moral condemnation in such a case: that this is murder that may take a decade to prove, and so the murderer cannot be condemned until then? Or would the act of execution itself be condemned, regardless of whether the person died instantaneously or later, having lived in fear and uncertainty of exactly when?

The reluctance or refusal to address the epidemic in conflict and postconflict situations may arise from this aspect of HIV infection, this stretching out of time between an act and its final direct consequence. It is arguable that the omission amounts to morally culpable neglect, in itself and because an HIV-infected person will most probably, unintentionally or otherwise, infect a number of other people before he or she dies. Yet this argument can only be made if effective HIV programming is possible in such circumstances.

Evidence indicates that this so. For example, Mozambican refugees arrived in Malawi with lower rates of infection than the surrounding population. Despite extensive economic and social interaction with the surrounding populations, the camp communities retained these lower rates by mobilizing to protect themselves. Also, organizations working among the Rwandan refugee populations in Tanzania helped the camp populations establish treatment programs for sexually transmitted infections (STIs), HIV education, and condom-distribution programs.

However, in the turmoil caused by conflict, HIV is usually eclipsed by other seemingly more pressing concerns.

HIV and Humanitarian Assistance

Humanitarian assistance concerns itself with the immediate: with palliation or treatment rather than prevention, with triage rather than complexity, with the short term rather than the longer term. Yet with HIV, even in situations of upheaval, scarcity, and chaos, the immediate is prevention. The psychology of emergencies may need to adjust accordingly.

HIV programs can best be established in crisis situations when effective programs have been put in place upstream—that is, in the preconflict period. Wherever people have the habit of talking about the difficult issues involved, of supporting the affected and protecting themselves, humanitarian programs can ensure that they continue to have access to the technology of protection: to condoms, diaphragms, and appropriate spermicides; soap and rubber gloves; sterile needles. They can, whenever possible, create spaces and occasions for discussion and the strengthening of mechanisms and habits of mutual concern and support. Whenever medical staff are already trained in the care and support of HIV-infected people, this training can continue to the extent possible in the circumstances.

Such programming is possible, but one should bear in mind that the response to the HIV epidemic to date has been of only limited efficacy: the epidemic continues to spread at an increasing rate (UNAIDS 1997). The lesson being learned is that *how* things are done is often more important than *what* is done. A sense of urgency has led to the use of more directive than interactive approaches, a tendency that often fails to mobilize local and national resources and frustrates the possibility of engagement and sustainability. The resource most needed for an effective response is people willing to converse with, and work supportively in partnership with, others on all aspects of the epidemic over time.

The task of humanitarian relief has been described as bringing a minimum of humanity into a situation that should not exist (Rieff 1995/1996: 6). Yet, in the fast-growing literature on the ethics of humanitarian interventions, the moral discourse has been predominantly focused on the response rather than on those who created the situations. Warnings have been sounded:

> In debates about humanitarian ethics . . . relief agencies and their critics have tended to overstate the moral burden on humanitarianism—perhaps because it is easier to accuse a relief agency than a warlord these days. But it should never be forgotten that relief agencies are always responding to the atrocities of others. . . . [T]he accusations of blame should be put squarely where they are most obviously due: with the killers, the rapists, the dispossessors and their political leaders who initiate and sustain the policies of excessive violence in today's wars and genocides. (Slim 1996: 2)

Similarly with HIV, attention has been focused on the rights and duties of the infected, less so on the moral questions raised by the adequacy of the response, rarely on the value systems that spread the virus, and virtually never on the behaviors and value systems that will enable communities and nations to survive it, whether in situations of conflict or otherwise (Reid 1995: 6).

Those who spread the HIV virus do so through behavior for which they may feel no shame or responsibility. Their sexual behavior is often socially tolerated or even encouraged, particularly in men. The spread of the epidemic through such social norms is not usually addressed, and it is rare indeed for those who spread the epidemic to be challenged to account for their actions.

In the same way, humanitarian assistance often focuses on the moral adequacy of the response rather than addressing itself to the warriors and warlords, the disciplined forces and the bandits, or the political economy that create or sustain situations of conflict. Strategies to confront the powerful and the conflict-hungry are difficult to advocate, more difficult to implement. Those who spread the HIV virus are powerful. It is they who determine or control the conditions under which sexual intercourse takes place.

The spread of the HIV epidemic reveals the nature of social and economic institutions and the systems of relationships, rules, traditions, and values that shape the behaviors of people within society. These same systems are also the causes and consequences of violence and conflict. The nature and complexity of this linkage between HIV and violence is not widely understood.

Humanitarian assistance is an attempt to protect the lives of and to ensure a future for those whose world has been uprooted and rendered asunder by conflict. Among those who survive the conflict and the camps, too many will die from HIV infections gained during the period of humanitarian assistance. Furthermore, the consequence of continuing rapid and extensive spread of the epidemic will be the exacerbation of conflict and lawlessness, and the rapid breakdown of the fabric of social relationships. Ironically, this situation will increase significantly the demand for humanitarian interventions in the future.

Moral Competition in Humanitarian Assistance

Any agency responding to situations of conflict will be faced with difficult programming choices. HIV programming is only one of many pressing imperatives, doing it well is difficult, and there are costs involved. Priorities will have to be set, and so the moral cost of not acting will need to be taken into account. How can it be determined whether HIV programs have a higher moral claim than other programs, if such choices must be made?

The impact in terms of lives, disruption, pain, violence, and suffering of not acting may be immense and its full extent not known for generations. The determination of the extent to which these consequences can be lessened by effective programs is extremely difficult.

Making difficult decisions about the use of scarce resources such as time and money in a situation of conflict, and in particular about whether to address the issues around HIV, will require both the imaginative capacity of prophecy or foresight to see the consequences of inaction, which capacity few yet have with respect to the HIV epidemic, and the technical capacity to know how to do whatever of value can be done in constantly changing circumstances or where to turn to for help. Such a situation is typical of the moral confusions that the HIV epidemic brings in its wake.

In such circumstances, there is no system of principles or rules by which such decision making can be made or judged. Nor do we need one. What is needed is understanding, which is a prerequisite for sensitive and constructive moral deliberation; imagination, which is a prerequisite for the moral skill of empathy; and the capacity to be responsible to one's self and to others.

The Symbiotic Relationships between the HIV Epidemic and Violence

The HIV Epidemic and Civil-Military Interactions

The spread of the epidemic through situations of conflict is not limited to the actual geographic or temporal dimensions of conflict. The web of social and sexual interactions between military and civil populations is dense and intricate, and HIV travels rapidly through its connecting threads: to wives, girlfriends, sexual partners, and rapees, and from them to the soldiers. One example of these dynamics can be found in the complex relationships among the past presence of a military base in Honduras; the political, economic, and other conditions that led to its establishment and extended presence there; and the fact that Honduras has the highest rates of HIV infection in the subregion and that the initial epicenters of the epidemic included the bars and brothels surrounding the base (Chelala 1990: 153–54).

The separation of soldiers from their wives and communities, low rates of pay, and a culture that does not encourage or ensure that remittances are sent home make it likely that the transmission may be from spouses to soldiers as well as vice versa. Further, those left destitute by pillage and wanton destruction by the military may become infected because of the strategies they adopt to try to re-create homes and livelihoods: outmigration, prostitution, and so on.

Brutality, arrogance, conflict, and violence are breeding grounds for the spread of HIV. Soldiers are trained for conflict. The capacity, and often the desire, for violence are drilled and marched into them. The marching songs of many armies are as abusive, crude, arrogant, brutal, and degrading to women as the men and their officers can make them. The exercise of this brutality is not limited to situations of conflict; the brutality is too often expressed sexually. Assaultive or nonconsensual sex often becomes a behavioral norm, as does nonprotected sex.

Some observers believe that since 1980, more U.N. peacekeeping troops have died of AIDS, or will soon die of AIDS, than have been killed in combat. In early 1996, over 50,000 U.N. troops were deployed on sixteen different assignments (*Alliance* 2, no. 1:1). Deployment, return, and demobilization create their own patterns of spread.

Infection rates among soldiers in Africa are now so high that they have a greater risk of dying from AIDS than from warfare (*Alliance* no. 1, 4: 3). Much, if not most, of this infection occurred in peacetime.

Conflict, peacekeeping, and troop deployment have in common two important factors. First, soldiers in camps often consecutively use the same women for sex. If condoms are not used, the seminal fluids may remain in the woman's vaginal tract, and the men may infect each other from their own sperm. Furthermore, different companies of troops are posted to the same place one after the other. They are serviced by the same group of women, and increasing infection in both the women and the following groups of soldiers ensues.

The Complex Relationships amongst HIV, Violence, and Gender: Rwanda

The complexity of these interrelations can be seen in a case study of Rwanda. Less information is available for other sites of bloody conflict, but the outlines of their dynamics will be similar.

HIV infection rates were extremely high in urban Rwanda long before the genocide of 1994: among the urban educated and wealthy possibly as high as 50 to 60 percent, among women who are sex workers virtually 100 percent. Infection rates were so high in the officer corps of the Rwandan army before the events in 1994 that some annual intakes reported that very few officers were left alive (Gordon 1991). Infection rates in the Rwandan army in early 1994 were thought to be as high as 60 percent (*Alliance* 1, no. 2: 3).

Nothing is known about the possible effects of the psychological and socioeconomic impact on people living within such an epidemic and the extent to which this might have affected what happened. Was the fear and paralysis generated by the epidemic a contributing factor to the behavior of the perpetrators of the genocide, or are the behaviors that spread the epidemic and the behavior of the perpetrators both causally related to other features of Rwandan society—population density, cultural values, social structures, poverty, memories, and so forth?

There is evidence, especially in the testimony of the women involved, that particularly toward the end of the genocide, a conscious strategy was adopted by the militia to infect women with HIV rather than to kill them outright. Militia members who were sick and suspected of having AIDS were used for this end. This tactic was often done within the women's own villages and so was known to their families and neighbors. The women were then left to live with the fear, shame, and other terrible social, psychological, and physical consequences of rape and HIV infection in these circumstances. It is estimated that over 250,000 women were raped, tortured, mutilated, and assaulted, and left to live (Royte 1997: 37). The rape and violence continued in the refugee camps (Munyemana and Muhongayire 1995: 9).

The rape and violence continue today in a social form. Seventy percent of the present Rwandan population is female, of whom 60 percent are widows. These figures are similar to those of postwar Cambodia, which now has one of the fastest-spreading epidemics in the world. Rwandan society has no place for these women, and their social marginalization is worsened by rumors and accusations of HIV infection in them and their children. Only in urban areas might some of these women find means of support. For the rest, virtually whatever strategies, social or economic, that these women adopt to support themselves and their children will place them at further risk of infection, reinfection, or progression to illness and death.

The direct outcomes of the spread of HIV in conflict and postconflict situations are psychological and social trauma, illness, and death. As this epidemic increases, the ensuing adverse impact on social relations and productive capacity leads to destitution, insecurity, lawlessness, political unrest, violence, and even conflict. Effective prevention, support, and care programs may minimize the extent of these dislocations.

Effective HIV Programming in Conflict, Postconflict, and Peacekeeping Situations

Upstream and Downstream

The nature of the epidemic and our responses to it mean that to be effective, programs must be intensively interpersonal, sustained over time, inclusive, participative, and generative of a sense of agency, and so of hope.

There are settings that are more conducive than others to the establishment of such programs: political and governmental stability, an effective legal system, a strong civil society, traditions of public debate and intellectual engagement, human rights activism, an openness to social critique and change. During conflict, the setting is nonconducive, and effectiveness will depend to a great extent on upstream work—that is, the programs that had been put in place before the conflict broke out.

This situation was seen vividly in the Rwandan refugee camps in Zaire, where it was those previously engaged in community-based HIV programs who argued strongly, but unsuccessfully, for their continuation in the camps (Desclaux and Raynaut 1997: 98). Similarly, where peer groups or buddy relations have been established among armed forces personnel, it is believed that the moderating influence of peer concern will assist in sustaining protective sexual behavior.

The kinds of programs that can be implemented in situations of conflict will depend on the nature of the conflict. Often HIV programs may best be integrated into existing programs. Even during bitter conflict, if food distribution is logistically possible, so too is condom distribution. The limitations of "condom aid" can be understood in the different signification of this phrase and the term "condom assistance" (Weir 1990: 1). This is the difference between a supply-side approach and interactive interventions. Although the success of most HIV programs depends on the quality of the interpersonal interface into which they are embedded, access to condoms is essential wherever there are people who want to use them.

Where drugs are being distributed, drugs for the treatment of STIs, reproductive tract infections, other genital trauma-producing conditions, and HIV-related opportunistic infections can be included. Wherever health and trauma services are being provided, all personnel should follow infection control procedures.

Human rights monitoring can also be used during conflict to raise and place in question certain practices. HIV-sensitive human rights monitoring during the Rwandan genocide could have clarified for the international community whether people with AIDS were being used by the militia and others as weapons of war. If so, the issue could have been brought to the attention of the international community in much the same way that, for example, the rape of women in Serbia and Croatia was. It could also be argued that, since the link between conflict and the rapid spread of the epidemic is so strong, it is a human right that HIV programs be established and that all such situations should be monitored for coverage and appropriateness of these programs and accountability required for them.

Human rights monitoring can occur at a number of levels: the existence or otherwise of effective HIV programs, the use of HIV as a strategy of war, the extent of HIV-transmitting behavior, especially rape. This monitoring could strengthen the capacity of the humanitarian community for HIV moral discourse and decision making.

In this time of HIV and AIDS, consideration must be given to the impact of other actions on the epidemic. Upstream efforts to contain or prevent conflict can have a detrimental effect on the spread of the HIV epidemic and programs to minimize its impact. Sanctions currently in place in Burundi have had an adverse effect on HIV and tuberculosis (TB) treatment and prevention programs in the military and the civilian populations. The voluntary testing and counseling services run for the general population by the associations of people living with HIV and a number of HIV/AIDS service organizations have had to stop because of the unavailability of testing kits. Treatment drugs, whether for HIV, STIs, or TB, are unavailable. Supplies for protection and prevention have run out. This is not a unique moral quandary. The same situation is found in Cambodia and Iraq, for example. But little moral discourse has occurred around the ethics and human cost of impeding HIV programs in such circumstances.

Learning Lessons: The Armed Forces and the Military Life Cycle

Within the contexts of the armed forces, much work has been done to identify effective approaches to behavioral change. These include a combination of forces-wide discussion and education programs, social support systems, and skills training, together with command support and leadership. Studies undertaken in the U.S. armed forces have shown that successful programs consistently employ several common elements, including skills building for condom use and alcohol reduction; social support systems, including peer educators and buddy systems; group problem solving and discussions, which establish supportive community norms; and programs sustained over time.

Within the context of sustained forces-wide interventions, subprograms have been developed targeting specific times in the military operational cycle. Studies have identified the postdeployment period as a time of high unsafe behavior, characterized by the highest rates of sex without a condom, sexual bingeing, and mixing sex with alcohol. In a study of troops returning from Operation Desert Storm/ Desert Shield, STIs increased to three times the predeployment rate during this period, followed by a gradual return to the baseline (Hendrix 1997: 5).

Demobilization is another time in the military cycle when special attention must be paid to targeted HIV programs. This point raises the issue of the responsibilities of the armed forces vis-à-vis the general population. Demobilization might be considered as the end point of military responsibility or, alternatively, as a transition point of intense civil-military interaction. The Bolivian armed forces, for example, train soldiers in simple health diagnosis and care and encourage them to work with local health services on their demobilization. Their names are sent to the health services, and continuing contact is kept.

Other armed forces—for example, in Togo (Bassabi 1997) and Thailand (Hendrix 1997: 7)—have also adopted an approach based on the establishment of peer norms of safe behavior and systems of mutual support on leave or deployment. The Senegalese peacekeeping forces in the Central African Republic (CAR) invited the CAR network of people living with HIV and AIDS to carry out sensitization, education, and discussion programs with them. The significance of this example of civil-military collaboration lies in its effective interlinking of care and prevention: the self-respect and sense of competency of the resource persons were strengthened, and the pertinence of the prevention programs was heightened for the troops.

Studies undertaken in the armed forces of the Central African Republic (Gondje et al. 1997: 159) and Ivory Coast (Lorougnon et al. 1997: 160) show a dramatic decline in HIV infection rates and STI rates with the introduction of HIV programs. However, the success of these programs is jeopardized by the poverty of the armed forces, which prevents them from making condoms reliably available. Although soldiers in the Ivory Coast are required to purchase condoms from their meager pay, condom usage rates have gone from 5 percent in 1994 to 10 percent in 1996. Evidence indicates a stronger willingness and desire to change that is shown in STI rates, which have dropped from 30 percent to 7 percent in the same period. Many development assistance agencies have been reluctant to fund the armed forces, but, as in so many ways, the HIV epidemic is challenging not only a somewhat simplistic dichotomy between civil and military populations but also between security and development.

Programs of support and care are beginning to be established for HIV-infected personnel and their families. The Malawi army recently walked from one end of the country to the other raising funds for such families. Military personnel in Malawi are extending their HIV protection and care programs into surrounding communities and so strengthening civil-military relationships in a country where the military, for budgetary reasons, must rely on families and communities to care for sick personnel who wish to return home to die.

The documentation, advocacy, and dissemination of these studies and experiences, and the catalyzing of attention to the epidemic in the armed forces and, more recently, the disciplined forces around the world, has been an important achievement of the Civil-Military Alliance to Combat HIV and AIDS. The alliance was started in 1994 by a colonel in the U.S. military, the editor of the *AIDS and Society* newsletter, and the U.N. Development Program (UNDP). Its Declaration of Principles was adopted at a meeting in Berlin later that year. Active regional and a number of subregional networks now operate in every part of the world.

Through the work of alliance members, the military commands and the medical corps of the armed forces are becoming engaged, partnerships are being established between the military and civil organizations, military epidemiological data are being released and discussed, personnel policies are being reviewed, the other disciplined or uniformed forces are being mobilized, U.N. peacekeeping policies and programs are being strengthened, and a focus is emerging on issues around women in the military.

HIV and Refugee Populations

The lessons learned within military situations are of value beyond these settings and could well be taken into account in the design of HIV programs in refugee camps and their surrounding populations. Few such programs have been set up despite the existence in these populations of most of the factors that place communities at risk of increasing levels of infection: the disintegration of community and family life, marital disruption and breakdown, weakening of social norms governing sexuality and social values, extensive dependency and poverty, increasing commercial sex, sexual violence and rape, and a lack of STI and other services and condoms.

The first large-scale HIV program established in a refugee population was in northeastern Tanzania (Msuya et al. 1996: 7–9). HIV testing and counseling were not included. This reveals another moral tension. The mass testing of refugees is against the policy of the U.N. High Commissioner for Refugees (UNHCR), and the nongovernmental organization (NGO) community in the camps feared that the information might be used against the refugees (Msuya 1997: 113). The UNHCR has opposed mandatory testing of refugees as a violation of the International Declaration of Human Rights (Article 14). Testing for HIV that leads to denial of refugee status, refusal of entry by third countries, forcible return, or barred entry to the country of origin is morally and legally suspect (Gostin and Lazzarini 1997: 90). However, the UNHCR has urged that refugees are given access to the same levels of voluntary testing and counseling, and care, that are available to nationals (UNHCR 1988).

The lessons learned from the Tanzanian program included the importance and feasibility of including HIV interventions from the onset of the crisis, drawing staff from the refugee populations, and involving community leaders who can facilitate access and encourage discussion of the issues. The involvement and inclusion of the surrounding communities and coordination among the participating organizations are also critical to the effectiveness of the program (Msuya et al. 1996: 9).

The participants at the 1995 Sociétés d'Afrique & SIDA workshop, *Urgence, Precarité et Lutte contre le VIH/SIDA en Afrique,* reached similar conclusions but identified further considerations: the need to take care in organizing people in the camps, not to create new types of social vulnerability; the encouragement of voluntary testing with counseling with adequate measures for confidentiality; legal measures to protect the rights of the most vulnerable; and the need to respond to the economic and medical needs of the communities (Desclaux 1995: 11–12).

Refugee camps provide greater opportunities for discussion than those available in civilian life. Lessons can be learned from the programs in military populations that could assist in establishing effective programs in the camps. In particular, approaches based on strengthening people's capacity to discuss these difficult issues and to find means of addressing them themselves can lead to a collective consciousness of the nature of the epidemic, a collective will to respond, and individual motivation to protect self and others.

Power, Conflict, and Morality

The basic tenet of this chapter is that HIV programs can, and should, be an integral part of all programs of assistance in situations of conflict, upheaval, and violence and their immediate and longer-term aftermath. The extent to which the issue will be addressed will vary from situation to situation, but, minimally, it should be mainstreamed into accepted emergency programs. In this way, false moral dilemmas ("we can feed them or we can protect them from HIV, but we cannot do both") can be rejected.

The grounded dilemmas are then exposed more clearly: to decide to feed such populations but to do nothing to minimize the spread of HIV may prevent immediate death from starvation but not immediate infection with HIV. The possibility of a future created by preventing starvation may be destroyed by the untimely death from the consequences of being infected. The person infected may in turn infect a number of other persons and leave children without care or financial and parental support.

For HIV to be addressed in situations of conflict may well require a psychological and political revolution. The capacity to see beyond the visibly immediate, to encompass prevention as well as treatment, causes as well as symptoms, will need to be developed for HIV, as it has been for conflict-traumatized children, for example. The moral imagination to acknowledge the dreaded, to deal with complexity and process rather than to promulgate solutions, and to make difficult choices between competing claims on scarce resources will be needed. The invisible will need to become a political priority.

The HIV epidemic rages in situations where power is exercised without regard for others, whether that power be economic, social, sexual, psychological, or the power of force. It spreads where there is a disregard for life, an intolerance of difference, a devaluing of women, a lack of a will to live, a breakdown of community values, violence, and conflict. Telling or forcing others to act in certain ways, even if done for their benefit, strips them of a sense of agency and rarely leads to change. The facilitating, supportive voice is more effective than the admonitory voice in these matters of intimacy, desire, passion, and life. The power required is catalyzing.

HIV then defines a limit of systems of authority and control and of ethical theories, based on concepts of rights, justice, and obligations. What is required to respond to it is a way of perceiving and construing social reality in its interconnectedness. Central to this morality would be the acknowledgment of interdependence and the exercise of trust. The paradox of the HIV epidemic is that to trust others in this matter is to be more vulnerable than one might otherwise have been to harm.

References

Alliance Newsletter: Newsletter of the Civil-Military Alliance to Combat HIV and AIDS (1995–   ).

Bassabi, K. Personal communication, Togo, 1997.

Chelala, C. A. "Central America: The Cost of War." *Lancet* 335 (1990).

Desclaux, Alice. "AIDS Prevention and the Fight against HIV in Health Systems in Crisis or in Emergency Situations." *Sociétés d'Afrique et SIDA* 10 (October 1995).

Desclaux, Alice, and Claude Raynaut, eds. *Urgence, Precarité et Lutte contre le VIH/SIDA en Afrique.* Paris: Editions l'Harmattan, 1997.

Gondje, S., et al. "Lutte contre les MST et le SIDA dans les forces armées Centrafricaines." *Round-Table on HIV/AIDS, the Military and the Security Forces.* Abidjan: Xth International Conference on AIDS and STD in Africa, Book of Abstracts, 7–11 December 1997.

Gordon, John. Personal communication, UNDP consultancy, 1991.

Gostin, L., and Zita Lazzarini. *Human Rights and Public Health in the AIDS Pandemic.* Oxford: Oxford University Press, 1997.

Hendrix, Craig. "Behavioural Surveillance and Intervention in the Military Environment." *Alliance Newsletter* 3, no. 4 (October 1997).

Lorougnon, F., A. Kouame, and Coll. "Evaluation des strategies de prevention du VIH en milieu militaire (Forces Armées Nationales de Côte d'Ivoire) de 1994 à 1996." *Round-Table on HIV/AIDS, the Military and the Security Forces.* Abidjan: Xth International Conference on AIDS and STD in Africa, Book of Abstracts, 7–11 December 1997.

Msuya, Wences. "Le programme de santé de la reproduction d'AMREF dans les camps de refugies rwandais du district de Ngara (Tanzanie)," in *Urgence, Precarité et Lutte contre le VIH/SIDA en Afrique,* ed. Alice Desclaux et Claude Raynaut. Paris: Editions l'Harmattan, 1997.

Msuya, W., P. Mayaud, R. Mkanje, et al. "HIV/STD Intervention in Rwandan Refugee Camps in Tanzania." *Société d'Afrique & SIDA* 14 (October 1996).

Munyemana, Sosthene, and Febronie Muhongayire. "Specific Risks of HIV Infection in Rwanda and the Refugee Camps." *Sociétés d'Afrique et SIDA* 7 (January 1995).

Reid, Elizabeth. "Towards an Ethical Response to the HIV Epidemic." In *African Network on Ethics, Law and HIV: Proceedings of the Intercountry Consultation, Dakar, Senegal, 27 June–1 July, 1994.* Senegal: United Nations Development Program, Regional Project on HIV and Development, 1995.

Rieff, David. "The Humanitarian Trap." *World Policy Journal* (Winter 1995/1996).

Royte, Elizabeth. "The Outcasts." *New York Times Magazine,* 19 January 1997.

Slim, Hugo. "Doing the Right Thing: Relief Agencies, Moral Dilemmas and Moral Responsibility in Political Emergencies and War." Background paper, Uppsala: Scandinavian NGO Workshop on Humanitarian Ethics, 24 October 1996.

UNAIDS. *Global Summary of the HIV/AIDS Epidemic, December 1997.* Geneva: UNAIDS, 1997.

UNHCR. *UNHCR Health Policy on AIDS.* UNHCR/IOM/21/88 and UNHCR/FOM/20/88. Geneva: UNHCR, 15 February 1988.

Weir, Kathryn. "Images of Emaciation: Representing AIDS and Famine in Africa." Unpublished manuscript. Australian National University, Faculty of Arts, Canberra, 1990.

16

The Stories We Tell

Television and Humanitarian Aid

Michael Ignatieff

T here are strict limits to human empathy. We make some people's troubles our business while we ignore the troubles of
others. We are more likely to care about kin than about
strangers, to feel closest to those connected to us by bonds of history,
tradition, creed, ethnicity, and race. Indeed, because moral impinge-
ment is always a burden, we may use these differences as an excuse
to avoid or evade obligation.

It is disagreeable to admit that instincts play a relatively small role
in our moral reactions. We would prefer to suppose that the mere
sight of suffering victims on television would be enough to rouse us
to pity. In fact, there is nothing instinctive about the emotions stirred
in us by television pictures of atrocity or suffering. Our pity is struc-
tured by history and culture.

The idea, for example, that we owe an obligation to all human
beings by simple virtue of the fact that they are human is a modern
conception. We still encounter tribal cultures in the world in which
such an idea seems nonsensical. Universality comes late in the moral
history of humankind, once Judeo-Christian monotheism and natural
law have done their work. Even when these traditions have established themselves, people go on finding ingenious ways to evade their
implications.

When we do make the misfortunes, miseries, or injustices suffered by others into our business, some narrative is telling us why these strangers and their problems matter to us. These narratives—political, historical, ethical—turn strangers into neighbors, aliens into kin. They also suggest some idea of reciprocal obligation: if we do not help them, these stories imply, they will not help us when our turn with adversity comes around.

Storytelling gives up pleasure, and the pleasures of moral stories are just as suspect as or at least as complex as the pleasures of, say, a dirty joke. Our moral stories usually tell us what we want to hear: that we are decent folk trying to do our best and that we can make good the harms of the world. We would hardly tell these stories if they did not make us feel better, and they make us feel better even when they make us feel guilty, because guilt endows us with capacity—it suggests that we have the power to make a difference and are failing to do so. The truth might be grimmer, after all: that we have less power than we suppose; far from being able to save others, we may be barely able to save ourselves.

Thus, if moral activity always involves the imagination, it is as much about imagining "us" as it is about imagining "them"; the stories we create always place us as their chief subject, and to the degree that this is so, our imagination is always susceptible to moral narcissism. The stories we tell lead us to think better of ourselves than we deserve.

Beside moral stories linking us and them, there are metastories governing the larger relationship between zones of safety and zones of danger. In the nineteenth century there were the stories of empire: the nexus of interest, economic, geopolitical, religious, and ideological, which bound the metropolis to the periphery. The imperial narrative—bringing civilization to the world of savagery—gave the media a metanarrative, a grand story into which each local event could be fitted and given its meaning.[1]

With the passage of the nineteenth-century empires and the creation of the postwar Soviet and American hegemony, the story that linked the two zones was the superpower rivalry for power and influence. What brought television to the war zones of these areas was the prospect of witnessing the proxy wars in which the world balance of power would be shifted. Now the superpower rivalry is over; "we" are no longer there, because "they" are no longer there, either. The proxy wars are no longer fed from Washington and Moscow, and while they continue—as in Angola—their salience and interest to the developed world has diminished. As for the parallel narrative of decolonization, some ex-colonies have made a successful transition to genuine independence and some degree of economic development, whereas others have foundered into tribalism, oligarchy, or civil war. Either way, there is no simple narrative to tell anymore. Instead, the narrative that has become most pervasive and persuasive has been the "chaos narrative," the widely held belief, only reinforced by the end of direct colonialism, that large sections of the globe, especially in central Africa and the fiery southern edges of the former Soviet empire, have collapsed into a meaningless disorder, upon which no coherent pattern can be discerned.[2] The "chaos narrative" demotivates: it is an antinarrative, a story that claims there is no story to tell and therefore no reason to get involved. Since the end of the Cold War, television has simply reproduced the chaos narrative. As it does so, it undermines even its own limited engagement in zones of danger.

These demotivating elements are reinforced by the collapse of two other narratives. In the first of these, liberals were interested in Africa and Asia because the narrative of colonial nations achieving freedom and independence after years of struggle seemed to confirm the liberal story of progress. Now that a generation or two has passed and many of these societies have either achieved independence or thrown away its advantages, the story has lost its moral gleam. There are few partisans of African and Asian independence left, and more than a few who are overtly nostalgic for the return of colonial rule.

Another metanarrative that sustained interest in the third world after World War II was socialist internationalism, the faith that newly independent states were a test bed for the possibilities of a socialist economy and way of life. Generations of Western leftists were lured to Cuba, Vietnam, and other places in the hopes of finding their dreams confirmed. The collapse of the Marxist and socialist project has ended this metanarrative of hope, and as it does, disillusioned and demotivated socialists turn away from developing societies altogether.

No new sinews of economic interdependence have been created to link zones of safety and zones of danger together. In the heyday of empire, there was at least ivory and copper, gold and timber. As the developed world entered the phase of permanent postindustrial revolution, based in knowledge and computers, it appears to stand in less need of the raw materials of the developing world. Large sectors of the world's population are not being drawn into globalized commerce but banished backward into sustained underdevelopment. The developed world is tied in ever-tighter linkage—the Internet, twenty-four-hour global trading, jet travel, global hotels, resorts, credit card networks, and so on—while sections of central Africa, Asia, Latin America, since they no longer even supply vital raw materials, cease to be of either economic or strategic concern.

This leaves only one metanarrative drawing zones of safety and zones of danger together: the humanitarian narrative. We are in one world; we must shoulder each other's fate; the value of life is indivisible. What happens to the starving in Africa and the homeless in Asia must concern us all because we belong to one species. This narrative, with its charter document—the Universal Declaration of Human Rights—and its agencies of diffusion—the nongovernmental humanitarian agencies and the U.N. system—puts a strong priority on moral linkages over economic and strategic ones. The question is how television mediates this moral linkage.

We should consider the possibility, first, that the media change little at all. Our best stories—from King Lear to Peter Pan—seem to survive any number of retellings. Why *should* the technology of storytelling change the story? We should beware of technological determinism in thinking about the moral impact of media. The claim that global media globalizes the conscience might be an example of technological determinism at work. It is certainly true that modern real-time television news-gathering technology has shortened both the time and the distance separating zones of safety—the small number of liberal capitalist democracies that possess power, influence, and wealth—from the zones of danger—the small number of collapsing states in Africa, Asia, Eastern Europe, and Latin America—where refugees and war victims stand in need of aid and assistance.

But it does not follow that media technology has reduced the "moral distance" between these zones. Real and moral distance are not the same. Real distance is abolished by technology; moral distance is only abolished by a persuasive story. Technology enables us to tell stories differently, but it does not necessarily change the story we want to tell. Indeed, one could say that the media follow where the moral story leads. To the extent that television takes any notice whatever of zones of danger, it does so in terms of a moral narrative of concern that antedates the arrival of television by several centuries. This narrative: that we are our brothers' keeper; that human beings belong to one species; that if we "can" help, we "must" help—all of this emerges out of the Judeo-Christian idea of human universality secularized in European natural law beginning in the sixteenth century. At best television merely allows us to tell this old moral story more efficiently. The medium is just a medium. The modern conscience had written its moral charter—the Universal Declaration of Human Rights—before television had even entered most of our living rooms. Television would not be in Kosovo or Kabul at all, if it were not for these antecedent moral narratives.

It may be the case that television cannot *create* any moral relationship between audience and victim where none exists already. If television's moral gaze is partial and promiscuous, it is because ours is no less so. The TV crews go where we were already looking. We intervene morally where we already can tell a story about a place. To care about one place is necessarily to cast another into shadow. There is no morally adequate reply to the charge that Europeans and North Americans, to the degree that they cared at all, cared more about Bosnia than Rwanda. The sources of our partiality were only too obvious. One was in Europe, the other in Africa; one was a frequent holiday destination, the other was off most people's map. For most white Europeans and North Americans this partiality was transparently a function of race, history, and tradition. But how can it be otherwise? Our knowledge is partial and incomplete; our narratives of engagement are bound to be inconsistent and biased. To lament this point is understandable, except when it is supposed that we *should* be capable of moral omniscience. We cannot be. It is simply unrealistic to expect that each of us should feel connection to every place in the world where victims are in danger. We are bound to care more about places and people we already know something about. It is certainly invidious to believe that white victims matter more than black ones, that coreligionists are more naturally a matter of our concern than nonbelievers; and we can counteract these biases where we can, but at the end of the day, we will care more about what we know something about, and if this is Bosnia, so be it. The media will simply reflect the biases intrinsic to their own audience: their coverage may indeed exacerbate them, but in itself, they are not responsible for them. Indeed, television coverage can do relatively little to counteract the inherent moral biases of its viewers. It follows where it and other media lead.

What is more to the point is that media ownership concentrates media power in mostly white European and North American hands, and their angle of vision determines the focus of world media coverage. For these reasons, natural partiality is grossly magnified, and the world's majority—nonwhite, non–North American, non-European—is forced to take the minority's moral priorities. This bias cannot be corrected by well-meaning gestures. It will only change as the majority takes economic power into its own hands and creates media institutions that reflect its own moral priorities. This is already occurring across southeast Asia, and there is no reason to suppose that it cannot happen eventually in Africa and Latin America.

The fact that television reflects but does not create moral relationships does not exclude the possibility that it may also distort these relationships. Three possible distortions are evident. First, television turns moral narratives into entertainment; second, television turns political narratives into humanitarian drama; third, television individualizes—it takes the part for the whole. All three forms of bias are interrelated yet distinct. Television news is an entertainment medium. It derives its revenue and influence from its capacity to make the delivery of information pleasurable. Pleasurable story lines are generally simple, gripping, and easy to understand. Now all moral life requires simplification, and all forms of moral identification proceeds by way of fictions. In framing up our moral world, we all seek for good guys and bad guys, innocent victims and evil perpetrators. Nothing is intrinsically wrong about this resort to fictions and simplifications. It is also puritanical to suppose that moral problems should never be mixed with entertainment values. Moral drama is always compelling, and television can be easily forgiven for seeking to build revenue and ratings on the production of moral drama out of news.

Dramatization only becomes problematic when the actors in our moral dramas stop playing the roles on which our identification with them depends. For moral roles frequently reverse: innocent victims turn perpetrators; perpetrators turn victims. In such circumstances, it may become difficult to alter the story line in the public mind. Serbs who were perpetrators of ethnic cleansing in Bosnia in 1993 turned out to be victims of ethnic cleansing in Croatia in 1995. But their demonization in 1993 foreclosed the possibility of empathy—and the assistance that rightly follows empathy—in 1995.

The distorting bias here is sentimentalization, because sentimental art, by definition, sacrifices nuance, ambivalence, and complexity in favor of strong emotion. Hence, it is art that prefers identification over truth. To the degree that television is an art form whose revenue stream depends on creating strong identifications, it is axiomatic that it will occasionally sacrifice moral truth. Occasionally, but not always: there are times when the sentimental is true, when we identify strongly with a story that happens to have got its facts straight.

The second distortion flows from the visual bias of the medium. Television is better at focusing on the consequences of political decisions than the rationale for the decisions themselves: hence on the thunder of the guns rather than the battle plans; the corpses in the ditch rather than the strategic goals of the ethnic cleansers. The visual bias of television has certain obvious advantages; it enables any viewer to measure the guilt that separates intentions from consequences; it allows a viewer to move, shot by shot, from the prevarications of politicians to the grimy realities these prevarications attempt to conceal. But the very intensity of the visual impact of television pictures obscures its limitations as a medium for telling stories. Every picture is *not* worth a thousand words. Pictures without words are meaningless. Even when pictures are accompanied by words, they can only tell certain stories. Television is relatively incoherent when it comes to establishing the political and diplomatic context in which humanitarian disaster, war crime, or famine take shape. It has a tendency to turn these into examples of man's inhumanity to man; it turns them from political into natural disasters, and in doing so, it actively obscures the context responsible for their occurrence. Its natural bias, therefore, is to create sentimental stories that by making viewers feel pity also, and not accidentally, makes them feel better about themselves.

Thus, television pictures from the Ethiopian famine in 1984 focused naturally on the pathos of the victims, not on the machinations of the elites who manufactured famine as a instrument of ethnic oppression or other long-term failures of the African economy or ecology. It did so simply because it chooses identification over insight, and it did so because television depends for revenue and influence on the heightened drama of this visual mimesis of one-to-one contact between the watching spectator and the suffering victim.

The third related difficulty is that television, like all forms of journalism, makes up its stories by means of *synecdoche,* by taking the part for the whole. Journalism is closer to fiction than to social science: its stories focus on exemplary individuals and makes large and usually tacit assumptions about their typicality. This is synecdoche: the starving widow and her suffering children who stand for the whole famished community of Somalia; the mute victim behind the barbed wire at Tranopole who stands for the suffering of the Bosnian people as a whole. Given that victims are numberless, it is natural that identification should proceed by means of focusing on single individuals. Synecdoche has the virtues of making the abstractions of exile, expulsion, starvation, and other forms of suffering into an experience sufficiently concrete and real to make empathy possible. But there are evident dangers. First, is the individual typical? Notoriously, television chooses exemplary victims, ones whose sufferings are spectacular and whose articulacy remains undiminished. Viewers trust experienced reporters to make these exemplary choices, but when viewers begin to question the typicality of the witness, they also begin to question the terms of their identification. When they feel that human suffering has been turned into entertainment cliché, they begin to feel manipulated: the ward full of abandoned orphans; the star-crossed Romeos and Juliets who loved each other across the ethnic divide and whose love shows up the folly of ethnic hatred; the plucky journalists who keep on publishing right through the shelling; the war-torn child whom the journalist adopts and spirits back to safety and endless interviews.[3] These forms of synecdoche forfeit any kind of complex identification with the whole panorama they are supposed to evoke.

The identification that synecdoche creates is intense but shallow. We feel for a particular victim, without understanding why or how he or she has come to be a victim; and empathy without understanding is bound to fritter away when the next plausible victim makes his or her appearance on our screen or when we learn something that apparently contradicts the image of simple innocence that the structure of synecdoche invited us to expect.

It may be, therefore, that television itself has something to do with the shallowness of forms of identification between victims and donors in zones of safety. Television personalizes, humanizes, but also depoliticizes moral relations, and in so doing, it weakens the understanding on which sustained empathy—and moral commitment—depend. The visual biases of television thus deserve some place in our explanation of "compassion fatigue" and "donor fatigue"—growing reluctance by rich and well-fed publics to give to humanitarian charities or support governmental foreign aid. Real distance has been drastically shortened by visual technology, but moral distance remains undiminished. If we are fatigued, it is because we feel assailed by heterodox and promiscuous visual claims and appeals for help coming from all corners of the world. Moral narratives have been banalized by repetition and in repetition have lost their impact and force.

Aid agencies, such as the International Committee of the Red Cross (ICRC), are waking up to the erosion of the narratives of moral engagement on which they depend to sustain both the morale of their field staff and the political support of donor governments. For aid agencies are moral storytellers: they tell stories to mediate and motivate, and they typically use television to get these stories and messages to pass from the zones of danger back to the zones of safety.

Typically the stories aid agencies tell are different from the ones television journalists tell, and these differences illustrate the moral dilemmas aid agencies characteristically encounter. Unlike journalists, aid agencies cannot point the finger of blame. They can name victims, but they cannot identify perpetrators, or if they do so, they must be careful not to do so in such a way as to jeopardize their access to victims. This limitation is especially the case for the ICRC, which has made moral neutrality its touchstone; but even groups such as Médecins sans Frontières (MSF), that have explicitly contested moral neutrality have learned that if they do engage in blame, they may gain credibility among victims, but they lose it among perpetrators and consequently lose the capacity to work in the field. If tables are turned, and victims become perpetrators and perpetrators victims, aid agencies that have told a blame-heavy story may find it impossible to change their line of response to the disaster.

Yet, if aid agencies refuse to tell a political story—one that attributes causation and consequences for the disaster they are helping to relieve—they risk falling back on a narrative of simple victimhood, empty of context and meaning. This disempowers the agencies when they appeal to governments and ordinary people for support. For purely sentimental, purely humanitarian stories create shallow identifications in the audiences they are intended to sway; such stories deny the audience the deeper understanding—bitter, contradictory, political, complex—on which a durable commitment depends. In the recourse to the pure humanitarian narrative of support for innocent victims, the aid agencies actively contribute to the compassion fatigue they purport to deplore.

Getting out of this contradiction is not easy. The pure humanitarian narrative preserves neutrality, and with it the agencies' autonomy and capacity to act. A political narrative commits the agency to a point of view that compromises its credibility with the group it has accused.

Aid agencies such as the ICRC have responded to this dilemma, in effect, by telling two moral stories, one in public, the other in private. The one reserved for public consumption preserves the neutrality of the organization and avoids attributing political responsibility for the disaster, war, or conflict in which it is intervening. The private message is more political: it is directed to governments, donors, and sympathetic journalists and does point the finger of blame. In the former Yugoslavia, the ICRC's public story offered emotionally charged but ethnically neutral descriptions of humanitarian tragedy, whereas the private back-channel story, told by its delegates and high officials, did not hesitate to attribute blame and responsibility and recommend political action. Its public statements about the Serbian camps in central Bosnia in 1992 preserved ethical neutrality; the private messages of its delegates on the ground did not mince words.[4]

Organizations that split their message in this way risk appearing duplicitous and hypocritical. The objective may be laudable: to preserve sufficient credit with perpetrators that access to victims can be preserved. But inevitably a certain credit is lost with victims and those who side with victims, notably journalists.

Faced with these challenges to their moral integrity, some agencies have tried to harmonize both public and private storytelling. Médecins sans Frontières has been most explicit: refusing to be even-handed as between perpetrator and victim; refusing to offer humanitarian assistance when the political conditions are unacceptable; denouncing both perpetrators and outside powers when they obstruct humanitarian efforts. In Afghanistan, likewise, Oxfam and UNICEF have refused to split their messages about Taliban treatment of women, publicly denouncing Taliban attitudes toward women. There are risks in this outspokenness—not merely that the Taliban may shut these agencies out but that these agencies themselves become more enamored of the politics of moral gesture than of reaching and assisting female victims themselves. So if the ICRC runs the moral risk of duplicity and hypocrisy by sharply distinguishing between what it says in public and what it says in private, agencies that refuse this distinction run the risk of moral narcissism: doing what feels right in preference to what makes a genuine difference.[5]

But these are not the only dilemmas that occur when aid agencies try to tell moral stories. Their humanitarian action is frequently exploited as a moral alibi. Aid agencies become victim of a certain moral synecdoche of their own. Thus, the fact that the ICRC has been doing humanitarian work in Afghanistan for a decade is taken, by the watching world, as a sign that "at least" "we" are doing something about the human misery there. The "we" in question is the moral audience of the civilized world, and this "we" has proven adept at taking moral credit for humanitarian interventions in which it has strictly no right to take credit at all. For there is no "we"; the so-called civilized world has no such moral unity, no such concentrated vision, and if politicians who represent its concerns claim credit for the humanitarian work of agencies in the field, they do so illegitimately.

Anyone engaged in humanitarian action in the field is indignantly aware of the extent to which his or her individual efforts are incorporated by the watching moral audience on television as proof of the West's unfailing moral benevolence. For television does not like to depict misery without also showing that someone is doing something about it. We cannot have misery without aid workers. They conjure away the horror by suggesting that help is at hand. This is synecdoche at its most deceiving, for if help is getting through in this instance, it may not be getting through in others, and sometimes help may actually make a bad situation worse—for example, if food assistance falls into the hands of combatants and enables them to continue a civil war. Television coverage of humanitarian assistance allows the West the illusion that it is doing something; in this way, coverage becomes an alternative to more serious political engagement. The Afghan civil war cannot be stopped by humanitarian assistance; in many ways, humanitarian assistance prolongs the war by sustaining the populations who submit to its horrors. Only active political intervention by the Great Powers forcing the regional powers bordering Afghanistan to shut off their assistance to the factions is likely to end the war. Aid workers in the region indignantly believe—and with reason—that their humanitarian presence allows the West the moral alibi to abstain from serious political engagement with the problem.

Thus, when humanitarian agencies bring television to a conflict site, they may not get what they bargained for. They may have wanted to generate stories that would focus the attention of policy makers on the need for substantive diplomatic or political intervention; what they get instead is the production of moral drama: sentimental tales of suffering, using a poor country as a backdrop, which, by stimulating exercises in generosity, simply reinforces donors' sensation of moral superiority.

This idea certainly goes against the received wisdom about the impact of television on foreign policy and humanitarian intervention. It has been generally supposed that television coverage drives policy and intervention alike, the pictures creating a demand that "something must be done." We have already questioned the technological determinism implicit in these assumptions, by arguing that it is not the pictures that have the impact but the particular story—moral or otherwise—that we happen to tell about these pictures. Where stories are wanting, television cannot supply them. Those who have examined the impact of television coverage on the propensity of governments to intervene in zones of danger would take this argument still further. After closely studying cases such as the Somalia, Haiti, and Bosnia interventions, most analysts come away with a marked degree of skepticism about the efficacy of the so-called "CNN effect."[6] Policy makers insist that they decide whether to commit their countries to action not according to what they see on the screen but according to whether it is in the stable, long-term national interest of their countries. According to these studies, three years of drastic and sometimes ghastly television footage did little to move European policy makers away from their reluctance to commit troops and planes to bring the Bosnian war to an end. At most, the television images stimulated a humanitarian response: aid agencies moved in, donations flowed, and some of the misery on the screen was alleviated. But television did little or nothing to drive the Bosnia policy of Whitehall or the White House. Here the determinant factor against intervention was Vietnam-bred caution about sinking into a quagmire. No amount of sentimental coverage of humanitarian disaster was able to shift the policy makers' and military analysts' basic perception that this was a "lose-lose" situation.

Both the victims themselves and the humanitarian agencies in Bosnia supposed that getting the cameras there would help trigger decisive military and political action. Both were angrily disillusioned when this action was not forthcoming. It was as if both believed that misery tells its own story, that pictures inevitably suggest the moral conclusions to be drawn from them. But, as I have argued, pictures do not tell their own story, and misery does not motivate on its own.

Yet skeptics go too far when they claim that television pictures had no impact on the foreign policy of states or the conscience of a watching public. Policy makers and military planners have an institutional stake in denying that they are at the mercy of television images and public pressure. It is essential to their *amour propre* and professional detachment to believe that they make policy on grounds of rational

interest rather than on the basis of inflammatory and sentimental television reports. Yet their disclaimers on this score are not entirely to
be believed. What the pictures from Bosnia undoubtedly did engage
was a small but vocal constituency of people who felt disgust and
shame and were roused to put pressure on the politicians who stood
by and did nothing. It was not the pictures themselves that made the
difference but the small political constituency in favor of intervention
that they helped to call into being. Television itself did not create this
constituency; rather, the images helped the constituency widen its
basis of support; it could point to these images and draw in others
who felt the same outrage and disgust as they did.

The numbers who care about foreign issues will always be much
smaller than for domestic ones, but their influence is out of all proportion to their numbers. Most of them—in the press, the humanitarian
agencies, the think tanks—have the power to create and mold public
opinion.[7] For three years, a small constituency pounded away at the
shame of Bosnia, and in the end their campaign worked—not, I hasten to add, because political leaders themselves felt any great shame
but because, in time, they were made to feel that they were failing to
exercise "leadership." Once a political leader feels his or her legitimacy and authority are put under sustained moral question, he or she
is bound to act sooner or later. Added to this, in the Bosnian case,
was the undoubted fact that prolonged inaction was beginning to
erode the cohesiveness of the NATO alliance and open up important
splits between Europe and America. In the end, the Clinton administration intervened and set the Dayton process in motion, not because
it had been shamed by television but because it felt, with good reason,
that at last an overriding political interest was at stake in Bosnia: the
coherence of the alliance structure and the continued hegemony of
America in European affairs. In other words, humanitarian pressure,
in the form of outraged editorials and gruesome television footage,
set up a train of consequences that only three years later eventually
helped to generate a national interest basis for intervention. This national interest drove policy, but it does not follow that the intervention was motivated solely by national interest considerations. The humanitarian, moral pressure was integral to the process by which a
reason for intervention was eventually discerned and acted on.

All of this suggests that the moral stories we tell through television are less influential than their visual impact would suggest, but they are not as unimportant as skeptics would imply; and that they do play a continuing role in structuring the interventions, humanitarian and otherwise, through which the zones of safety attempt to regulate and assist the zones of danger.

As humanitarian agencies confront the question of how to use television more effectively to sustain engagement, by donors and governments, and to counter "donor fatigue," they need to address the general breakdown of metanarratives linking the developed and developing worlds. We have two metanarratives on offer, globalization and the chaos narrative: economic integration and collapsing time and distance constraints for the wealthy few in the northern world; state fragmentation, ethnic war, and economic disintegration for the unfortunate citizens of as many as twenty-five nations in Africa, Asia, and Latin America. The rhetoric of globalization—and especially the globalization of media—altogether conceals the fact that this promise is withheld from the majority of the world's population. Indeed, as the developed world integrates still further, it is reducing, not extending, its contacts with the worlds of danger. Highly mediatized relief operations, such as Somalia, Goma, and Afghanistan, conceal the shrinking percentages of national income devoted to foreign aid, just as highly mediatized charitable campaigns such as Live Aid conceal the shrinkage of private donations to international humanitarian charities. The metanarrative—the big story—is one of disengagement, while the moral lullaby we allow our humanitarian consciences to sing is that we are coming closer and closer.

Notes

1. See my *Warrior's Honour: Ethnic War and the Modern Conscience* (New York: Henry Holt, 1998), chap. 4.

2. See Robert D. Kaplan, *The Ends of the Earth* (New York: Vintage Books, 1996).

3. Gilbert Holleufer, "Images of Humanitarian Crises: Ethical Implications," *International Review of the Red Cross* (November–December 1996): 609–13.

4. See Roy Gutman, *Witness to Genocide* (Middleton, Wisc.: Lisa Drew, 1993).

5. Michael Keating, "The Reality Gap," *Geographical Magazine*, September 1996, 23–24; also M. Keating, "Painting It Black: Who's to Blame?" *Crosslines* 18–19 (December 1995): 21–22.

6. Nik Gowing, "Real-Time Television Coverage of Armed Conflicts and Diplomatic Crises: Does It Pressure or Distort Foreign Policy Decisions?" Joan Shorenstein Center, Kennedy School of Government, Harvard University, occasional paper, June 1994; see also Steven Livingston, "Clarifying the CNN Effect: An Examination of Media Effects According to Type of Military Intervention," Joan Shorenstein Center, Harvard University, occasional paper, June 1997; see also Nik Gowing "Media Coverage: Help or Hindrance in Conflict Prevention?" report for the Carnegie Commission on Preventing Deadly Conflict, New York, 1997.

7. Larry Minear, Colin Scott, and Thomas G. Weiss, *The News Media, Civil War and Humanitarian Action* (Boulder, Col.: Lynne Rienner, 1996).

Index

Afghanistan, 35, 90, 297, 298
African Great Lakes region, xiii. *See also* Somalia
aid, 21; concentration of, 97; definition of, 239–40; minimum, 90–91
aid misappropriation, 141, 145–46; in Cambodia, 179, 180; in Rwandan refugee camps, 160
aid providers: conditions for, 150; separation from aid recipients, 149–51. *See also* humanitarian organizations
aid recipients, interactions with, 88–91, 96, 149–51
AIDS. *See* HIV
alliance building, 93
alliances between states, 20
ambiguity: in aid provision, 138, 148; moral use of, 23
amnesty, 104, 220, 225; in South Africa, 218, 225, 226
anarchy, 11, 29
Angola, 59
Annan, Kofi A., 233
apartheid, 57
appropriateness, 23
Arendt, Hannah, 192
Argentina, 211, 218
Arias, Oscar, 265
Aristide, Jean-Bertrand, 99, 102–3
armies, private, ix, 110. *See also* military

arms: categories, 264; removing from circulation, 265; small/portable, 265–66; uses of, 260
arms embargos, 251, 262–63
arms trade, 5, 97, 257; banning, 258–59, 263–64, 266; consequences of, 252, 263, 266; criteria for limiting, 260–63, 267; dilemmas of, 256–57; economics of, 261–62, 263; extent of, 254–56; free market approach, 258; illicit, 266; intermediaries, 257; international controls on, 265–66; limiting, 255–56, 257, 259–66; morality of, 258, 263; recordkeeping re, 265; suppliers, 260, 264–65, 266; types of weapons, 257
Aron, Raymond, 11
assistance. *See* aid
authoritarian states, 14
authorization, 26; multilateral, 44
autonomy: communal, 40; of humanitarian agencies, 95, 296; individual, 31; state, 30, 31, 32
awareness, 3

balance of power, 31, 36, 40
Bertram, Christoph, 23
blame, 272, 296. *See also* impartiality; neutrality
Bosnia, 20, 38; aid in, 190–91; arms

About the Authors

MARY B. ANDERSON is an economist and president of the Collaborative for Development Action, Inc., in Cambridge, Massachusetts. Since 1995, she has directed the Local Capacities for Peace Project, which is a collaborative effort of donor governments, international and indigenous nongovernmental organizations (NGOs), and multilateral aid agencies to learn more about the relationships between humanitarian and development assistance and conflict. She has written extensively on rural development strategies that build on local capacity, gender analysis in development programming, the relationships between emergency relief assistance and long-term development, and educational policies as they affect access to primary education in developing countries, including *Do No Harm: Supporting Local Capacities for Peace through Aid* (1996).

KOFI A. ANNAN is the secretary-general of the United Nations, serving in this post since January 1, 1997. He was special representative of the U.N. secretary-general to the former Yugoslavia in 1995–1996. He served as undersecretary-general for peacekeeping operations during 1993–1995. He was U.N. comptroller and head of its Office of Program Planning, Budget and Finance in 1990–1992. Previously, Annan served in a variety of finance, management, and personnel positions at the U.N. He has also worked for the Office of the U.N. High Commissioner for Refugees in Geneva, the U.N. Emergency Force in Cairo, the World Health Organization in Geneva, and the U.N. Economic Commission for Africa in Addis Ababa.

RONY BRAUMAN is a senior lecturer at the University of Paris XII. He was president of Médecins sans frontières from 1982 to 1994 and is a member of its foundation. A doctor himself, he has carried out many humanitarian assignments in crisis situations worldwide. Between 1992 and 1997, he ran a postgraduate seminar at the Institute for Political Studies in Paris. Brauman's latest publications include *L'action humanitaire* (1995), "Humanitaire: le dilemme" (interview with Philippe Petit in *Textuel,* 1996), and "Les médias et l'humanitaire" (in cooperation with René Backmann, *CFPJ,* 1996).

ROMEO A. DALLAIRE is Lieutenant General in the Canadian Army and the Assistant Deputy Defence Minister (Human Resources— Military) in Ottawa. From July 1993 to August 1994 he commanded the United Nations Observer Mission—Uganda and Rwanda (UNO-MUR) and the United Nations Assistance Mission in Rwanda (UNA-MIR). Following his service in Rwanda, he assumed simultaneously the positions of deputy commander of Land Force Command in St. Hubert and commander of the 1st Canadian Division and later command of Land Force Quebec Area. Dallaire is a recipient of the Meritorious Service Cross, the Vimy Award, and the U.S. Legion of Merit.

RICHARD J. GOLDSTONE is justice of the Constitutional Court of South Africa. From August 1994 to September 1996, he served as the chief prosecutor of the United Nations International Criminal Tribunals for the former Yugoslavia and Rwanda. Before that, he had served as chairperson of the Commission of Inquiry Regarding Public Violence and Intimidation, which came to be known as the Goldstone Commission. Goldstone heads the board of the Human Rights Institute of South Africa, is the chancellor of the University of the Witwatersrand in Johannesburg, and is a member of the International Panel to Monitor the Argentinian Inquiry to Elucidate Nazi Activities in the Argentine Republic since 1938.

COLIN GRANDERSON is executive director of the Organization of American States (OAS)/United Nations International Civilian Mission in Haiti. He has held this position since May 1993 and was appointed head of the OAS Election Observation Mission in Haiti for the presidential elections that took place in December 1995 and the partial legislative and local government elections in April 1997. Granderson worked in prior OAS assignments in Haiti since 1992. Previously, he had been director of the Political Affairs Division in the Ministry of Foreign Affairs, Trinidad and Tobago, after diplomatic postings to London, Geneva, and New York.

PIERRE HASSNER is a philosopher and historian. He is research director, Centre d'Études et de Recherches Internationales, Fondation Nationale des Sciences Politiques, and professor at the Institut d'Études Politiques in Paris. He is the author of many articles and books on international relations and political philosophy, particularly on the theme of war and peace. These include: *Violence and Peace: From the Atomic Bomb to Ethnic Cleansing* (1997), *Totalitarismes* (with Guy Hermet and Jacques Rupnik, 1984), *Europe in the Age of Negotiation* (1973), and *Change and Security in Europe* (1968).

J. BRYAN HEHIR is professor of the practice in religion and society at the Divinity School and the Center for International Affairs at Harvard University. He also serves as counselor to Catholic Relief Services in Baltimore, Maryland. From 1973 to 1992, Hehir served in Washington, D.C., at the U.S. Catholic Conference of Bishops, where he was director of the Office of International Affairs, and at Georgetown University, where he was Joseph P. Kennedy Professor of Christian Ethics. Among his publications are "Intervention: From Theories to Cases," *Ethics and International Affairs* (1995) and "Just-War Theory in a Post–Cold War World," *Journal of Religious Studies* (1992).

MICHAEL IGNATIEFF is a historian and author. He is a regular contributor to the *New Yorker* and the *New York Review of Books*. In 1994, he wrote *Blood and Belonging: Journeys into the New Nationalism*, and his most recent book, published this year, is *The Warrior's Honor: Ethnic War and the Modern Conscience*. Ignatieff has worked as a journalist for the *Toronto Globe and Mail* and the *Observer* (London); taught at the University of British Columbia, Cambridge University, and the École des Hautes Études in Paris; hosted various BBC television shows; and written two novels and a screenplay.

IAN MARTIN is Deputy High Commissioner for Human Rights in Bosnia-Herzegovina. He is a fellow of the Human Rights Centre at the University of Essex, and was secretary-general of Amnesty International from 1986 to 1992 Martin was director for Human Rights of the U.N./OAS International Civilian Mission in Haiti in 1993–1995, and after that served as chief of the U.N. High Commissioner for Human Rights' Field Operation in Rwanda. He was Special Adviser to the High Commissioner in 1998. His writings include "Haiti: Mangled Multilateralism," *Foreign Policy* (1994).

LARRY MINEAR is codirector of the Humanitarianism and War Project and senior fellow at Brown University's Thomas J. Watson Jr. Institute for International Studies. He has worked on international humanitarian and development issues since 1972, including assignments in Africa and in Washington, D.C., where he headed the advocacy office of Church World Service and Lutheran World Relief. His recent coauthored books include *Political Gain and Civilian Pain: The Humanitarian Impact of Economic Sanctions* (1997), *Soldiers to the Rescue: Humanitarian Lessons from Rwanda* (1996), *The News Media, Civil War, and Humanitarian Action* (1996), and *Mercy under Fire: War and the Global Humanitarian Community* (1995).

JONATHAN MOORE (Editor) is a senior adviser to the administrator of the U.N. Development Program and associate at the Shorenstein Center on the Press, Politics and Public Policy at Harvard University. He was U.S. coordinator of refugee affairs and ambassador to the U.N. Economic and Social Council. He previously served in senior positions in the U.S. Departments of State; Defense; Health, Education and Welfare; and Justice, and he also was director of the Institute of Politics at the Kennedy School of Government at Harvard. His writings include *Morality and Interdependence* (Dartmouth College, 1994) and *The U.N. and Complex Emergencies: Rehabilitation in Third World Transitions* (UNRISD, 1996).

MU SOCHUA is a member of the Cambodian Parliament from Battambang, elected in the 1998 legislative elections. She is chief of cabinet for the FUNCINPEC party. Mu worked as education and social service coordinator for fifteen camps for Cambodian refugees for the United Nations Border Relief Operation in Thailand from 1982 to 1986. She founded and led the first Cambodian nongovernmental organization in Cambodia to assist urban poor women from 1991 to 1995 and was appointed the following year as adviser on women's affairs to the first prime minister.

ELIZABETH REID is the U.N. Resident Coordinator and U.N. Development Program (UNDP) Resident Representative in Papua New Guinea. From 1989 to 1997, she directed programs at UNDP headquarters in New York on HIV/AIDS and Women in Development. Previously she was senior consultant in development assistance for USAID in Kinshasha and ESCAP in Bangkok, adviser to Princess Ashnaf Pahlavi of Iran on international programs for women, and adviser to the prime minister of Australia on the welfare of women and children. She has degrees in philosophy from Australian National University and Oxford University and is an honorary fellow of the Academy of the Social Sciences of Australia.

MOHAMED SAHNOUN is special envoy of the U.N. secretary-general in Africa. During 1997, he served as joint United Nations/Organization of African Unity (OAU) special representative for the Great Lakes region of Africa. From April to November 1992, he was special representative of the U.N. secretary-general to Somalia. Sahnoun has been a member of the Brundtland Commission, senior adviser at the U.N. Conference on Environment and Development, and deputy secretary-general of both the OAU and the League of Arab States. He also has served as Algeria's ambassador to Morocco, the United Nations, France, and the Federal Republic of Germany.

ROGER WILLIAMSON is policy and campaigns director of Christian Aid, London. He worked as international affairs specialist for the Church of England (1994–1998); as director of the Council for Arms Control, London, and the Life & Peace Institute, Uppsala, Sweden; and on peace and human rights for the British Council of Churches. Williamson has written and edited many articles and books, specializing particularly in the arms trade, peace research, and social ethics. Most recently, he has edited *Some Corner of a Foreign Field: Intervention and World Order* on behalf of the Council on Christian Approaches to Defence and Disarmament (1998).

JOSÉ ZALAQUETT is a professor of human rights and public ethics at the University of Chile. He has been active in human rights since 1973 when the military regime took over in Chile, first as a lawyer for political prisoners in Chile and later as an international human rights activist. He has served as chairperson of the International Executive Committee of Amnesty International and as a board member of Americas Watch, the International Commission of Jurists, and other human rights organizations. In 1990–1991 he was appointed to the Chilean Commission on Truth and Reconciliation. Zalaquett has written extensively on human rights issues.